Winning Ways of Coaching Writing

A Practical Guide for Teaching Writing, Grades 6–12

Edited by
Mary L. Warner
Western Carolina University

Foreword by
Leila Christenbury
Virginia Commonwealth University

Allyn and Bacon

Boston ▪ London ▪ Toronto ▪ Sydney ▪ Tokyo ▪ Singapore

To the memory of my parents,
Harvey and Agnes Warner—two extraordinary teachers

Vice President: *Paul A. Smith*
Senior Editor: *Arnis E. Burvikovs*
Editorial Assistant: *Patrice Mailloux*
Executive Marketing Manager: *Lisa Kimball*
Editorial Production Service: *Maes Associates*
Manufacturing Buyer: *Julie McNeill*
Cover Administrator: *Jennifer Hart*

Copyright © 2001 by Allyn & Bacon
A Pearson Education Company
160 Gould Street
Needham Heights, MA 02494

Internet: www.abacon.com

Between the time Web site information is gathered and published, some sites may have closed. Also, the transcription of URLs can result in typographical errors. The publisher would appreciate notification where these occur so that they may be corrected in subsequent editions.

Library of Congress Cataloging-in-Publication Data

Winning ways of coaching writing : a practical guide for teaching writing, grades 6–12 / edited by Mary L. Warner ; foreword by Lelia Christenbury.
    p. cm.
    Includes bibliographical references and index.
    ISBN 0-205-30851-1
    1. English language—Composition and exercises—Study and teaching (Middle school)
  2. English language—Composition and exercises—Study and teaching (Secondary)   I. Warner, Mary L.

LB1631 .W55 2001
808'.042'0712—dc21

                                           00-030608

Printed in the United States of America

10 9 8 7 6 5 4 3 2 1   05 04 03 02 01 00

CONTENTS

13 **Learning to Diagnose and Prescribe for Success in Student Writing   211**
Stewart Bellman

PREFACE

As recently as the late 1980s when I began teaching English methods courses, there were no courses devoted solely to the teaching of writing in middle and high schools. By contrast, the number of courses and textbooks available for teaching college composition continued to multiply. In the history of secondary English, writing or composition has received slow recognition because of so much segmentation into topics such as grammar, spelling, and mechanics. The study of literature was frequently privileged. With the current focus on writing as a process and as integral to reading, response, and thinking, however, the need has grown for pre-service English teachers to be prepared to be writing teachers.

Winning Ways of Coaching Writing is by teachers *for* teachers. In many ways it replicates the underlying philosophy of the National Writing Projects, which relies on teachers teaching teachers. It is also addressed to teachers in the field who have had very little direction in the teaching of writing, and who now struggle even more as they face a barrage of issues, not the least of which is state-mandated writing tests. The authors of this book have a composite of more than 300 years of teaching, and this experience is the greatest gift they offer: years of coaching student writing and years of learning with and from student writers. Most of the authors, however, unlike you, the readers and users of this book, never had a formal course in the teaching of writing for middle- and high-school-aged students. Most learned by doing in the challenging environment of experience on the job.

The aim, then, of this text is to meet a need for teachers of writing to talk with new teachers of writing or to other colleagues out in the field who are struggling with real writing issues: How to integrate grammar? How to help ESL students? How to encourage student writers to find and use their own voices? How to respond to writing? How to motivate those who say they hate writing? How to respond to the many publics criticizing English and language arts teachers for the many problems in education that go far beyond spelling errors? The issues of coaching writing are many, and each is complex. Our purpose is to share practical teaching strategies, building on what many of you already know about writing as a process and about the integration of reading, writing, thinking, and literacy skills.

The design of *Winning Ways of Coaching Writing* presents a range of topics connected with writing in grades 6–12, although these topics do not necessarily follow sequentially through the writing process. The logic behind the book's arrangement, however, is the presentation of topics that arise for teachers and writers throughout the writing process.

Stephen Tchudi, widely recognized for his expertise in the field of English and language arts, launches the book with a discussion of writing's place in the humanities. Tchudi grounds the philosophical in English and language arts (as he grounds all his writing) in numerous practical writing activities.

In Chapter 2, Mary Warner focuses on thesis statements and definitions to help students learn to create and control this essential tool for beginning writers. Kathyrn Klintworth's chapter on audience and voice follows. Klintworth discusses ways to bring a sense of audience and a realization of personal voice to the writing done by middle and high school students, recognizing that the leap to academic writing done in postsecondary contexts can more likely be enriched by the honest and real voices our writing students have developed.

Mark Honegger presents two chapters on ongoing issues that are consistently controversial. In Chapter 4, Honegger examines two approaches to teaching grammar; he offers two perspectives, hoping that readers will weigh the advantages and disadvantages of each in order to select the one that fits their teaching context and their students. In Chapter 6, Honegger looks at the ESL (English as a second language) and dialect-speaking students, covering two important areas with sensitivity and knowledge gained through experience with ESL students and through his studies in linguistics.

No school can successfully move into the new millennium without more understanding of the place of technology in learning. In Chapter 5, Nancy Zuercher expertly provides a practical guide for the integration of technology and writing. Zuercher's suggestions are devoted to stable principles, although textbooks can hardly keep pace with the rapid changes in technology.

In Chapter 7, Ellen Shannon examines a growing need—the ability to address writers who have attention deficit disorder (ADD) or attention-deficit/hyperactivity disorder (ADHD). Shannon's application of the Theme Park of the Writer's Mind provides insights into a variety of teaching strategies to reach those student writers with hidden disabilities.

Dan Madigan and Deborah Alvarez also address a special population of student writers present in most schools who confound teachers with all levels of experience: the nontraditional ninth grader. The point Madigan and Alvarez emphasize is not to stereotype a group of learners as noncollege bound; rather, they examine the challenge of student writers who do not have the motivation to continue in academic settings. The nontraditional ninth grader, can anticipate at least 3 years more of writing in school settings. Thus, these authors provide strategies to meet the needs of this unique group of student writers.

Carla Verderame explores the reading and writing transaction; her discussion in Chapter 9 will be most applicable to teachers working with college-bound student populations. The appendix following Chapter 9 provides guidelines for any group of students writing about literature.

In recent years many contexts for writing about literature have been in the state-mandated test arena. Chapter 10, then, follows Chapter 9's discussion of writing about literature. In Chapter 10, Mary Warner integrates ideas from a range of practitioners and emphasizes the need for student writers to find connections with literature that will encourage them to write. This chapter also acknowledges the inherent drawbacks of mandated testing while encouraging cooperation among English and language arts teachers in grades K–16.

No text related to the teaching of writing can avoid the topic of responding to writing and the often unpleasant issue of grading. Knowing that most teachers cannot have the utopia they desire of abolishing grades altogether, Stephen Tchudi guides them through a range of options.

Chapter 12 is the most unusual of this text; it is addressed to *teachers* of writing. Teresa Berndt and Donna Fisher, both in-the-field teachers of English and language arts, bring both credibility and tested practice to bear as they write about the collegial journal, which can be used first, and often most successfully, by the student teacher and mentor. Both writers strongly believe that their journal writing gives them credibility with their students; as teachers who are "right there, right now," their voices powerfully convey their passion and urgency to other coaches of writing.

Stewart Bellman's chapter closes the book with real-life examples and seasoned wisdom about coaching writing successfully. A major contribution of this chapter is the student writing samples for a series of writing assignments. Through these, Bellman again offers writing teachers practical strategies for coaching writing.

In my teaching of courses such as "Composition for the English Teacher" and "Fundamentals of Teaching Writing," I have met many future writing coaches. And in more than 10 years of supervision in public schools, I have met many practicing coaches of writing. These two groups are the audience I have focused on and have encouraged all the book's writers to consider. I have also had the students in "Fundamentals of Teaching Writing," spring 1999, serve as responders and reactors to many of these chapters. These students, like many of you using this text, wanted to see practical pedagogies, and they have helped each of the authors to produce a book that can make you a successful coach of writing.

Acknowledgments

I owe deep gratitude to a special group of preservice English teachers. These are the Western Carolina University students of ENGL 414: "Fundamentals of Teaching Composition," spring 1999, who read and responded to many of the chapters and provided the authors with realistic and valuable feedback. Tyler Faetz and other former students have also read and responded to chapters, helping my fellow writers and me to make the book practical in their teaching contexts.

Jan Williamson of the North Carolina Department of Public Instruction, Dee Grantham of Smoky Mountain High School in Sylva, North Carolina, and Mike Lodico and his English department colleagues from Tuscola High School, Waynesville, North Carolina, are among the practitioners who have contributed their perspectives on the complexities of state-mandated writing assessments.

I am also grateful to the authors who have been faithful to deadlines, who have been willing to revise and improve their texts, and, above all, who have the dedication to teaching English and language arts and are truly coaches of writing. My colleague, Mark Honegger, deserves special recognition since he has been the on-site author on whom I've depended for advice and help in reviewing editorial components. Each of the book's authors has also worked with students and colleagues in the work of coaching writing; I acknowledge their contributions as well.

Gratitude goes to Leila Christenbury, Virginia Commonwealth University, for taking the time to review the book and write the foreword.

Keith Stiles, a graduate student at Western Carolina University, and my former English education student, performed a valuable service in preparing the index. He also provided careful editing and technical assistance.

I also acknowledge the support of the other members of the English department at Western Carolina University, especially the administrative assistant, Nancy DeSain. Michael Dougherty of Western Carolina's College of Education and Allied Professions offered direction for creating this edited volume; he also provided constant support as my faculty mentor.

I express gratitude as well to my family members, to friends, and to the School Sisters of Notre Dame, especially of the Mankato, Minnesota Province, for their moral support and prayer.

Finally, I appreciate the efforts of Bridget Keane, editorial assistant at Allyn & Bacon, Virginia Lanigan of Allyn & Bacon, who contracted the project, and the current Allyn & Bacon editor, Arnis Burvikovs, for their guidance through this project. Reviewers Marylyn E. Calabrese, St. Joseph's University, Christian Knoeller, University of Wisconsin at Eau Claire, Karl Matz, Minnesota State University, and Karen Stinson, Upper Iowa University, also provided valuable insights for the text.

CONTRIBUTORS

Deborah Alvarez, coauthor of Chapter 8, was born and raised in the Midwest. She has taught English and language arts in secondary schools for 15 years, from rural Kansas to city schools in Colorado and Wisconsin. Deborah graduated from the University of Wisconsin, Madison, with a Ph.D. in Composition Studies; her field of research is in the writing strategies of adolescents. She is presently an assistant professor in the Department of English at Bowling Green State University, Bowling Green, Ohio, where she teaches a variety of rhetoric and composition courses, as well as the English Secondary Language Arts methods course for the College of Education.

Stewart Bellman, author of Chapter 13, is a cofounder of the Dakota Writing Project. He practices the principles of the National Writing Project; as a teacher of written composition, he writes with and for his students. Stewart has been an active partner with elementary and secondary teachers in advancing the writing, reading, and thinking skills of students. Subscribing to the belief that the best teachers of teachers are other teachers, he has recruited successful practicing teachers to participate as consultants and guest instructors in his college English Methods and Composition for the English Teacher courses.

Stewart served as president of the South Dakota Council of Teachers of English. Prior to his retirement in 1996 from college teaching, Stewart directed the Bush Foundation, supporting faculty development programs at Black Hills State University and the South Dakota School of Mines and Technology. He was an active member of the Collaboration for the Advancement of College Teaching and Learning, a five-state consortium of colleges and universities headquartered in St. Paul, Minnesota, and served as board chair in 1995–1996.

Teresa Berndt, coauthor of Chapter 12, has taught eighth grade language arts at the Mitchell Middle School, Mitchell, South Dakota, since 1994. Besides teaching language arts, she has been the yearbook advisor and National Junior Honor Society advisor and has created a new curriculum utilizing creative dramatics in the classroom. She completed an externship with the Friends of the Middle Border Museum, which provided a connection to regional authors and literature for her classroom.

In 1998, she was nominated for *Who's Who Among American Teachers;* she was also a participant in the Dakota Writing Project. Teresa serves as a committee member for the South Dakota Teacher Forum and has represented her district at the State Writing Assessment Conference. Teresa has presented papers at both the South Dakota Teacher Forum and the South Dakota Council of Teachers of English conferences. Beyond the classroom, Teresa has been both a counselor and dean for summer church camps.

Teresa holds a B.A. degree from Dakota Wesleyan University with majors in English and journalism; she graduated summa cum laude and was named Outstanding Secondary Student Teacher. Teresa's continuing studies have focused on writing, reading strategies, and technology.

Donna Fisher, coauthor of Chapter 12, has spent 11 years as a classroom teacher of English and journalism, plus 13 years in school library media. Since 1988, she has taught English and journalism at Mitchell High School, Mitchell, South Dakota; Donna is currently teaching Junior English, Advanced Placement English, and literature electives. She has edited newsletters and newspapers for more than 15 years, currently serving as chief communications officer and editor-in-chief of *Dakota Connections,* the official news organ of the United Methodist Church of the Dakotas. With another teacher, Donna has developed the first literary map of South Dakota and an accompanying web site as part of a cooperative project for the South Dakota Humanities Council and the South Dakota Council of Teachers of English.

Donna has been named 1999 Carl F. Sprenger Outstanding Educator by the Mitchell Rotary Club and Rotary Scholars; South Dakota Language Arts Teacher of the Year—1996; has been a member of U.S. West Teachers and Technology Team—1997–1998; was a member of the English Standards Writing Committee and a participant in the South Dakota Initiative for Challenging Standards; served as chairperson of the South Dakota Teacher Forum in 1994, 1995, and 1997; represented South Dakota Forum at the Goals 2000 Teacher Forum in Washington, D.C., in 1993; represented South Dakota at the White House Conference on Libraries and Information Services in July 1990; and was a Fellow in the Council for Basic Education/National Endowment for the Humanities Summer Program in 1993.

Donna earned a B.A. degree from Drew University with majors in English and sociology. Her graduate studies have focused on library media, journalism, computers, and American literature. She earned an M.Ed. from South Dakota State University in 1987. Continuing graduate studies have focused on writing and literature, as well as technology classroom integration.

Mark Honegger, author of Chapters 4 and 6, is an assistant professor in the Department of English at Western Carolina University; Mark teaches courses in linguistics and English as a Second Language. He holds a Ph.D. in linguistics from the University of Illinois, Urbana–Champaign. Mark taught for 3 years in Malaysia at Stamford College and Universiti Kebansaan Malaysia. His research interests include the application of current syntactic theories to the teaching of grammar and ESL.

Kathryn Klintworth, author of Chapter 3, has been a teacher of English for almost 25 years. She taught elementary, junior high, high school, and college in Hawaii, Washington, Idaho, California, and Michigan. Kathy holds a Doctor of Arts degree in English Language and Literature from the University of Michigan, Ann Arbor. She is presently an associate professor of English at Concordia College in Ann

Arbor, Michigan, where she teaches first-year composition and courses for secondary education students on how to approach reading and writing in their majors and minors. Kathy also is the director of the Academic Resource Center, which includes a Writing Center. She has been a presenter at National Council of Teachers of English conventions and at the Conference on College Composition and Communications conventions.

Dan Madigan, coauthor of Chapter 8, taught high school English for 14 years before receiving his doctorate in English Language and Literature from the University of Michigan, Ann Arbor. Since 1990, Dan has been a faculty member in English at Bowling Green State University. His areas of research include literacy issues and the integration of technology into teaching and learning. Dan has been the Director of the Center for Teaching, Learning, and Technology at Bowling Green State University since 1996.

Ellen Shannon, author of Chapter 7, earned an M.A. and a B.A. in American Studies/Women's Studies from Case Western Reserve University. Ellen also has a Certificate in Technical Communication and Writing from the New York Institute of Technology and an Associate's Degree from Sinclair Community College. She has been employed in the field of Residence Education at the University of Michigan, Ann Arbor, where she has taught writing and intergroup relations; at the State University of New York at Stony Brook; and at the State University of New York at Farmingdale. Her work includes course design in writing across the curriculum and for student athletes in the writing classroom. Ellen has actively tried to raise awareness of hidden disabilities and learning disabilities. She was diagnosed with attention-deficit disorder and an auditory deficit as an adult.

Stephen Tchudi, author of Chapters 1 and 11, is professor of English and chair of the English Department at the University of Nevada, Reno, where he teaches and writes in the composition and rhetoric program. He received his B.A. in chemistry from Hamilton College, Clinton, New York, before shifting gears and earning his M.A.T.E. and Ph.D. in English Education from Northwestern University. Stephen taught for 21 years at Michigan State University, where he received the Distinguished Faculty Award in 1990.

As a member since 1990 of the English Department at the University of Nevada, Reno (UNR), his primary responsibility has been developing graduate programs in composition and rhetoric. He is also codirector of "Reading and Writing the West," a summer institute for teachers and is the coordinator of UNR's University Seminar program, which offers interdisciplinary experiences for first-year students. He recently directed a new interdisciplinary program for UNR in "Reading and Writing about London." He has also developed internship programs that place undergraduate and graduate tutors at Washoe High School, Reno's alternative high school. In 1997, he received the Mousel–Felter Award for Research and Creative Activity from the UNR College of Arts and Science. In 1998, he was named a foundation professor for long-term research efforts.

Stephen is the author of some 40 books for the general public, for teachers, and for young adult readers. Among his recently published books are *The English Language: An Owner's Manual* with Lee Thomas (Allyn & Bacon, 1999); *The Interdisciplinary Teachers' Handbook* with Stephen Lafer (Heinemann/Boynton Cook, 1996); *The New Literacy* with Paul Morris (Jossey Bass, 1996), and *Community in the American West* (Halcyon, 1999).

He especially enjoys writing for readers ages 8 through 15, and his young adult books include two novels: *The Burg-O-Rama Man* (New York: Delacorte, 1984) and *The Green Machine and the Frog Crusade* (Delacorte, 1986). The latter has also been published in France as *La Croisade des Grenouilles* (Castor Poche, 1998). His most recent nonfiction book for young readers is *Lock and Key: The Secrets of Locking Things Up, In and Out* (Scribner's, 1993). A new young adult novel, *The Valedictorian* was published in 1999 by Royal Fireworks Press.

Stephen is a past president of the National Council of Teachers of English, as well as past president of the Michigan and Nevada Councils of Teachers of English. He was an editor of *The English Journal*.

Carla L. Verderame, author of Chapter 9, received her Ph.D. from the Joint Program in English and Education at the University of Michigan, Ann Arbor, in 1998. Before returning to graduate school, Carla taught English and language arts at the secondary level. She currently teaches English and English Education courses at West Chester University of Pennsylvania. In addition to her teaching responsibilities at West Chester, Carla supervises prospective teachers of secondary English in their student teaching assignments. She has presented numerous papers to national and international audiences; her research interests include teacher education, writing and literature pedagogy, Southern women writers, and Native American literature.

Mary L. Warner, editor of this textbook and author of Chapters 2 and 10, holds a Doctor of Arts degree in English Language and Literature from the University of Michigan, Ann Arbor. Mary taught English in junior high and high school in Iowa and North Dakota for 9 years and has taught for 15 years on the postsecondary level at Creighton University, Omaha; Mount Mary College, Milwaukee; the University of Michigan, Ann Arbor; and Black Hills State University in Spearfish, South Dakota. She is currently an assistant professor of English at Western Carolina University, where she also serves as director of the English Education Program. Mary teaches courses in Methods of Teaching English, Fundamentals of Composition, Grammar for Writing, the Bible as Literature, and composition and literature liberal studies courses. She also supervises interns and student teachers in secondary English education.

Mary has published articles in *Christianity and Literature* and in *The ALAN Review*. She has presented extensively at the National Council of Teachers of English (NCTE), the Conference on College Composition and Communication (CCCC), the ALAN Workshop of NCTE, and the South Dakota and North Carolina Council of Teachers of English. Her research interests include Literature as a Site of the Sacred, with particular focus on Jessica Powers and Graham Greene; Young Adult Literature; and English education.

Mary is a member of the School Sisters of Notre Dame, an international congregation of women religious dedicated primarily to the education of women and youth.

Nancy Zuercher, author of Chapter 5, works with middle and high school teachers in the Dakota Writing Project, which she has directed for 10 years, and in the South Dakota Council of Teachers of English. An honors graduate of Ohio Wesleyan University, she earned her M.A. in American Studies at the University of Wyoming, and her Ed.D. from the University of South Dakota. As an English professor at the University of South Dakota, she teaches advanced composition in a networked Macintosh classroom, English methods, and composition theory. She is a past president of the South Dakota Council of Teachers of English and a scholar-discussant for the South Dakota Humanities Council. Her best ideas for writing occur during her early morning runs.

FOREWORD

The metaphor of *coaching* writing, not teaching, is a useful one that may endure well into this new century. The image of *coaching* acknowledges that the major actor in the business of writing is the writer and that this person's activity is the appropriate focus. Certainly, writing is a lonely act that is never really performed alone; but it lends itself more to encouragement and aid than to direct instruction. Explicitly *teaching* writing is something that cannot be efficiently done; writing is a skill acquired messily and idiosyncratically and must be practiced, shaped, formed by the individual writer, not transmitted wholesale by the teacher.

What is it about writing that necessitates a book such as *Winning Ways of Coaching Writing*? What is it about writing that makes it difficult?

One reason that writing is difficult is that it is not as immediately natural as its communicative twin speaking, and teachers who try to encourage their students by telling them that the two activities are indistinguishable are not telling the truth. Little in the average piece of writing can match the immediacy of even highly pedestrian speech. Oral discourse uses inflection, gesture, volume, rhythm, pronunciation, and even facial expression, all of which help speakers to convey and their listeners to understand a message. Although humans of almost any age can make their complex needs quickly understood orally through vocalization and attendant body gestures, it takes years of practice before an individual's writing can begin to match the communicative and emotional effectiveness of speech. Confronted with the dreaded blank and silent page, most students understand this fact and, unlike their optimistic but not entirely truthful teachers, rarely confuse their spontaneous, self-reinforcing talk with their often laborious writing.

Another reason that writing is difficult is that many teachers and students don't write frequently or even a whole lot. Most of us talk every day, to different audiences, for different purposes, and in different forms of discourse. Writing, however, is an activity reserved for isolated segments in the classroom, for homework, or for semester examinations, and, if we are adults who yearn to write the great American novel, for that ever elusive moment when we will have the "time to write." Most students beyond elementary school don't write more than 30 minutes in any given week, and few write outside school tasks. Most adults, including we, their teachers, write much less than that. It's difficult to improve at something that you don't do frequently or for long periods of time or, truth be told, for any reason other than a grade or an assignment.

By addressing these drawbacks and talking about them with our students, we can encourage them and help them improve their writing. But if we are smart about coaching our students in their writing, we also need to remind them of writing's special appeal.

The special appeal of writing is centered in the self, one of the most powerful motivators we possess. As American essayist Joan Didion reminds us in a piece about her writing ("Why I Write"), it is the central vowel sound of her title, *I*, that is at the center of writing. When we write, we take a stand, paint a picture, insist on an interpretation, tell a story as *we* know or recollect it. We tell our readers this is what *I* think; this is what happened to *me*; this is *my* story, *my* example; or *I* feel this way. We are thus egocentric in a way that speech can hardly afford to be, and accordingly we have a unique investment in making what we write clear and powerful.

Didion tells us, "In many ways, writing is the act of saying *I*, of imposing one-self upon other people, of saying *listen to me, see it my way, change your mind*." Using the ego, this *I*, can help students come to care about their writing in a way that may surprise us.

Perhaps more than speech, writing is the medium to tell others what we think, why we believe, how something affects us. It is an accepted form in which we are allowed, even encouraged, to be energetic and in which our persuasive words, our compelling ideas carry a formality and permanence that no sponta-neous speech can equal. Once this connection is established, once we give students writing topics and writing environments that help them use their egocentricity, we encourage students to produce more effective writing.

As the title of this book emphasizes, there are indeed *winning* ways of coach-ing writing. They embrace, as the contributors detail, a wide variety of strategies and approaches, including the use of interdisciplinary writing, writing to learn, and multigenre writing, and can involve journals, creative dramatics, and the read-ing and example of literature. To keep students writing, the authors suggest assess-ment, not grading, putting correctness in perspective, and, as a crucial modeling activity, teachers writing with students. Attention to audience and voice and to the needs of the individual is also paramount, as well as the warning that students must know that someone outside the grade giver (that is, the teacher) will read their writing. These strategies can all help students write effectively and with enjoyment, and these strategies are clearly delineated by the authors.

The act of writing can be one of the most satisfying of human endeavors. Making time in our classrooms for frequent practice, helping students to under-stand the connection between their speech and writing, and giving them the opportunity to tell *their* stories and take *their* stands are all winning ways of coach-ing writing. You will find many others in the pages of this book.

Leila Christenbury
Virginia Commonwealth University

1 The Philosopher's Stone: Writing and the Humanities

STEPHEN TCHUDI

This introductory chapter blends the philosophical view of writing with practical application; it describes writing as "*the* quintessential language art" and the essential discipline of the humanities. In his discussion of writing, Stephen Tchudi uses a powerful metaphor: the philosopher's stone. That is, writing will turn "base learning into gold." Following his brief introduction, which clearly defines such terms as *grammar, rhetoric,* and *logic* and discusses their roots in the learning process, Tchudi discusses four categories of writing in the humanities: *experiential, interdisciplinary, constructivist,* and *multimedia and multigenre*. Although these four terms are abstractions, he grounds each in a series of practical writing activities applicable to any writing classroom.

Tchudi describes seven areas in which writing becomes experiential:

- Writing for personal growth
- Writing to learn
- Writing to make a difference
- Creative writing in action
- Writing in and about a second language
- Writing in the applied arts
- Writing for evaluation and self-assessment

Finally, Tchudi provides a model for structuring interdisciplinary humanities units that fully integrates writing, or *composing*, a term that more aptly describes all the forms of making-things-in-language. This chapter is indeed a writing coach's guide to developing the philosopher's stone of the human mind, with its extraordinary power to transform experience into language. It will assist English language arts teachers, who have the joy and opportunity to be writing's defenders and promoters, to prepare the literate and humane people that our world desperately needs.

The Philosopher's Stone

I would like to open *Winning Ways of Coaching Writing* with a brief note on the place of writing in the history of education; for even as we think about concrete ways of working with children in grades 6–12, it's important to recognize that writing is important beyond the language arts classroom and schoolhouse, that it is important for both life and education.

Medieval education divided the curriculum into two major parts: the *trivium* and the *quadrivium.* The basic part, the trivium, consisted of three language-related components: *grammar, rhetoric,* and *logic.* The *quadrivium* continued education in the fields of astronomy, arithmetic, music, and geometry—the arts and sciences, for practical purposes. Thus we see that language was the base of the curriculum: the keystone that supported other subjects and the key to unlocking other learning.

Medieval education in language was different from the best practices of language education today. The medieval method of study was primarily by rote and repetition, a method that has been largely discredited in our time. But language study continues to be at the heart of education today, and, in my judgment, it deserves to be restored to its former place of honor and primacy.

Grammar looms large and frightening in the minds of many people, but at its best, grammar is not just parts of speech and the rules for talking properly. As a descriptive science, grammar concentrates on the system of language: how it works, how it signals meaning, how it puts words and ideas together, and how it reveals the intricacy and sophistication of human thinking and expression.

Rhetoric, unfortunately, has been degraded in the popular mind to represent the puffery of politicians and salespeople. But rhetoric has long held the potential to examine how language functions in human affairs and to help people learn to use their words more aptly.

Logic (from the Greek *logos,* or *word*) is the essence of critical thinking and is inexorably bound up with language. Human thought depends on language for its expression. Thus both our internal monologues and external speech and writing are wrapped in a package of grammar, rhetoric, and logic.

Writing, the topic of this book, is the modern-day manifestation of the classical *trivium.* Contemporary writing theory and practice bring together grammar, rhetoric, and logic in lively combinations. Writing is vibrant; it is the way we do business in words. In education today, writing is *the* quintessential language art, the essential discipline of the humanities. By this bold assertion, I mean that the critical and creative use of language is probably the most important subject and skill that students will ever master.

However, in making this generalization, I do not mean writing in the traditional sense of mere spelling and grammar or the writing of five-paragraph essays or job applications, important as these may be in context. At its best, writing (or composing) is a way of seeing and responding to our universe. It's how we make sense of what's going on around us: We compose our ideas and our universe, and we do so in *language.* This is why writing is found in the humanities, rather than in, say, the business department. Writing teachers must show that writing is a liberal art as well as a practical skill, a creative act, not simply the skill of record keeping.

In the schoolhouse, this means that writing should *infuse* the curriculum, making English language arts the natural cauldron for a rich amalgam of fields and disciplines. To develop my title metaphor (a medieval example made modern), I believe that writing is the philosopher's stone in the curriculum, turning base learning into gold. Through writing, students can transform their understanding of textbooks into synthesized learning; they can compose perceptions of their own experience as personal essays or poems; they can write their lives into drama and their schooling into true *education.*

To show how writing can effect these kinds of dramatic changes in learning, I want to suggest that writing in the humanities is *experiential, interdisciplinary, constructivist,* and *multimedia* and *multigenre.* I'll explore each of these abstract concepts briefly and suggest practical ways to use these characteristics of writing to transform student learning into gold.

1. *Writing is experiential.* Perhaps the major way in which contemporary composition teachers differ from their predecessors is in their view that language skill is acquired through *experience with language,* rather than through *learning of the forms of language.* Whereas in earlier historical periods students might have memorized long lists of figures of speech or the structures of speeches and essays, or might have diagrammed sentences as a way of understanding the architecture of grammar, research in language learning over the past several decades has identified the *naturalistic* nature of language learning. People immersed in language learn that language through imitation and synthesis.

For example, a baby learns a language not through direct parental instruction in grammar, but by listening to others, figuring out how language works, and testing it out in new circumstances. Babies learn far more about language than even a master linguist could teach them, and they master the essentials of grammar by age 3 or 4. Infant language is a miracle akin to turning base metal into gold.

Learning processes are much the same for the rhetorical and logical structure of language: From hearing and telling stories we pick up and refine the idea of narrative; from engaging in dialogue and dialectic we pick up the conventional forms of discussion and debate; from reading and writing journals and essays we come to understand how the personal essay is composed. While the formal teaching of structures may be necessary in the schools, by and large contemporary composition theorists urge us toward immersing our students in language. To learn to use words well, students should use them in situations in which communication matters. To learn to use language better, our students mainly have to use it *more.*

In some respects, this experiential view of pedagogy simplifies the task of the teacher because we no longer have to teach figures of speech or sentence forms or assume that we must lecture on narrative structure or the features of imaginative nonfiction. On the other hand, our task becomes more complicated in a naturalistic learning model because our task becomes one of helping youngsters to truly engage with ideas and language.

Fortunately, the discovery that one learns to write by writing allows us to understand that writing is *experiential* in another way: Writing grows from and as a result of people's *experience* with the world. If we want our students to write, we don't really have to tell them *what* to write; we simply have to tap their experiences and show them ways to get experiences on paper. The best way to do that, to mine the gold of experience, is to recognize that . . .

2. *Writing is interdisciplinary.* The three- and four-part structures of trivium and quadrivium reveal the traditional dominance of a discipline-centered model in education, which continues to this day in our departmental and subject organizations. In medieval teaching the disciplines did not cross lines: The student learned grammar and then moved on to rhetoric; music did not mix with arithmetic, nor geometry with astronomy. In today's schools the "big four" disciplines generally include English and language arts, science, mathematics, and social studies. Too often they are isolated from one another, with art, music, and the applied arts as fringe disciplines that are even further isolated.

Although the structuring of disciplines functions successfully for scholars, educators have increasingly come to question whether organizing instruction for novices is best done from a disciplinary perspective. Does it make sense to instruct students in the basics of history while ignoring the literature of a period? Should biology really be introduced independently of the appropriate concepts from physics, math, or chemistry? Is it logical to isolate geometry from trigonometry and the calculus from both?

In today's schools, educators are recognizing the value of the *integrated* curriculum, where knowledge and inquiry flow to, from, and around the topics at hand, rather than being dictated by disciplinary boundaries. Writing is a natural partner in the integrated, interdisciplinary curriculum, for when students are on the track of an idea, the written word can carry them off in many directions, into multiple disciplines. In their language arts class, students can write about science and society, about global issues past and present, about numbers, about words and ideas, about sports, hobbies, computers, boyfriends and girlfriends, parents, mentors, idols, dreams, and visions—all these comfortably erasing disciplinary boundaries.

Since English and language arts teachers are regularly blamed for what goes wrong in education (a single misspelled word in print can generate a storm of criticism in the press), we might as well claim the *entire world* for our domain. If a topic can be expressed in words, it's *ours*—a legitimate topic for writing. No longer must English teachers concentrate solely on the canon of literature, the niceties of grammar, and the five-paragraph theme. Our students can read and write about any topic under the sun (and even those beyond). In other words, any subject, discipline, or field is fair game for the writing program, for . . .

3. *Writing is constructivist.* Constructivism is educational/socio-jargon for "meaning making," which is pedagogical–linguistic jargon for the notion that people create their vision of the world through words. Constructivism is an increasingly accepted theory of education; it recognizes that people generate interpretations of experience, rather than passively accepting whatever comes along. Reading involves reader response, not just passive comprehension or acceptance of an author's supposedly intended meaning. Writing is an inherently constructivist, meaning-making activity.

A few forms of writing are concerned solely with recording data: grocery lists, legal descriptions, or the fine print in an advertisement or lease. But most writing involves an active writerly mind that collects data and ideas and meditates on their significance, which leads to a newly forged set of meanings. Although some people would limit the term *creative* to the writing of poetry, fiction, and drama, teachers increasingly recognize that any good piece of writing is creative, whether a memo or essay, a poem or ultimatum, a play or call-to-arms. School assignments that merely call for students to regurgitate facts and figures are rapidly disappearing; the best activities allow plenty of room for students to synthesize ideas and to generate new meanings for themselves and their audiences. In turn, writers must seek out different ways to structure and send their constructivist messages, for . . .

4. *Writing is multimedia and multigenre.* Writing is not limited to pencil and paper; it may encompass sending messages in a variety of forms and media. We "write" photographs, paintings, and drawings; we "compose" in dance, video, and web site. In the traditional writing class, students wrote things called variously *themes, compositions,* or *papers.* But, curiously, these forms are not often found in the real world. We write editorials, not papers; we draft letters, not compositions; we create poems or stories or essays, not themes. In addition, whereas themes and compositions were often addressed to a single person—the theme reader or composition grader (better known as the teacher), contemporary composition theory calls for the use of real-world genres and media. Our students should write for audiences other than the teacher: An editorial reaches the general public; a drama deserves an audience; videos are shown on television and photographs are hung in a gallery so that people can read and respond.

Writing and the Humanities: Implications and Activities for the Classroom

It should be clear from the preceding four concepts why writing can be a curricular philosopher's stone, transforming ideas and people. Without going into the fine details of teaching methodology, I now want to offer a range of teaching ideas to demonstrate just a small portion of the spectrum in which writing can be used in the liberal arts and humanities. I've tried and tested most of these in my own classes, from fourth grade through graduate school. Other ideas I've unabashedly stolen, borrowed, or adapted from other teachers, K–college. These ideas will, of course, need to be adapted to individual classrooms; the intent is to describe the immense ballfield in which writing and the humanities can play. [To emphasize the need for teachers to generate their own approaches, I supply a brief self-test (see The Midterm Examination on page 9).]

Writing for Personal Growth

Professional writers often discuss ways in which writing allows them to discover and construct their own personalities. They acknowledge that most good writing comes from their personal experiences, which they turn into fiction, nonfiction, and poetry. As an aid to this evolution, students create the following:

■ Journals and diaries reflect day-to-day experiences and, especially, the response to experience. Most teachers whose students write journals allow the students to keep some aspect of these journals private, and they never correct grammar or spelling, since the journal is a personal document for exploration. Nevertheless, teachers are often surprised by the excellent quality of writing in journals, a by-product of the fact that in journals writers write from the heart.

■ Autobiographies are bits and pieces of lives reflected through writing, such as autobiographical poems or one-act plays based on humorous or serious moments in their lives.

■ Fiction about "somebody a lot like me" allows students to gain distance from their own experience and to live their lives through an imaginary other.

■ Letters may be personal and friendly, to classmates, friends, pen pals, parents, or significant adults, a task nicely augmented by e-mail, which has revived interest in the letter as an art form.

■ Personal essays and memoirs may be written on wishes, dreams, adventures, powerful experiences, moments to relive, moments to forget, heroes and heroines, and the like.

■ Responses to fiction are, again, stories about "somebody a lot like me" or stories about people very different from oneself who may live in distant lands and different cultures in the past, present, or future.

Writing to Learn

Composition theorists persuasively argue that writing is a way of helping people not only to recall what they learn, but also to *synthesize* what they know. When you write about something, you *learn* it. Students may participate in writing to learn with the following:

■ Active note taking, in which they not only write down "the facts," but may also question these facts—challenge them or puzzle over where ideas come from and why they are important.

■ Learning logs, in particular, the "split column" log, in which they record "the facts" in one column and their appraisal of these facts in the other.

■ Records of research and observation: how dogs learn, the arrival of spring, how people age.

■ Imaginary letters to people in a field or discipline: a letter to Plato, Descartes, Marie Curie, or Napoleon Bonaparte, or real letters with genuine inquiries to Henry Louis Gates, Jr., Stephen Jay Gould, or Barbara Tuchman.

■ Rewriting those dull study questions at the end of the chapter to reflect active learning, for example, designing "story problems" with a contemporary twist.

■ Role-played talk shows and discussions on topics from the textbook.

Writing to Make a Difference

A student recently reminded me that the pen really is mightier than the sword, because a person who can write can get things done in society. Your students may write the following:

- Letters to the editor or columns and articles for the school or local newspaper or other print media.
- Proposals for action or reform around the school.
- Letters to political leaders requesting explanation or advocating action.
- Journal entries about their plans and ambitions and the ways to achieve them.
- Soapbox oratory on current events, either scripted or *ex tempore.*
- Debates on crucial and emerging issues around school and town, and circling the planet.

Creative Writing in Action

Creative writing is important because it permits new avenues to explore important ideas in our time. Students may use the following:

- A poem designed to dramatize a cause or injustice or a short play on the same topic.
- Science fiction on a current issue or problem, such as population growth, media entertainment, or human values, projected one hundred or one thousand years into the future.

- Parody and satire in which almost anything is fair game for a laugh and critical analysis.
- Combinations of visual and verbal media, in particular, taking advantage of computer technology to develop visual–verbal slide shows, posters, photo displays, commentary on their own work, illustrated stories, and photo essays.
- A one-act play with alternative endings, perhaps with the "best" ending selected by the audience or improvised by actors and actresses.

In and About a Second Language

Americans are notorious for being monolingual, in part because it is so difficult in our country to find active uses for the foreign language studied. We learn the grammar, but we never practice and soon forget it. English and language arts teachers can form an alliance with language teachers to promote the following:

- Composing *for real* in a language that the student is studying in school, because writing anything in the target language teaches more than the usual schoolbook composition exercises.
- Keeping journals or diaries in the new language.
- Translating stories and poems from the second language into the native tongue (or from first language to second language), with license to do idiomatic translation, not just literal.
- Interviewing a non-native speaker of English to write about the grammar of that person's language. How does it work? How does it differ from English?
- Interviewing non-native speakers in the class to write about the coping strategies that second language students master to survive in school.
- Writing the model for a perfect or world language. How can we improve on English or any other natural language?
- Reading, researching, and then writing an understanding of another culture as gleaned through the language—not the usual recipes or holiday traditions from another land, but by looking at the kinds of literature produced in or by a language.

Writing in the Applied Arts

The old adage that you don't understand something until you write it is especially true when it comes to hands-on arts and crafts. Possible projects for students are the following:

- Writing a how-to manual for a hobby or skill or something that the student can do well: building a model, sewing a seam, teaching a bird to talk, rebuilding a hemihead automobile engine with dual turbo blower intakes.

- Learning how to do something new through reading; writing about one's reading; exploring a new skill in words and assessing successes and failures in one's learning.
- Designing architectural plans for a building and then writing a short story about the building.
- Drafting a home repair manual, a first aid manual, or a troubleshooting manual for an automobile.

Evaluation and Self-assessment

One of the most useful applications of writing in school and in life is as a source of reflection. Writing is a unique way to let people preserve their ideas for future inspection and rumination. In an age of accountability, students may write the following:

- Periodic assessments and self-assessments in any class. What are my goals in this class? What have I learned? What don't I know? How do I learn most successfully? How can the teacher help me more? How can I be a better learner?
- Reflections on collected work. In portfolio assessment, students collect what they regard as their best or most representative work and write about it — an annotated guide, an introduction, a description of what has been learned, or a discussion of what might come next.
- Assessments of career and educational possibilities, including research into possible futures, the educational requirements, and the possibilities for growth and development.
- Evaluations of society and the world around us. Where do I fit in as a member of humankind? What does society seem to be doing right? What wrong? How can this be changed? How can I make a difference?

The Midterm Examination

At this point, I've given you a sampler of the possibilities for writing in the humanities. Pause for a moment now and jot down some ideas centered on your present or future teaching. How might writing and your students interact with the following areas?

The mass media
Important school and community issues
Future-casting and prophesy
History
Current global issues and affairs
Ethics
Science and technology issues
Economic issues

You catch my drift: When we perceive of writing broadly as a way of learning, the possibilities for topics are infinite.

Structuring Interdisciplinary Humanities Units

Instruction in writing needs to be more than a potpourri of ideas of the sort I've offered in the previous section. How should we organize writing? How can we make writing something more than the occasional event or a Fridays-only ritual? At its (and our) best, composing should take place almost daily in our classes (not necessarily writing to be "graded" or marked). Writing will ebb and flow with the intellectual content of the class.

For me, the best (but not only way) to do this is through the thematic inter-disciplinary unit. By *thematic* I mean centering instruction on an issue, topic, idea, or problem, rather than on the components of a particular field or discipline. For example, it's conceivable that we could create an interesting, writing-centered unit around a single disciplinary topic, such as simple machines in physics, or Roman-tic poetry in English, or South America in social studies–history. But it is much more interesting to choose ideas as a starting point, such as "Moving Large Objects," an interdisciplinary unit that could include machines, but would allow us to explore the moving of minds as well as objects; "Visionaries and Dreamers," which might allow us to integrate the visions of pyramid builders, those movers of large objects, with those of the people of any generation who have had a romantic vision of the future; or "Global Issues and Concerns," which would not only let us discuss South America, but also push us into multiple cultures and, to stretch my point, permit us to integrate our concerns with the dreams, visions, and moving objects and minds as we talk about the common concerns of humanity worldwide.

The point I want to make is that through thematic or topical teaching we can range farther than we can if tied to disciplinary topics. In the English language arts class, because the universe of discourse is our playground, we can make a wide range of thematic topics work.

Topics can, in fact, have apparently humble or concrete beginnings. In *The Interdisciplinary Teacher's Handbook* (Tchudi and Lafer), my colleague Steve Lafer shows how one can take a topic as simple as the common *shoe* and spin it into a unit that bridges history, sociology, geography, technology, literature, and language (How many common expressions or sayings can you come up with based on "feet" and "shoes"?). We can also take grand themes, such as the traditional theme of the humanities, "What is humankind?", and come up with an equally broad range of possibilities.

My preferred approach is to thumb through the daily newspaper, looking for topics. The day of this writing I spent twenty minutes looking at the paper and came up with the following list, all of which I'd like to teach: *political ethics, air pollution, water supplies and clarity, adult crime, youth crime, gun control, educational aims and issues, renovation* (cities and people), *re-creation* (cities and people re-creating themselves), *land use, activities for teens, tobacco and drug control, radio and TV entertainment, libraries and reading, information access, sports* (including the subthemes of *competitiveness, violence, ethics, economics,* and *education*), and *music and the fine arts.* I was looking for topics because at the moment I'm engaged in an interdisciplinary writing project with area high school students that will illustrate the process of interdisciplinary unit planning.

My grand theme that unites all the topics above is called "Quality of Life." The *Sparks Tribune,* for which I write a Sunday column, has invited me to work with area high school students to produce a tabloid on this topic, timed to precede the city elections. Although this will not be a class in the usual sense, I am following a series of stages that are very similar to unit planning:

1. *Choosing a topic.* I've already suggested the range of thematic topics available. I chose "Quality of Life" for this one, first, because it has been an area of considerable community concern and, second, because it provides a kind of umbrella that allows young people to explore everything from the arts to sports.

2. *Creating subtopics and divisions.* I've already done this with my list of newspaper topics, but the first step in any thematic unit is to brainstorm with the students: What do *you* see as the important subdivisions and topics? Jotting down ideas on chalkboard, butcher paper, or overhead transparency, we will see how many related topics we can find, principally to make certain that every participating student has a point of entry into the topic. Thematic topics permit that breadth; sooner or later we will find an area or subtopic that will be of interest to just about any student. (Note the role of writing here: jotting, list making, using writing as a tool, but creating writing that does not have to be graded!)

3. *Framing questions.* What do we want to know about a topic or subtopic? Again we pull out pen and paper or go to the chalkboard to explore the subtopics. What do we already know? What do we want to find out? If we are exploring fine arts, our questions might range from the relatively concrete "What's going on in town?" to the more difficult and abstract "So who cares about 'fine arts' and why?" Reading specialists talk about "surveying prior knowledge," and this is an important part of the process—even as we raise questions about what's to be learned, we also pool group knowledge and experience.

If the *Sparks Tribune* project were based in a classroom, especially an English language arts classroom, I'd also prime the pump with some literature. Emily Dickinson's "I'm Nobody, Who Are You?" might trigger a discussion of anonymity in society. William Blake's poems of innocence and experience raise questions about the quality of life that are vital today. I might bring in some of Kurt Vonnegurt's short stories from *Welcome to the Monkey House* to dramatize quality of life issues, such as the real meaning of *equality* or the potential effects of overpopulation. (Note again the possibilities for writing here: response to literature, imaginary dialogues, responses to writers, and commentaries on themes and issues.)

Generally, in a thematic unit, I'll encourage enough reading to demonstrate the range and possibilities of the topic. Eventually, I want to get each student or small groups of students to the point where they will adopt a part of the topic for more detailed study and writing.

4. *Exploring resources.* For this newspaper project, with its focus on civic concerns, young people will find most of their resources close to home: either in the newspaper "morgue" or from knowledgeable people. We have put city officials on alert that they will be receiving phone calls from student reporters; we have advised leaders in various city agencies that young people will want to learn from them.

In a classroom version of the Quality of Life unit, we'd employ an even broader range of resources:

Reading all types of literature. I suggested earlier that I like to bring in literature to prime the pump; beyond that, an individualized reading program becomes important, with help from the teacher (and perhaps even sparked by a book cart prepared by the librarian). Reading leads to writing, everything from notes and responses to original compositions. This chapter is not the place to explore the details of such a reading-to-writing program, but the thematic, humanities, multicultural, interdisciplinary approach opens the doors to the broadest range of print resources, as well as . . .

Film, television, media, Internet, and the like. These are what I call *preserved* or *archival* resources; like books, they preserve and save what we value in society. Although as English–language arts teachers we may have a personal preference for paper-and-print, our students increasingly learn from multimedia sources. I think we need not only to draw on such materials, but should also rejoice that they are available. (Teaching at the university level, I'm interested to note that my TV/video/Internet students are writing at least as articulately as print-era students once did and are doing so with an astonishing range of information and resources, thanks to their multimedia backgrounds.)

People and institutions. People know an incredible amount about a wide range of topics, and I like to send my students to the human sources and resources, coupling the assignments with lessons on interviewing strategies. Writing that grows out of the interview includes workaday notes and transcripts, as well as summaries-cum-essays about what has been learned.

Individual research. In my classes I describe *research* as what you do to answer your own questions after the archival and human resources have been consulted. That is, after you've learned what there is to learn from others, you generate knowledge for yourself. In the English–language arts class, surveys and polls seem to be the most manageable kind of research; I include some discussion of questionnaire design and even the principles of statistical sampling and drawing of conclusions. But I've also had students do informal "kitchen science" experiments, as well as projects in behavioral science and conditioning. I want my students to move beyond the traditional school research paper and to develop confidence in writing up their results.

5. *Writing or composing.* Having sketched out the range of writing possibilities earlier, I'll simply mention that in a thematic, interdisciplinary unit the final outcomes or student projects can take a wide range and wealth of forms. In my experience, if students have done considerable writing-as-preparation in stages 1 through 4, they are often well positioned to make original, even literary contributions. For the *Sparks Tribune* project, the students will be limited to journalistic forms, mostly writing short feature articles with the possibilities and restraints implied by that. In a classroom unit, the forms of discourse are endless, and the same students might compose any of the following:

- A video showing quality-of-life trouble spots in our town.
- Poems of innocence and experience on quality-of-life issues.
- Proposals to various city officials about needed projects.
- A volunteer project for themselves. (Is volunteering a writing or composing project? I argue yes.)
- Historical studies of important town sites.
- Position papers on community development issues.
- Posters to display around town as a way of building community interest and commitment.

Beyond Teaching Units: Writing and Humanity

The pattern of thematic units that I've described here grows from my own teaching and experiences, using styles of instruction that I feel work successfully with my own students. The larger pattern, however, is one that I see reflected in all areas of human inquiry. Human beings are curious critters, and we're uneasy when we don't know the answers. Thus we reach out to learn more. As we find answers, even partial or tentative ones, we compose our ideas in language to test our experiences against those of other members of society. The outline of thematic teaching I've given here is an effort to duplicate that cycle, to make it come alive in the classroom:

People question.
People seek answers.
People compose their ideas for an audience.

The philosopher's stone in the humanities, then, is not a magical teaching method to be found "out there"; it's not a gizmo or machine or chemical process of permutation. The genuine philosopher's stone is the human mind, with its extraordinary power to transform experience into language. To repeat my earlier claim, writing is *the* quintessential language art, the essential discipline of the humanities. English language arts teachers have the joy and opportunity to be its defenders and promoters in a society that desperately needs the kinds of literate, humane people who, with the aid of writing, can emerge from our classrooms.

REFERENCES AND RESOURCES

Abbs, Peter. *English within the Arts.* London: Hodder and Stoughton, 1982.

Boomer, Garth. *Metaphors and Meanings.* Sydney: Australian Association for the Teaching of English, 1988.

Brooks, Jacqueline G., and Martin G. Brooks. *The Case for Constructivist Classrooms.* Alexandria, VA: Association for Supervision and Curriculum Development, 1993.

Burke, James. *The Day the Universe Changed.* Boston: Back Bay, 1995.

Christenbury, Leila. *Making the Journey: Being and Becoming a Teacher of English Language Arts.* Portsmouth, NH: Boynton/Cook, 1996.

Courts, Patrick L. *Multicultural Literacies.* New York: Peter Lang, 1997.

Gardner, John. *Multiple Intelligences.* New York: Basic Books, 1993.

Holbrook, David. *Children's Writing.* New York: Cambridge University Press, 1967.

Jackson, David. *Continuity in Secondary English.* London: Methuen, 1982.

Mayher, John. *Uncommon Sense.* Portsmouth, NH: Boynton/Cook, 1990.

Morris, Paul, and Stephen Tchudi. *The New Literacy.* San Francisco: Jossey Bass, 1996.

Purves, Alan. *How Porcupines Make Love II.* New York: Longman, 1990.

Tchudi, Stephen, and Stephen Lafer. *The Interdisciplinary Teacher's Handbook.* Portsmouth, NH: Boynton/Cook-Heinemann, 1996.

Weaver, Constance. *Understanding Whole Language.* Portsmouth, NH: Heinemann, 1990.

2

Thesis, Thinking, and Tying Together

MARY WARNER

Moving from the groundwork established by Stephen Tchudi about the place of writing in the humanities and, indeed, in all learning, Mary Warner begins a discussion of the specific components that beginning writers need to know. Being able to formulate a thesis statement and topic sentences for the paragraphs that follow are two such skills; both skills are desired by writing teachers. However, these skills are not often the most intuitive for student writers, particularly those in middle and high school who are novices in the world of academic writing. An opening vignette emphasizes one of the great challenges for writing coaches: We can't "open heads and rewire." In the face of writing that lacks coherence or logic and of young writers struggling to get their experiences into language, this chapter provides first a series of definitions of thesis. Students need to know about thesis statements as one of the important things in writing, one of the tools for success; the definitions become clear with the aid of Margaret Wise Brown's picture book, *The Important Book*.

Warner also provides a discussion of the qualities of strong thesis statements: they are *limited, precise*, and *unified*, they *take a stand*, and they *matter*. In a follow-up activity, *Thesis Recognition*, readers are able to test their comprehension by working with sample statements and determining their suitability as thesis statements. The *Classroom Consensus Activity* can be used in workshops with the entire class to fortify students' comprehension of thesis statements and to emphasize the concept that all the students form a community of writers.

The *Write-Around* is another way to coach student to student and can be used to help formulate stronger, clearer thesis statements and to focus paper topics. This activity can be modified to "computer hopping" if the technology is available. A sample interest survey to help with paper topic selection and formulation is another of the chapter's teaching ideas; again, these tasks frequently require good coaches with the skill to tap their student writers' expertise and interest.

The final section of the chapter focuses on thinking and tying together; a swimming analogy provides a coaching tool for analysis in peer reviews and workshopping.

When I began my first teaching at the postsecondary level at Creighton University, I was concerned that I would not know how to teach college freshmen in courses such as strategies of composition or expository writing. I had been teaching high school English for 9 years and should have realized that college freshmen were not significantly different from high school students. I should also have realized that the writing process for them is not significantly different, although the means by which we help students work through and with the process vary in depth and development. I had never taught *just* a writing course before, though; outside of the occasional quarter of research writing for twelfth graders or of basic composition for ninth graders, on the high school level, I had simply included a range of writing assignments in literature classes. I offer this disclaimer because I realized when I began teaching on the college level that most of what I knew about the teaching of writing came from teaching English and language arts in grades 7–12. The following scenario will demonstrate how important teaching thesis, thinking, and tying together is on so many levels of learning.

The day came when I was struggling with an essay by a Creighton freshman who assured me he was intending to be a doctor, a surgeon, in fact. The paper lacked coherence and organization. I could not imagine that this young man, who could not present his ideas clearly and logically, would one day be able to operate on a person and do the necessary reordering to heal the patient. Unfortunately, that young man's difficulties with logic and coherence in writing are not uncommon, as is the case for many students. That day I formulated a phrase I've used since in my teaching of writing and in the methods courses in which I teach future teachers of writing: "I can't open the head and rewire."

Precisely because we can't open the head and rewire, one of our greatest challenges as writers and coaches of writers is to facilitate organization and tying together. Also, as should be evident from this scenario, clarity of thinking is not only one of the main issues of school writing, but it is also of first importance to students preparing primarily for the workplace.

As I share ideas about thesis, thinking, and tying together, I emphasize that teachers of writing in grades 6–12 have critical foundation-building responsibilities. We are the ones who help students get their initial experiences in expository writing. So we begin at the beginning, helping students learn just what a thesis is, how to create thesis statements, and how to recognize thesis statements in the writing of their peers or in other texts.

Margaret Wise Brown's wonderful picture book, *The Important Book*, can provide an excellent introduction to thesis statement work. Brown presents a series of objects, each time beginning with the phrase "The important thing about . . . is. . . ." The brief description of each particular object, which also offers an excellent model of the details that show rather than merely tell, provides additional elements of importance. The culminating sentence reiterates the initial statement, with the words "But the important thing about . . . is. . . ." Since my introduction to *The Important Book* during the Dakota Writing Project, in the summer of 1995, when a third-grade teacher in the Writing Project shared her strategies for using this excellent picture book, I have used it with preservice teachers and college freshmen; it can be used effectively with students in grades 6–12 in teaching the primary purpose of a thesis: it is *the important thing* about. . . .

Once having used something like *The Important Book* as the lead in, the following provides information and methodology for teaching how to formulate a thesis statement.

Definitions of Thesis

- A thesis is a summary in a single sentence of what the writer wants to say about a subject.
- A thesis helps us define and express what we want to say.
- A thesis makes an assertion about the main idea that will be developed in our writing. (Some sixth or seventh graders may not know the word *assertion*. Be ready to offer the vocabulary that the reader can comprehend.)
- The thesis, in a sense, summarizes conclusions about the subject and our view of it.
- An effective thesis is derived from the material we work with, and it makes a compelling statement about the material.
- The thesis is the basic stand we take, the opinion we express, and the point we make about our limited subject.
- The thesis is the controlling idea, tying together and giving direction to all other separate elements in the paper.

These are definitions to offer; students take ownership of words or ideas when they can express them or teach them to others. Having presented these definitions, have students create their own definitions. You can compile these student definitions or in some way display them in your classroom so that, when you and your students are working with thesis in paper assignments or in preparing for writing tests, you will have visual reminders of just what the thesis is.

A second phase of defining thesis or thesis statement includes description of what a thesis is and is not. (Much of the information that follows is adapted from Joseph Alvarez's *Elements of Composition*.) An effective thesis is marked by five qualities: it is *limited*, it is *precise*, it is *unified*, it *takes a stand*, and it *matters*.

It is limited. This quality implies that the thesis narrows the subject down to manageable proportions, often focusing on a specific aspect of the subject. A thesis must limit the scope of an essay to what can be discussed in detail in the space available, the length of the paper as assigned. It will not be merely a title; instead, it will give the focus of the paper.

Broad	*Limited*
The Olympics	The Olympic games are hypocritical nonsense.
Schools are failing to educate our children.	Students today test lower in reading than their parents did.
Professional athletes are overpaid.	The salaries of baseball players bear little relation to their skill.

Note in each of these examples (and again these are examples to adapt to your class context) that you can help students see what it means to focus the topic at the stage of the thesis. We have no doubt read more than our share of essays that say nothing because they are simply a series of broad, general statements, each of which could function as the topic sentence of a paragraph or the thesis for a separate paper. Here is where thesis work can be integrated with focus on critical thinking. When we show students that a statement such as the one about professional athletes being overpaid could be speaking of baseball, hockey, basketball, or football—to name a few of the options—and that even with a focus on one sport, a thoroughly developed text will surely be more than three or four pages, as are most of the assignments given at the high school or middle grades level, then we are assisting them with the concept of limitation of topic.

It is precise. This quality means that the thesis lends itself to only one interpretation. The key is to use specific words that clearly express what you want to say. Words like interesting, colorful, exciting, unusual, or unique are too vague for a good thesis.

Vague	*Specific*
People are too selfish.	Human selfishness is seen at its worst during rush hour.
New York is an interesting city to visit.	The New York theater is overrated.
Vitamin C is good for you.	Large doses of vitamin C help fight colds.

Once again, take your students through the examples to see the vagueness. I caution my classes, in particular, not to use the word *society*. I repeatedly stress that society means people and this means each one of us. So who are we speaking of when we use the word? Or help students to see the many vague uses of a word like *interesting*. Examples connected to friendship are powerful. When your best friend appears with an awful or outlandish haircut and you are asked whether you like it, the safe and harmless answer is "It's interesting." Once students are reminded by such everyday examples of the weakness of such words, they can become more alert to imprecise wording in thesis statements.

We also need to show that even the examples of more specific statements can be considered broad, depending on the length of the paper we will write. What is key is that each example does give a statement that can be proved or shown or demonstrated; that is what a thesis must lend the paper.

It is unified. This quality is one of the more obvious: the unified thesis expresses a single governing idea. A good thesis may sometimes include a secondary idea if it is strictly subordinated to the major one; but without that subordination, the writer will have too many important ideas to handle and the structure of the paper will suffer.

Not Unified
Nuclear power plants pose health hazards to the community and create problems of waste disposal.

Unified
Nuclear power plants pose health hazards to the community.

The new health program is excellent, but it has several drawbacks, and it should be run only on an experimental basis for 2 or 3 years.

The new health program should be run only on an experimental basis for 2 or 3 years.

Again, I assure you that the characteristic of single focus is one of the easiest for students to see and to use in their writing. The final two qualities of strong thesis statements are more abstract and are not as easily comprehended.

An effective thesis takes a stand. This quality expresses the writer's point of view, claim about, stance, or attitude toward the subject. It is not merely an announcement nor is it only a statement of absolute fact.

Weak
The income tax structure.

Effective
The income tax structure favors the rich at the expense of the poor.

One out of two marriages ends in divorce.

The current high divorce rate is destroying the traditional nuclear family.

This quality of thesis statement calls into question something many English teachers have taught. A very common outline for a paper was the three-step process of "telling them what I am going to tell them," "telling them," and "telling them what I told them I was going to tell them." Strunk and White in the seminal work *The Elements of Style* encourage writers to avoid the "I think" or " in my opinion" or "I feel that" phrase since people know when reading a text that they are getting the perspective of the writer. Furthermore, there is nothing to prove in a thesis statement that proclaims, "I am going to tell you about the most important event in my life." What the statement says is that you are going to do a certain thing and that is "tell." You may or may not manage the task, but the point is that announcement-type statements hold nothing provable or debatable. (Note that this statement also violates the characteristic of precise words.)

The other aspect of this characteristic suggests that thesis statements cannot merely state a fact. The sentence about the divorce rates, albeit a sad reality, is a fact. When something is a given, a fact, there is nothing to prove or demonstrate; there is nowhere for the writer to go in the paper. My caution to writers for avoiding this trap is to make sure you have some word or phrase that signals a debatable or provable point.

An effective thesis matters. This quality requires that the subject be engaging enough to be worth writing about—and reading about. The person to whom it should matter most is the writer. If it doesn't matter to the writer, it is not likely to matter to anyone else. An interesting subject not only engages the reader, but also prods the writer to explore his or her ideas about it, making the writing process a learning process as well. Thus, the thesis should help establish a "so what" for the paper: What is it that is really of value for you as writer and for others as readers to discuss? I like to tell students that, discounting the fact that I am not much of a pet person, I still probably won't find much significance in an essay about the death of a cat or dog, particularly when the essay does not surpass emotionality. What can work with such a topic is to demonstrate some points of significance. If you have an elderly relative living with your family and the pet is a major companion for this relative during the day when the rest of the family is out at school or work, then the death of the pet can be a topic worth writing about. Or if a family member has a heart condition and must exercise daily, and the family pet helps this member get out and walk, again you have a point to make as you relate the death of the pet. Build your own examples for students; do teach them, however, to think about ways to lend significance to the topic.

Thesis Recognition Activity

To decide how well you grasp the qualities of thesis statements, determine which of the following would be a good thesis for a paper of two to three pages. Be prepared to identify the words or phrases that weaken the statement. Decide how you might revise those that are not workable as thesis statements.

1. I want to tell you about the many defects in the administration's proposals for decreasing the budget deficit.
2. Japanese management techniques can improve the efficiency of some American industries and also their safety.
3. Andrew Jackson gave American democracy its distinctive character as a *popular* democracy.
4. Those students make best use of college who pursue a double major, one major for fun, one major for profit.
5. The climatological phenomenon known as *el niño* created many hardships.
6. Unlike the game of 30 years ago, professional football today is a showplace of technology.
7. The Grand Canyon is a major tourist attraction.
8. My grandfather's method of lighting a fire is the surest I have ever seen.
9. By making the issue of the American family so public and political, demagogues jeopardize the privacy and intimacy on which the family depends.
10. Hardware improvements have made downhill skiing safer over the years, but recent changes in skiing style have increased skiing's hazards.
11. As new facts and theories come to light, history must be rewritten, even if such revisions ruin our traditional heroes and destroy our popular myths.

In using this activity in your classroom, you will want to create statements based on applicable content. Let's analyze each statement to see if you have assimilated the characteristics of strong thesis statements.

If you have noted the words "I want to tell you about" in statement 1, *I want to tell you about the many defects in the administration's proposals for decreasing the budget*, then you have realized that this sentence *announces.* The writer will either manage to tell or not, but the statement as worded does not take a stand nor make an assertion about the administration's proposals; there is no place for the writer to take this topic.

Statement 2, *Japanese management techniques can improve the efficiency of some American industries and also their safety*, is a fairly obvious nonunified thesis. The *and also their safety* clause signals the second topic; clearly too much to handle in a short paper.

Some of the eleven examples are open to discussion; statement 3, *Andrew Jackson gave American democracy its distinctive character as a* popular *democracy*, is one such example. Most groups doing this activity agree, though, that statement 3 fits most of the qualities of a workable thesis, particularly since the word *popular* is set off, signaling that it will be discussed in a particular context.

Statement 4, *Those students make best use of college who pursue a double major, one major for fun, one major for profit*, is similar to statement three: the heart of the statement is the portion preceding the first comma. What follows identifies the double major; it does not take the statement in two directions.

Statement 5, *The climatological phenomenon known as* el niño *created many hardships*, merely states a fact; if the writer made the point that *el niño* caused the worst weather-related disasters of the decade, then there would be an assertion. This sentence as is, however, does provide a teachable sample with which students can be guided to more careful wording.

Statement 6, *Unlike the game of 30 years ago, professional football today is a showplace of technology*, offers something workable; the sentence is not set up to take on everything about professional football. The writer's task is clear: to show the increasing technological aspects of the game.

Statement 7, *The Grand Canyon is a major tourist attraction*, is a parallel example to statement 5. Here again the statement is fact; it is true as written with nothing further for the writer to do. The statement of absolute fact merely short-circuits the writer, who simply has nowhere to go, having given a point of reality. Again, if the statement is reworded to build in a comparative element, for example, with other tourist attractions located west of the Mississippi, the writer might have the potential for a paper.

Statement 8, *My grandfather's method of lighting a fire is the surest I have ever seen*, offers challenges to students assessing the statement. It is limited and unified; it takes a stand. This example, though, presents a case for the quality *it matters.* Much would depend on the type of assignment or topic given, but the statement itself does not provide a "so what" kind of focus. Remember my earlier point about the topic of the death of a pet. What underlying or deeper issue can be brought into play?

The final three examples each have some obvious problems. In statement 9, *By making the issue of the American family so public and political, demagogues jeopardize the privacy and intimacy on which the family depends,* there is *dual focus.* Statement 10, *Hardware improvements have made downhill skiing safer over the years, but recent changes in skiing style have increased skiing's hazards,* has too many words requiring contextualization, thus limiting the depth of development the writer could achieve. Statement 11, *As new facts and theories come to light, history must be rewritten, even if such revisions ruin our traditional heroes and destroy our popular myths,* provides a good example for discussion; challenge your students to articulate their comprehension of the workable thesis as they determine this statement's potential.

A major emphasis in the preceding activity is articulation. Students need an understanding of the language of response or evaluation. Several activities allow practice in evaluating and formulating thesis statements. One involves total class response; the other involves individual peer response.

Classroom Consensus: Determining Workable Thesis Statements

When you have assigned a paper or any writing task that requires formulation of purpose, have students come to class the next day with their thesis statements. As students enter the classroom and before they are seated, have them write their statements on the board. If they get their statements on the board before the period begins, they have a certain anonymity; no one need know whose statement is whose. This allows for a safer climate for class discussion of the thesis. When you go through each statement, analyzing it for the qualities of strong statements, you can involve everyone working together to decide whether the thesis will work. Such activity gives practice in student response, helps them grow in their sense of analysis, and builds the sense of a community of writers. This activity can also deflate some of the competition for grades as well. I urge students to do all they can to assist the writer; questions such as "How can this writer develop a stronger thesis?" or "Where do we as readers expect the paper to go from the thesis as given?" signal that teacher and students are united in the common goal of improving the student's writing or of solving the writer's struggles with focus.

Until they have drafted a paper, many writers do not know precisely what they want to prove; thus, for those who raise the objection that they don't know their thesis until after they have written a substantial amount, simply encourage students to compose as much as possible of the statement or to bring the beginning paragraph or brainstorming for the paper. Again you will have the opportunity to foster a sense of community here; when the thesis is not totally formulated, encourage the total class to collaborate in creating an effective thesis.

Remember, too, that students in middle grades, in particular, are beginners in the writing process. Frequently, they need help as they begin learning about the structure for expository writing. This is why so many of us were taught the five-paragraph theme structure. We needed that structure as the skeleton for future well-developed writing. Here's an analogy. When you first learned how to ride a bike, someone may have given you specific directions about how to get on the bike, how the pedals should be positioned, and how you could achieve and maintain balance. Once you were a confident rider, you did any of these steps from pre-riding subconsciously or automatically. The same is true for writing: get students to see and employ the structure automatically; then they can be freer and more creative writers and thinkers.

The Write-Around and Topic Selection

The second activity for practicing the formulation and analysis of thesis statements is an activity I call the *write-around.* I adapted this activity from my experience in the Dakota Writing Project; a high school teacher, Dennis Larsen, provided the original idea. The activity can be used for clarifying and developing the thesis, as well as for generating ideas for the paper. Each student, and you as the teacher, should come to class with an idea for the thesis or paper topic. Each student writes out a thesis on a sheet of paper and signs his or her name. The student then passes the paper to the person to the left. This next writer adds comments of explanation or clarification, such as "The thesis needs more of a claim" or "I know something about gargoyles" or "Have you thought about interviewing . . . for help with this topic?" or "I know that you can find more information in. . . ." The subsequent writers must include their signatures so that the original writer can go to those who have offered ideas. The signatures also provide a check for the teacher—you can monitor inappropriate remarks or gauge students' abilities to provide feedback or assign a participation grade based on the comments you see. The write-around provides a good composition strategy on several fronts. students become engaged in conversations with other writers and there are seldom behavior problems, since everyone, including the teacher, is busy reading and writing. I have been amazed at how willing students are to offer ideas; the activity helps to verify ways that students become "authorities" when they can share their knowledge or further ideas on topics. I frequently have my classes move desks so that the students are in one large circle or U-shaped formation. For this activity, I sit in the circle as well, and I become one of the contributors to the dialogue created as the papers are passed around and each member of the class writes additional comments that clarify or question or add information. I also sign my name and frequently work at connecting with a previous writer's comments. Students love it when the teacher has signaled that their advice is workable. Additionally, the write-around subtly expands students' notion of audience: now they see that their peers are among the audience, not only their teacher. The write-around fosters a sense of community; again students can see that they have an investment in helping their peers with topics, ideas, or thesis formulation.

If you have access to a computer lab or electronic classroom, the write-around activity can be modified to *computer hopping.* Each writer brings up a document and begins with the thesis or topic idea and signature; the writer then moves to the next computer and types a response. Students can save to disk if they've brought their own or can print out a copy at the end of class. In either case, they take with them comments from at least ten or so readers; in my experience you cannot manage more response than this in a 50-minute class simply because you want each student to give thoughtful responses; and remember that when you receive a paper that has been responded to by several others, you are now reading extensive dialogue. Because the write-around engages students, offers them many hands-on aspects for strengthening their writing skills, and provides built-in assessment, the time involved is well worth it.

Because selection and narrowing of a topic are steps that precede the formulation of a thesis, and because so many students struggle with this stage of the process as well, you might consider creating interest inventories or surveys. These can be used at the beginning of the year or the semester to get to know students, but they can also be used to help your writers work with topics of greatest interest to them. Consider the following inventory:

> From the following major themes or issues, select three that you find important and valuable to you, that you are interested in and want to learn more about, and that you want to do more thinking and writing about. Rank these in order of importance by numbering them 1, 2, 3, . . . , with 1 being the theme of greatest interest to you.
>
> _____ Death and afterlife/burial rites
> _____ Belief in God(s), religious customs, rituals
> _____ Marriage customs/selection of spouse
> _____ Fame, honor, glory, immortality
> _____ Role of women/rights of women
> _____ War as glory, valuable to manhood
> _____ Peace and harmony (national, familial, individual)
> _____ The place of family/home/homeland
> _____ Heroism/courage/bravery
> _____ Freedom/patriotism/nationalism
> _____ Value of the land and natural resources
> _____ Friendship/loyalty/trust
> _____ Love (specifically that leading to marriage)
> _____ Wisdom figures/respect of elders
> _____ Sense of identity/coming of age/rites of passage
> _____ Effects of pride/jealousy/greed
> _____ Justice and human rights

_____ Psychological and emotional health

_____ Physical strength/body prowess

A survey such as this will provide a good foundation for interest level. You can also survey your students' reading interests: do they read magazines, newspapers, or books, and, if so, what types? Or other literacy issues are do they watch TV, do they watch or listen to news, what types of music do they enjoy, do they listen to NPR? Build on the students' bases of knowledge and engagement; remember the wise premise of good writing—it comes from topics in which the writer has an interest.

One quality of strong thesis statements is that the thesis must _matter._ This abstract quality is not easily comprehended. Integral to the "so what" notion of the thesis is the level of thinking involved in composing the paper and articulating ideas or arguments. Daphne Swabey, a former colleague at the University of Michigan's Composition Program, offered a superb analogy to help students grasp levels of thinking: the swimmer analogy. The analogy uses lap swimmer, lake swimmer, snorkeler, and scuba diver to parallel levels of thinking.

Begin by asking students how many of them have ever done lap swimming. Then ask them to describe what lap swimming is like, where it is done, and in what conditions. You may get the simple response that lap swimming is boring. Amazingly, you can do a great deal with this response, since indeed this kind of swim requires little imagination. You are in a swimming pool with highly predictable water temperatures, depths, and conditions. Students can easily grasp that thinking on the lap swimming level is equally simplistic or unimaginative. It is truly just working on the surface. Yes, it is true that lap swimmers do make some plans; they are creative about dodging swimmers in their lanes and they do solve problems. Chances are, though, that these are lower-level concerns that are parallel to writers who focus mainly on the surface.

Moving to the lake swimmer level, again ask about the conditions of lake swimming. Here students will tell you that lakes have varying temperatures, surfaces, and water conditions; they will comment that there may be things that bite—minnows or crab—or things that surprise or shock, like a drop-off or some object for you to run into or try to avoid. When students suggest all these and more, they see that the lake swimmer level of thinking is stronger and deeper; writers who are lake swimmer thinkers will write papers that are more appealing and readable.

If you have students who have been snorkeling, they are the best ones to help everyone grasp the strength of thinking on this level. The obvious point to emphasize is that with an air source, as snorkelers have, they can go deeper into the water and can stay for a time below the surface. Below the surface or beyond the surface or, to use the colloquial, "out of the box" thinking involves more complexity, imagination, and creativity. Snorkelers and scuba divers are best able to scour the ocean depths or any topic's depth. Scuba divers, of course, are best equipped for reaching the deepest levels of discovery or thought; your writers want to aim for becoming Jacques Cousteau types of thinkers.

This swimming level or thinking level discussion allows for excellent critiquing during peer reviews or writing workshops. When a peer tells another that "You are doing lap swimmer thinking here, can you get some more depth?", this comment achieves more than much of the commentary that a teacher invests significant time offering. You can easily select a number of analogies to help students comprehend the distinctions in levels of thinking. I have found success using the swimmer analogy and am indebted to Daphne for her suggestion.

Children's books provide another venue for conveying the importance of varying levels of thinking. Dr. Seuss's creative play with language has led to many fun books; try using Seuss's *Oh, The Thinks You Can Think!* This delightful book has great potential even if just in the words of the title, which is repeated throughout. "The Thinks You Can Think" could be a powerful coaching mantra. The point is, coach for the thinking that grounds good writing and good work habits in employment circumstances. At the same time, realize that strong and clear thinking must underlie everything in the writing process, from the creation of texts to the response to others' texts. The analogy analyzing levels of thinking offers one vehicle for looking at the kind of thinking that is done. As we move to the final subject of the chapter, *tying together*, we examine another facet of the thinking and writing process.

The skill of tying together was referred to earlier as I spoke of the future surgeon with seemingly little skill at organization and coherence. Recall from the definitions of thesis that one description says, "the controlling idea tying together and giving direction to all other separate elements in the paper." Tying together can also be achieved by transitions; tying together is about making connections that help your readers to know how to follow. Just as no teacher can literally "open a head and rewire," neither can readers get into the mind of the writer. A fairly safe assumption is that you have more than once commented on student writing as being "unclear" or that "I don't know what you mean here." Similarly, one challenge in working with texts of any sort is that all that readers have is what is on the page; this point can never be emphasized enough to writers.

One activity here relates to the *prediction* we often use in teaching literature. Just as you might begin teaching a short story or drama by reading a first paragraph or few lines of dialogue and then asking students to make predictions about characters or plot, you can work similarly with papers in a writing classroom. Cover everything except the first line or first paragraph of the essay; ask others in the writing community to explain what they expect to hear next, or what they expect the writer to do, or, even more significant, what they must know next for the text to have coherence. What kind of evidence should follow a claim? What kinds of details are needed to "show" a general statement or topic sentence? Or, working solely from the thesis or moving sentence by sentence, again ask students to anticipate what will come next. If the text does not follow predictions or expectations, readers may be lost. Remember, we cannot fit inside the writer's head; we cannot fill in, particularly with integrity to the writer's intentions, what we have not been given.

One instance that works well for clarifying what is meant by a lack of coherence is peer response to writing. If such response is to be helpful and concrete, students need the language to articulate what constitutes strong writing. When generating the qualities of strong writing, students frequently name *flow*. When I ask exactly what they mean by flow, they provide the description of coherence or of tying together. Sometimes they do not have the language, but the point is that flow translates into a quality of writing in which each idea links to the next, or in which we can predict as we read because the writer moves coherently from sentence to sentence, from topic sentence to proper development.

A student writer that I coached could not organize ideas and raised the same desperate plea that so many students raise: "I just can't get what I want to say down on paper. I know what I want to say, but it doesn't come out." I urged her to try making an audio tape, to "talk out" her paper and then do a playback. Or, I suggested, she might talk to her roommate or a friend and explain what she wanted to say in her paper. If students have someone they can "talk the paper to," maybe a writing partner, a friend, a parent, they can have someone else provide the playback. Coaches earn that title because they are capable of encouraging and guiding. As you work with students whose minds you sometimes wish you could simply "rewire," offer them guidance that leads them to a solid formation of thesis and encourage scuba-diver thinking, and tied-together ideas.

REFERENCES AND RESOURCES

Alvarez, Joseph A. *Elements of Composition.* New York: Harcourt Brace Jovanovich, 1985.
Brown, Margaret Wise. *The Important Book.* New York: Harper & Row, 1977.
Flower, Linda. *Problem-solving Strategies for Writing.* New York: Harcourt Brace Jovanovich, 1985.
Matz, Karl A. "The Important Thing: Connecting Reading and Writing in the Primary Grades." *Reading Teacher* 47.1 (September 1993): 70–72.
Seuss, Dr. *Oh, The Thinks You Can Think!* New York: Random House, 1975.
Strunk, William, Jr., and E. B. White. *The Elements of Style.* New York: Macmillan Company, 1972.

As I review this list of sources, I am confirmed in the rationale for this textbook. There are not many sources directed to teaching writing in middle schools and high schools. Also, our best resource is frequently other teachers, our colleagues. Journals like *Language Arts* and the *English Journal*, with *Notes Plus* and *Ideas Plus*, are some of the best sources for teaching ideas.

3

Audience and Voice

KATHRYN KLINTWORTH

Two crucial aspects of writing are (1) the audience and (2) voice, or how the writer must express himself or herself to assure that the writing will be "heard." Kathryn Klintworth surveyed students who remembered that in middle and high school they never really thought about audience. The "teacher was the only one who read anything" some remarked; others were told never to put "I" in a paper. Klintworth's chapter offers a series of activities to help writing coaches meet these two challenges. From addressing the "one" phenomenon to helping students realize they *will* have a voice when they have something to say that truly matters, these writing strategies promote the value for students in discovering their voice—indeed, their identity.

As I read through another year's stack of papers by the incoming first-year students, I was struck by how lifeless many of them seemed to be. The first day of the term I ask students to write a short paper on a personal topic so that I can assess their writing strengths. This year's topic was "What has been most significant about your college experience since you arrived on campus three days ago?" I hoped the topic would generate some lively text that showed great relief in discovering that your roommate doesn't snore or have a wardrobe that takes up all of her space and one-fourth of yours; that being on your own was exhilarating; that the rumors about cafeteria food were unfounded (at least for now); that leaving home was difficult, but exciting; that emotions were brought to the brink when your family, having unloaded all your stuff, finally left. A few papers met these expectations. However, as I read my way through the entire stack of papers, written by these new high school graduates, two areas of writing that many of the students seemed unaware of were audience and voice.

Discussions with my students confirmed the fact that these aspects are often glossed over in junior high and high school. Among the comments students made about audience and voice were "I never did much about audience. The teacher was the only one who read anything." "I was told to stay so far away from 'I' in my paper that I never thought to stick myself in a paper." "In junior high and high school I never thought of myself as an authority." "I really didn't know who I was.

I was defined by other people, like my parents." The omission of voice and lack of attention to audience in writing in English, as well as in other classes, is certainly understandable, given all that teachers are asked to teach and how abstract the topics of audience and voice are. However, closer attention to these topics can empower students to have greater control of their writing. But how do you address audience and voice with students?

Audience

"The Teacher Is the Only One Who Reads Anything"

Much of the writing students do should probably be stamped CONFIDENTIAL in large red letters at the top of the paper, since the teacher is the only one who ever sees it. Although this writing experience may be good training for students who go on to college to write papers that only their professors read, a great deal of writing exists outside of "only teachers read papers." Junior high and senior high students also engage in writing to audiences other than the teacher when they write e-mail messages to friends they have made in chat rooms in cyberspace, thank you notes for birthday gifts from a grandparent, job applications, gossipy notes to friends in class, and the like. Each of these examples has a real audience that students do not often have the chance to write for in school assignments. Yet these kinds of audience will receive a large part of the writing in a student's life. So part of our task as people who hand out the writing assignments is to give students opportunities to develop the sense that we write for people other than the teacher and that audience counts when we write.

How can we help students see someone else as audience? An activity that I have used frequently to make students aware of audience and writer is a puzzle that brings together two different ideas about what something is, which is a problem writers often face when they assume that the audience to whom they are writing is approaching the topic with the same mind-set as the writer. My husband brought this puzzle home from a leadership training course. For him, it had something to do with trusting people with whom you work. However, I saw it as a wonderful metaphor for what happens in writing. With a few changes, I adjusted the exercise for a totally different audience and gave it a new meaning.

Two puzzles are constructed in the shape of an upside-down T (see Figure 3.1). Each puzzle has pieces that are the same shapes. However, the pieces in each puzzle are not the same colors.

Two people are selected to leave the room. While they are gone, two desks are placed back to back. On one of the desks, one of the puzzles is correctly assembled in the shape of an upside-down T. The pieces of the second puzzle are placed unassembled on the second desk. The two people are brought back into the room and asked to sit back to back in the desks. The person whose puzzle is put together (essentially the writer) then verbally instructs the second person on how to place the puzzle pieces on the second desk so that they fit together in the same way as the

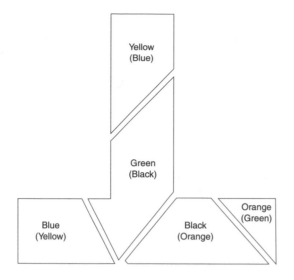

FIGURE 3.1

correctly assembled puzzle. While the first person explains how the pieces fit together, the second person is not allowed to ask the first person any questions, which in essence simulates a writer–audience experience. When the writer does not give the audience a general focus ("This puzzle is in the shape of an upside-down T"), which frequently happens, and uses only the colors as a way to put the puzzle together, there is no success in assembling the pieces correctly. When the second person is able to ask questions to clarify the first person's directions, often there is success if the audience can figure out that the writer has a different perspective than the audience. This exercise usually helps students to realize that, because the reader cannot directly ask the writer any questions, the writer needs to keep the audience in mind when writing, to anticipate questions a reader might have, and to be as clear as possible.

Another exercise with which I have had great success in helping the writer to be aware of the audience is an experience I call "Ties and Jewelry Tell You Something about the People Who Wear Them." The original idea stems from the Dakota Writing Project. Like so many good ideas, I heard about the idea from a teacher friend and eventually adapted it for my own use. First I have students write down three issues in which they are interested. Topics have included child abuse, gun control, overpaid athletes, animal testing, binge drinking, destruction of the rain forests, bilingual education, and hate groups, to name a few. Next each student selects a tie and pin (grab bag style) from a selection of ties and costume jewelry that I have collected. After studying the tie for several minutes, students are asked to describe the person who would wear this particular tie. My original collection of ties came from the men in my husband's office, who are all engineers, so my original collection of ties was somewhat conservative. However, I have managed to pick up a number of ties that are fairly wild in color and print to give me an eclectic collection. In the past, students who have selected one particularly gaudy orange, black, and gold tie inevitably say it would belong to a used car salesman.

Next each student creates a profile for the person who would wear the pin. My collection of pins is also fairly eclectic; it includes such items as a locket-size silver cross and a two-inch tall wooden duck with a green bill. If the tie and pin themselves do not stir students' imaginations enough to invent a profile, I may help them by giving the following prompt:

For both the tie and the pin, give the following information:

    Name of the person

    Age

    Occupation

    Religion

    Salary

    Marital status: single? married? divorced? engaged?

    Children: ages? sex?

    Pets: kind?

    Political party

    Favorite music

    Magazines (the person reads or subscribes to)

    Level of education

    Values

    Relationship to you

The next step is to decide, based on the profiles created, how to persuade this person to become involved with the issue he or she has chosen. I ask students to think about how they might adjust their vocabulary and sentence structure to fit the audience and what characteristics in the person's profile they might appeal to. For example, the used car salesman may have children or grandchildren and could be persuaded to vote yes on a tax that was designed to provide funds for drug education. If the man did not have children, he might be persuaded to vote yes so that youths who were breaking into his cars to steal radios to support their drug habits could be helped. The same process is used with developing an argument for the woman that students say would wear the pin. Using a woman as audience provides an opportunity to discuss how and if a female might respond differently from a male to a message.

After students have constructed an argument, I divide them into groups of two or three to try out their arguments on each other and then to decide if their peers think the points of argument fit the audience.

Students can also use their peers as audience. Students can then write on "hot topics," but take a stance opposite of what most of their peers support, in an effort to convince their peers of the worth of their positions. It is a good idea to let the class generate subjects that interest them. If they need priming to come up with a list, you can suggest such topics as the drinking age, the driving age, legalization of marijuana for medical purposes, curfews, or mandatory service to the government. In no time, students will come up with a comprehensive list of issues about which they feel strongly. Having students write on hot topics for their classmates increases the opportunity that students have to write without necessarily increasing the grading tasks. When peers serve as audience, they can give each other feedback about whether a paper has meaning for them.

Another way students can be made aware of audience is by addressing writing to a partner. The idea of a writing partner often helps students to focus their voices and registers for a real audience. The writing partner may be someone in the same class, someone in another grade, or even an adult. E-mail opens up many possibilities for having writing partners in other places. Whatever the pairing, it is important that both partners share writing with each other, even if there is an age difference or difference in level of education, keeping in mind the people for whom they are writing.

Voice

"I was Told to Stay So Far Away from Using 'I' in My Paper That I Never Thought to Stick Myself in a Paper"

In addition to helping students be aware of audience when they write, it is also beneficial to their growth as writers to discuss the concept of voice. Research done by Zoe Keithley at Columbia College, Chicago, in her composition classes showed that "Seventy-five percent of students questioned had *never* been told to use their own voice in their writing; the remaining 25 percent, except for one, said one or two teachers out of twelve years of schooling encouraged them to do so" (84). When I asked my English Methods students what they thought of as voice in writing, they had a hard time coming up with a definition. However, understanding what is meant by voice is important in helping students to find theirs.

Voice is the *writer's identity*. It may include style, which as William Zinsser notes, "is organic to the person who is doing the writing" (20). However, style is not the same as voice, although style may be a part of voice. I like Donald Murray's distinction between voice and style. "[S]tyle seems to get related to fashion. Style sounds like something you buy off the shelf. It is made by someone else and it changes with the season" (21). The speaking style of young adults who are seeking to fit in with their peers may be filled with the current slang and jargon of their classmates. "Like" and "ya know" and "I mean" and "awesome" may be the fillers in their sentences when they are speaking, and just as these expressions are not necessarily used in their writing, often neither are their own voices present. The honesty that Murray notes (21) is part of good writing is missing and thus the writing in many instances appears voiceless. The writing typifies that of the student who told me, "I was told to stay so far away from using 'I' in my writing in high school that I never thought to stick myself in a paper." When students eliminate the "I-ness" in papers, the result is often a kind of voiceless prose, as in the following example from a student paper.

> Teen violence is a major problem in many cities. This problem is growing as more and more teens join gangs, buy guns and get into trouble. There has not yet been found a solution to these problems, but they have come up with laws that have helped to reduce them.

This student's writing lacks the honest voice and truth that good writers strive for. Contrast the previous student's writing with that of another student who wrote on a similar topic.

> To know the extent of gun violence in Detroit is to truly hate it. To grow up in a world so demented is reality. I have observed through my own eyes that Detroit has a big time gun violence problem . . . I have been recently directly hurt by gun violence in Detroit. An old friend of mine was in a neighborhood that he hadn't grown up in alone at night, and he was shot in the back.

This second example has the honest voice and truth that is lacking in the first. In this example, the student was not writing only for the teacher, but was also talking to his peers.

Teachers can also help students get voice into their writing and acknowledge that someone is actually out there listening by getting rid of the *"one"* phenomenon ("one sees," "one does," etc.). Frequently, my freshmen composition students say that an English teacher in ninth grade told them *never* to use "I" in more formal kinds of writing, especially in academic papers. Well-meaning teachers who themselves were probably admonished to never use "I" have passed this rubric on to their students. At one point in my teaching career, I too held students to this tenet. Although this may be an acceptable approach for very formal papers in some disciplines, for junior high and high school students, the rule is probably overly prescriptive. The result will basically be voiceless compositions that put the audience somewhere "out there" where the writer cannot see them and where it is very difficult for the audience to hear the writer. Teachers can also help students to see how clinical writing can become by showing them examples of the agentless prose that is found in some textbooks. For example, some science texts have sentences such as "It has been seen in the past that . . . ," as if no person had done the seeing.

A good activity related to agentless prose is to have students bring in examples of such writing. When you have a collection of such voiceless prose, let your students rewrite selections and test these revisions out on their classmates to see if the revised texts have voice.

What I tell students about voice is that it should have an immediate presence to it and make writing sound as though we are sitting together talking over pizza. Sometimes people eat pizza with a knife and fork, which is a bit more formal than with your fingers. But it's still pizza. If this analogy doesn't make sense to them, I use one about a tea bag. I tell them voice is like tea. You immerse tea in hot water, and it flavors and colors it. When you drink the tea, you may use a Royal Dalton china cup and saucer, or a black mug with a Siamese cat on it, or one of those stainless steel thermal cups that fits in the drink holder in the car, or even the dreaded white Styrofoam cup. Each of these containers has a different level of formality, but they can all hold the same tea. Your voice is like tea. It colors and flavors the writing, and no matter who your audience is, the flavor and color of you should be in your writing. You may approach a topic with a different register depending on the audience, but it should still have the sound of you in it in order to keep your involvement in the topic present in the writing. Without this presence, writing becomes merely a string of flat, tasteless words.

Sometimes students can be made more aware of their voices by listening to the voices of others. When discussing voice, Peter Elbow defines it as "what most people have in their speech but lack in their writing—namely, a sound or texture—the sound of 'them'" (288). He also notes that people "adopt a voice in order to face an audience" (292). To help students hear the "texture—the sound of 'them'" and to understand the various voices that people assume depending on the situation, students can engage in listening exercises. Listening to other people's voices, students can hear the characteristics of language that give an individual his or her voice. Dona J. Hickey notes, "The melody of real talk includes wide pitch intervals, loud stresses, and most importantly, a variety of timbres (the subtle shades of feeling we identify as wry, ironic, mock serious, and so forth). It is the timbres of speech that are difficult to encode in printed symbols" (30).

Students can either listen to conversations, listening especially for those timbres in individual voices that identify them as belonging to a certain person, and immediately record what the people involved in the conversation said, or, with permission, they can record and later transcribe conversations. Students should be given a topic, such as curfews, driving age being tied to grades, or teens and guns, and then discuss this topic with three different groups. One group should be made up of people the student considers friends. Another group should be people the student does not know very well. The third group should include a teacher. As students listen to the conversations, they may discover that individual voices change depending on who the audience is and that conversations with close friends tend to reveal a voice that is closest to what Elbow calls the "real voice" that people have.

Another exercise students can engage in to help them discover their voices is to write in the voice of someone they know who has a voice very different from their own. A student can assume the voice of a parent, friend, relative, teacher, coach, or supermarket clerk. The student might also try to write with a man's voice if female or a woman's voice if male. Students can also assume the voice of a character in a story and write about an incident or react to an event from this character's perspective. These are fairly nonthreatening experiences because they do not ask students to reveal anything about themselves. Such exercises serve to introduce students to the idea of voice.

Topics for Composition

"I Never Thought of Myself as an Author"

The idea that a student might be an *authority* on some topic and thus be capable of being an author is not a way in which most high school or middle grade students perceive themselves. But students *are* authorities on many kinds of topics that they can write about with some degree of confidence. They may be authorities on malls, tennis shoes, music groups, fast food, movies, fashion, television programs, media stars, computer games, lawn mowing, baby sitting, comic strips, science fiction, the house they live in, the school they attend, their friends, racing bikes, basketball, or turtles. To help students realize that they are authorities, ask them to list ten topics on which they think they are authorities. These topics can become the grist to be refined in future compositions. And, because they are authorities on these topics, they can speak with clear, discernible voices and make the topics come alive for an audience.

Encouraging Students to Find Their Individual Voices

"I Didn't Know Who I Was in Junior High and High School"

In middle and high school, students may need encouragement to find and include voice in their writing when they are in the midst of trying to discover who they are in the first place. One young woman commented, "I didn't really know who I was in junior high and high school. I was defined by other people, like my parents." For some it is also a challenge to find an inner voice that is unique to the student when he or she just wants to fit in. Dona Hickey notes, "developing voice depends on risk taking" (27). Students may need convincing that taking the risk to find their voices is a worthwhile endeavor, especially since students work hard to be just like everyone else, and being an individual often subjects a student to ridicule and ostracism. However, students at these ages are also extremely passionate and energetic, and helping them to find their voices in order to infuse their writing with this passion and energy is definitely worth the time it takes.

To help students find their voices, they need to examine their own lives. John Schultz in *Writing from Start to Finish* claims "individual voice—'my voice'—incorporates ALL the language of personal background, includes 'the powers of the conscious and unconscious . . . is the articulation of all perceptions including the so called nonverbal. . . .' " It is " 'person-centered/generated' . . . the expression of the whole person, an extension of speech, an extension of the body" (quoted in Keithley 84, 85).

Examining their own backgrounds is a way to help students find their individual voices. A simple way to get students to think about their own lives is to give them writing prompts that encourage them to think about who they are and what is special about them. The enchanting picture book *If You're Not from the Prairie* by David Bouchard is a good way to get students to think about how the culture and landscape in which they have grown up may have affected who they are. Bouchard shows how the prairie helps to define the people in the book, which can be used as a prompt to help students think about how the culture and landscape in which they grew up have influenced their lives and who they are now. An example from that book begins with the repeated line coming from the title: "If you're not from the prairie, / You don't know me." Then the narrator asserts the special qualities of prairie life: hair is windblown, eyes are frequently filled with grit, skin is tanned and lips chapped. After students have read this book, they can begin to write their own examples. If you did not grow up on Columbus Avenue in a middle class, mostly white neighborhood, you do not know. . . .

Two books by Sandra Cisneros, *The House on Mango Street* and *Woman Hollering Creek* are also useful as students think about voice. *The House on Mango Street* has a chapter entitled "My Name" that you can read to students to prompt them to write about their own names.

> In English my name means hope. In Spanish it means too many letters. It means sadness, it means waiting. It is like the number nine. A muddy color. It is the Mexican records my father plays on Sunday mornings when he is shaving songs like sobbing. (10)

To find information about their names, students may talk with parents, grandparents, or namesakes. These conversations can also help students develop a sense of their own identity.

Woman Hollering Creek has a section describing what it feels like to be eleven.

> What they don't understand about birthdays and what they never tell you is that when you're eleven, you're also ten, and nine and eight, and seven, and six, and five and four, and three, and two, and one. And when you wake up on your eleventh birthday you expect to feel eleven, but you don't. You open your eyes and everything's just like yesterday, only it's today. And you don't feel eleven at all. You feel like you're still ten. And you are—underneath the year that makes you eleven. (6)

After reading this chapter aloud to students, have them write about the particular age they are and what it feels like to be that age and what is special about them.

William Zinsser, in his now classic *On Writing Well* observes, "Getting writers to use 'I' is seldom easy" (22). Beginning writers often think they do not have anything to say that anyone will want to read. Zinsser notes, however, that readers will "care if you tell them something interesting, and tell them in words that come naturally." One way to help students discover their "I-ness" is to give them the opportunity to free write in class on topics of their choice. (It's a good idea to have lists of topics available for the inevitable "I don't know what to write about" response that some students will give.) Students can be prompted, also, by observing, for example, a video clip on teenage smoking and then responding to the following questions: What do you know about this topic? What do you think about it? What do you feel as you watch this?

Although voice is an illusive quality, teachers must encourage students to "Believe in your own identity and your own opinions" (Zinsser 25). When students who are developing authors face an audience other than themselves, they may feel a lack of confidence in their own authority and language. Happily, however, students do know the stories of their own lives and can readily share these if teachers provide writing activities that bring together these stories and writing. Using prompts that ask students to describe events in their lives is one way students can begin to discover their natural voice. When free writing on the following prompts, students will undoubtedly write in the first person. This is important, because a writer is obviously "most natural and relaxed when writing in first person" (Zinsser 22).

What is the earliest memory you have of your childhood?

What is the best advice you were ever given?

Describe the best vacation you ever had.

My favorite television show is _____. I like it because _____.

Describe the birthday that you liked the best (the least).

Aside from your mom and dad, who is the person in your family who has had the most influence on you? How has that person influenced you?

Who is a person not of your family who has influenced your life?

What is the funniest event that has happened to you so far in your life?

What is the saddest event that has happened to you so far in your life?

Describe why you like the music of your favorite group. (If possible, avoid the word *awesome.*)

What are your dreams?

What are your secret wishes?

What is the one thing about you that you hope will never change?

What is the biggest problem you are facing today?

What has been the best part of your life so far?

What has been the worst part of your life so far?

If a favorite relative sent you $100.00 for your birthday, what would you do with the money?

What is your favorite outfit?

How well do you understand the opposite sex?

How well do you think you know yourself?

How well do you know your best friend?

What is your best quality?

What is your worst quality?

If you could live at any other time than the present, when would it be? Why?

Describe your most prized possession. Where did you get it? Why is it important to you?

Describe the biggest problem you think is facing the world today. What do you think you can do about this problem?

If your best friend offers you a joint to smoke, what would you do?

What do you think should happen to kids who commit crimes with guns?

Does someone in your class have a tattoo? Look at it (providing it is in a place that is easily visible and if the person will let you). What do you think about the tattoo? How does it make you feel to look at a tattoo? What would your parents do if you got a tattoo without their permission?

Describe your best friend. Why do you and this person get along so well?

What is your favorite music group? How would you describe their music? Why do you like their music? Have you ever gone to a live performance of this group? What was it like?

How much power do you have in the family decisions that affect you? (money, curfews, cars)

These prompts help students to focus on their "I-ness" in preparation for including themselves in academic writing.

Journals are also an excellent place for students to find their personal voice, especially if the journal can be used like an ongoing conversation between the writer and reader, whether the reader is another student or the teacher. In responding to journals, I try to encourage writers to see their journals as places for more writing and thinking. For each journal I read, I try to ask at least one question. This doesn't mean that students necessarily have to answer the question (although some do). In journals the real voice of the writer becomes evident. I have had students who had difficulty doing academic writing because they have the voice of the textbook or source authors in their heads and think that this is how they should sound. The result is that the texts students produce do not make much sense. When this happens, I point students to how they write in their journals. The register of academic writing is usually more formal than what a student uses in a journal, and the students' real passion, voice, personality, inner self, and angst are all apparent in journals. This is the voice that I encourage students to find and use in all their writing.

To further encourage students to write freely in their journals, I assure them that I do not disclose anything they write in their journals unless it reveals risky or self-destructive behavior. If such a situation occurs, I promise students that I will talk to them about it before I try to get them help. I also tell them that if they write something that they don't want me to read, they can fold the pages and I'll skip them.

It takes time to discover who you are and what your voice is. The voices of students will change as they mature and have more life experiences that influence their sense of self. I know that my voice has changed as I have matured into the person I am today. My voice has even changed in this text. After reading an early draft, I realized that although I was writing about voice, my own voice was not in the writing. For writing to sound honest and truthful, voice needs to be evident.

Once students have gained some sense of voice, encourage them to keep inserting themselves in their writing. If at times they feel that they have lost their voices, they need to know that "voice is always there," as Diane Wakoski notes in her poem, "The Neighbor's Cat." Wakoski's speaker explains that as she wakes in the morning she sometimes thinks she has lost her voice and maybe will never speak again. Then she adds that the neighbor's cat wanders into her room, and because of her allergies she can't have this cat in the room and she needs to yell at it. The poet's key lines proclaim "you always have a voice / when there is something you really need to say."

Using this poem to talk about voice is another way to make students aware of theirs. Ask students if they have ever lost their voices in the literal sense. How did they feel? What was the worst thing about losing their voices? How did they compensate? What happened when they got their voice back again?

Perhaps the best encouragement we can pass on to our students is that, when they have something that they really need to say, their voices will be most authentic. To help students realize the authentic part of their voice and who they are, read Diane Wakoski's "My Neighbor's Cat." Then ask each student to think of an argument or disagreement that she or he recently had with a parent, brother or sister, friend, grandmother, boyfriend, ticket taker at the movies, and so on. What was the argument about? Was it an issue about which you feel strongly? What did your voice sound like? Was it loud? Did the words tumble from your brain and out of your mouth rapidly, like gushing water from a fully opened faucet, or did the words seem to be clogged up somewhere in your brain and refuse to come out? Were you stuck when trying to make the other person understand your point of view? How close do you think the voice that came out in the argument was to your real voice? Do you think Wakoski is right when she says that "you always have your voice / when there is something / you really need / to say"?

A writing experience that considers both voice and audience that works particularly well around Thanksgiving involves a letter writing exercise. During Thanksgiving week, when students are often restless in anticipation of Thanksgiving vacation and the Christmas events that will follow, I read the class Alex Haley's piece "Thank You." It was written about a Thanksgiving Haley had at sea when he was in the Navy. Haley relates how, after cooking Thanksgiving dinner for the crew, he began to think about people in his life who had taught him something that in some way made him who he was. He ended up writing to several people, including his father, his grandmother, and his grammar school principal. He thanked his father for teaching him to "love books and reading"; his grandmother for teaching him "to tell the truth, to be thrifty, to share and, to be forgiving and considerate of others"; and his principal for the motivating and positive influence the morning school prayers had on his life (Haley 5).

After reading this essay, I ask students to think about people who have been influential in their lives and who contributed in some way to making them who they are today. I ask them to limit their choices to people they have had actual close contact with, rather than someone like a rock star or president whom they have not met personally. What specifically did this person teach you? What difference does what the person taught you make in your life today? I ask students to share their stories of people who have had an effect on their lives with the class.

Following this discussion, I ask students to write a thank-you letter to the people who made specific contributions to the students' lives, personality, outlook, and/or moral development. Even reluctant students can come up with at least one or two people who have influenced them. This exercise has the benefit of making students think about both audience and voice in very specific ways. Not only do students address the letter to a specific well-known audience, but also, in the process, they think about who they are as individuals.

At the risk of glossing over the topic too lightly, I must at least touch on students for whom finding voice may be particularly confusing. The matter of voice and audience is doubly complicated for the ESL and/or dialect speakers and writers in your class. (Chapter 6 addresses many other issues involved in teaching ESL and dialect speakers and writers, so here I am focusing solely on voice and audience.) They may have two different voices, both of which are authentic. My sister-in-law, who was born and raised in Illinois and who spent several years in the Peace Corps in South America, speaks Spanish fluently. When I discussed the matter of voice with her, she said that she is a different person when she is using Spanish than when she is using English. Part of this probably has to do with the fact that culture is bound up in language, or maybe it's that language is bound up in culture. She commented that she has noticed this phenomena in her Spanish-speaking junior high students who seem to have a different voice in Spanish than they do in English. This characteristic is something that teachers who have L2 students need to consider, especially those who are at various stages on the continuum of English.

These students are caught between two worlds, those of their home language and culture and the language and culture of school; and they may have an especially difficult time finding their individual voices. It is therefore important that students have the opportunity to discover the voice inside them that is part of their cultural histories and that they have the opportunity to share that voice and history with their classmates. Students may need to think about how race and culture may influence voice not only in the way their voice sounds, but also in the way that they may develop an argument.

It is important not to discourage the voice that a student who comes from another culture may have. A writing assignment that asks students to interview family members to discover their cultural histories in order to share them with the rest of the class is a good way to help students discover their voices. Reading a personal history to the class provides the opportunity for class members to get to know each other better and also provides an authentic audience for the writer. It is important for students negotiating more than one language to realize that the teacher is not the only audience for their writing and that they have valid and engaging ideas to share with their classmates.

Discussing audience and voice can be a positive experience for both students and teachers. In fact, one great pleasure of teaching writing is helping students to become aware of audience and to discover their own voices. Using a few simple activities, such as those suggested in this chapter, may help students to discover their unique selves and the people for whom they write. Empowering students to discover their own voices and encouraging them to write for an audience can also increase the pleasure that students take in writing, the pleasure that students take in hearing each other's writing, and ultimately the pleasure that teachers take in teaching writing and reading student compositions.

REFERENCES AND RESOURCES

Bouchard, David. *If You're Not from the Prairie.* Vancouver: Raincoast Books, 1994.

Cisneros, Sandra. *The House on Mango Street.* New York: Random House, 1984.

———. *Woman Hollering Creek.* New York: Random House, 1991.

Elbow, Peter. *Writing with Power.* New York: Oxford University Press, 1981.

Haley, Alex. "Thank You." *Parade Magazine,* November 21, 1982.

Hickey, Dona J. *Developing a Written Voice.* Mountain View, CA: Mayfield Publishing, 1993.

Keithley, Zoe. " 'My Own Voice': Students Say It Unlocks the Writing Process." *Journal of Basic Writing* 11.2 (1992): 83–102.

Macrorie, Ken. *Searching Writing.* Rochelle Park, NJ: Hayden Book Co., 1980.

Murray, Donald M. *A Writer Teaches Writing, Second Ed.* Boston: Houghton, 1985.

Reed, Janine. "Self-orientation in 'Expressive Writing' Instruction." *Journal of Teaching Writing* 13.1,2 (1994): 109–126.

Schultz, John. *Writing from Start to Finish.* Portsmouth, NH: Boynton/Cook, 1990.

Wakoski, Diane. "The Neighbor's Cat." *Virtuoso Literature for Two and Four Hands.* Garden City, NY: Doubleday, 1975.

Zinsser, William. *On Writing Well.* New York: Harper & Row, 1980.

4

No-Grammar and Grammar Appreciation: Two Approaches to the G-Word

MARK HONEGGER

One issue in teaching writing in grades 6–12 that is constantly and most intensely debated is the teaching of grammar. In this chapter, Mark Honegger presents two very different approaches to the issue of grammar in the writing classroom: the no-grammar approach and a grammar appreciation approach. Teaching strategies are included to illustrate how grammar instruction might actually be realized in each of these classrooms. Honegger intends readers to compare and contrast these approaches so that they might be well informed as they choose the approach best suited to their own style and philosophy of teaching.

Two Approaches to Teaching Grammar

Jamie's paper came in on time, and his teacher, Julia Denton, picked it up to read with curiosity. Jamie had struggled with his writing the entire semester. He had average interest in the writing process. Julia was thankful that he wasn't one of the many students who disdained writing. Yet she knew you couldn't expect everyone to love writing like Natalie Parker did. In some assignments, Jamie seemed to have an authentic message to convey, but he never managed to convey it clearly. His words always got in the way of his thoughts. In other assignments, Jamie was totally lost, and the last one had been a disaster. Julia had sat down with Jamie and had a long talk with him. She had encouraged him to use language that he was comfortable with and to try and use words that he spoke with, and Jamie had dutifully promised to give it his best effort on this next essay.

The paper started like this:

Going down the highway. Kevin noticed smoke around the back of his car, and losing speed. He shook his head, his car was always acting up and he was discussed at it. Why couldn't cars be like people like their cars a lot?

Julia winced. In her own preparation for teaching, she had been exposed to very little grammar instruction. A few of her professors had assured the class it was of limited value to directly teach grammar to their students. After all, the research had shown that grammar instruction did not improve students' writing. Julia had picked up her explicit grammar knowledge in dribs and drabs and "in the streets," as the occasion arose. She wished now that she had been given more explicit instruction; she didn't know where to start to address Jamie's problems.

Enter stage left, the dreaded g-word—grammar. Julia's story represents a generation of teachers, many of whom have come through the educational system with a general uncertainty about the importance of grammar in language and literature studies. It is not the fault of the teachers themselves. The field of composition has been ambivalent for a number of years about the value of grammar in writing pedagogy, and this ambivalence has led to doubts and confusion for many students, in general, and teachers-in-training, in particular.

Teachers in the field have sharply divergent views about grammar as well. Some are very thankful for research that dismisses grammatical training altogether; others swear by the value of patiently working through grammatical analysis and exercises. In light of this state of affairs, this chapter will present two dramatically different approaches to the problem of grammar instruction: a minimal- or *no-grammar approach*, and *a grammar-appreciation approach*. My goal is to contrast these different pedagogies so that readers can think through the issues in a way that lets them choose a method that fits their own developing role as teachers and lets them think about the pluses and minuses of each. Hence, it is important that readers read the entire chapter, because each approach is meant to be read against the other.

The No-Grammar Approach

The no-grammar approach is something of a misnomer, because it doesn't mean that grammar is absent from the classroom. Rather, the teacher assumes an attitude of benign neglect: she uses no grammatical terminology, she refrains from red-inking grammatical and punctuation mistakes, and she eliminates all lessons that require the analysis of sentence structure. She does this not out of haphazardness, but out of a conscious effort on her part to let her students develop their writing abilities by encouraging a love of writing and reading. As students write and read more, it is hoped they will unconsciously improve their mastery over the conventions of writing, much as a child unconsciously develops his spoken language without massive corrections.

There is research that can be read as favorable to the no-grammar approach (although see Kolln, 1981, for a more detailed critique of the research). Such studies support the contention that the teaching of grammar has absolutely no benefit for the teaching of writing and may even be harmful because it detracts from spending time on other more important matters. A number of factors explain why this would be the case.

First, language is an extremely complex phenomenon, and the structure of language is part of that complexity. Consequently, writing classes are encountering a difficult task when students try to learn grammar and writing at the same time. This difficulty manifests itself in two ways. For starters, teachers may lack the training and knowledge to teach grammar well, and they may not know how to present grammar in a way that students can transfer their grammatical knowledge to the challenge of writing. Teachers may also struggle with a corresponding lack of confidence in teaching grammar. This can be true even for experienced teachers who value the overt teaching of grammar. Anyone who works with language long enough runs into sentences and expressions that do not fit into the neat categories that we use for grammar, and when these kinds of sentences come up in the course of a grammar lesson, it can be frustrating, if not embarrassing, for the conscientious teacher. Students also face a daunting task trying to master a subject that has occupied many minds for millennia. While some students warm to the systematic nature of grammar and enjoy the kind of analysis it promotes, other students find it baffling and never gain any permanent understanding, even after years of exposure. Part of the motivation for keeping grammar instruction out of the classroom is that the difficulty of the enterprise requires a lot of class time to make any significant headway, and the devotion of the many contact hours to grammar may not be warranted, compared to the many other aspects of writing that can be profitably dealt with by the teacher.

Second, many teachers dislike teaching grammar. This dislike *may* be due to the difficulty mentioned in the previous paragraph. It's normal to dislike things we find hard to do. I remember how much I disliked Shakespeare the first time I read one of his plays in high school because I couldn't easily understand his language. But dislike may also stem from the nature of the subject material. The study of grammar can appear rather sterile and confining compared to the creativity and expansiveness of the act of writing itself. Many people who teach writing are attracted to the profession because they value creative self-expression and wish to stay far away from any domain where lifeless rules hold sway. It is no great surprise then that if teachers are bored with a subject students will be bored and dislike the subject, too. This presents a challenge to writing teachers. If they wish to overtly teach grammar, they must try to develop a positive attitude in the classroom toward their subject matter. However, another solution is to look for ways of teaching by which the subject is avoided altogether. For teachers who have a complete antipathy toward the g-word, I recommend a no-grammar approach.

Many students also dislike learning grammar, in particular, the drills and rote memorization that have often been the backbone of grammar instruction. Negative student responses are a problem, because one thing we are trying to do is promote a love of learning and a love of writing in students, and so there is a desire to make the classroom experience as fun as possible. Numerous other, more enjoyable activities can be done in place of grammar drills, so getting rid of formal grammar instruction looks to be a good way of jazzing up the writing classroom.

How to Teach No-Grammar

There are a number of things that teachers can do to address the sentence-level abilities of their students without mentioning the dreaded g-word. The first thing that comes to most teachers' minds is the general benefits of encouraging lots of reading. We know already that students pick up many pieces of language by reading. For example, children pick up a tremendous amount of vocabulary throughout their elementary school years, an estimated 600 to 5,000 words annually (Nagy, Herman, and Anderson). There is a general consensus that the more students read the more they are likely to pick up the feel of good style, the more their own grammatical competence increases, and the more they pick up the punctuation conventions of formal writing without the punitive nature of going through dreary drills. It must be remembered though that reading is a long-term solution to increasing general writing competence. It won't put bandages on students' difficulties in the course of a semester. Hence, if you want to use reading as your primary means of addressing students' writing problems, you must also assume the role of benign neglect, not commenting on students' grammatical errors because you don't wish to distract them from more important writing issues and you don't wish to kill their delight in the writing process.

Not surprisingly, the second major tool the no-grammar teacher has is to encourage writing, lots of writing and lots of different kinds of writing. Teachers should look for a variety of writing tasks in different genres that can elicit the need for different types of grammatical constructions from the students. Again, the teacher does not correct the mechanics of the prose that students produce, but trusts the process of students' growing written fluency to eventually issue in prose with fewer mistakes and missteps. What is crucial again is that the students' conscious goals always be writing goals, that their motives always be to produce a certain kind of writing that has the potential to affect the audience in the way the writer desires.

Teachers can also take this general emphasis on writing to design very specific writing activities that more or less compel students to practice a specific kind of grammatical construction. However, the activity is presented in such a way that the student's focus is not on the particular grammatical construction, but on some rhetorical purpose. Still the teacher can choose rhetorical purposes that lend themselves well to certain kinds of sentence structures.

For example, instead of teaching a unit on run-on sentences and comma splices, a teacher can set up a writing situation that encourages students to combine many clauses into coordinate structures within a single sentence. In doing so, the teacher also demonstrates to the students how long and short sentences affect the reader. A possible scenario could be the following: the teacher directs the students to write an identical narrative in two ways, the first in a way that makes the story move very slowly and the second in a way that lets the story move quickly. The teacher also supplies a model for students to see and discusses the model with students and asks for their reactions. The first version would consist of many short sentences that lend a choppy effect to the writing. It might read like the following.

> The night was cold. I was tired. Ten days had passed. Still there was no word from my friend. My courage was failing. My heart was sick with impatience. Suddenly, a noise came from the front walk. My breath stopped. Could it be? Was it now? Is she here?

The second version would be revised so that the short clauses were combined into longer compound sentences using a variety of means.

> The night was cold; I was tired. Ten days had passed, and still there was no word from my friend. My courage was failing, and my heart was sick with impatience. Suddenly, a noise came from the front walk—my breath stopped. Could it be, was it now, is she here?

Crucially, the teacher would make no direct reference as to how the sentences should be combined: no instructions on the use of punctuation and no corrections of student errors. Rather, the teacher would keep her comments focused on the rhetorical effect that the students produced with their own paragraphs. It is very useful to compare alternative ways of writing the same material, for example, the three versions of the following two clauses:

> The night was cold. I was tired.
> The night was cold, and I was tired.
> The night was cold; I was tired.

The teacher can begin by reading the sentences aloud and then encouraging her students to listen to the sound and rhythm of these three versions so that students may appreciate how the sentences affect them. Much enjoyable writing comes from people who have a taste for and appreciation of the music of language. It is well worth classroom time to slow down students to simply listen to language and begin to imbibe its melody. When the teacher reads these sentences aloud, she could slightly exaggerate their effects to make more obvious the typical rhetorical effects of the prose. For example, she can read the first with a slightly longer pause between the two sentences. "The night was cold. [long pause] I was tired." The second sentence can be read with a single melody. The third sentence can be read with two separate melodies, but no significant pause between the two clauses. Then the teacher can ask questions: In which version do the sentences have the strongest connection to one another? In which version do the sentences seem the most unconnected to one another? In which version do the sentences seem like they're simply part of a story? The teacher can also comment on how these versions speed up or slow down the story. For example, the second version with *and* makes the story move more quickly than either of the other two. All the while, the teacher continues her benign neglect. Students are encouraged to play around with the punctuation and sentence structure in the hope that proficiency will come over time as students read and write more.

Another example of a writing task that is geared toward a particular problem of mechanics would be to have students construct narratives that manipulate active and passive sentences. For example, students could be shown a short film that involved physical action between two characters or a series of pictures that portrayed the same thing. Then students are directed to write sentences that focus on a different character, sometimes the doer of the action and sometimes the recipient of the action. This will encourage students to write both active and passive sentences as the participant does or receives the action.

Suppose, for example, that students are shown a series of picture in which Jane picks up a glass and gives it to James. Then students are asked to write sentences that focus on Jane and are encouraged to describe the situation in as many ways as they can. Creativity is encouraged. The teacher might encounter the following sentences:

> Jane gives/gave James the glass.
> Jane hands/handed James the glass.
> Jane picks up/picked up the glass for James.
> Jane is helpful. She sees James and gives him a glass. Etc.

Then students are told to reverse roles and make the other participant the topic of all the sentences. The second set of sentences might look like the following:

> James is/was given a glass.
> James is/was handed a glass.
> James receives/received a glass from Jane.
> James looked thirsty, and Jane gave him a glass.

After the class has produced a nice set of sentences for each task, the teacher can engage the students in a discussion about the effects of the different expressions they have created. For example, the teacher can compare an active sentence with its passive version and ask the students what effect the sentence makes on readers. Which one is longer? Which one is more direct? What are writing situations for which either could be used successfully? Instead of grilling and drilling students in the mechanics of active and passive sentences, students are taught to be sensitive to the uses and effects of active and passive sentences. The teacher can continue the exercise by presenting paragraphs in which a sentence is missing and then present an active and passive sentence as possible completions of the paragraph. Or the teacher can construct paragraphs in which a passive sentence or an active sentence could be replaced by its opposite.

These serve as examples of how specific kinds of grammatical issues can be addressed by gearing assignments to those problems. Yet there are still other exercises that can, so to speak, limber up the overall language muscles of students. Killgallon lists four that he has used successfully: sentence imitating, sentence unscrambling, sentence combining, and sentence expanding. All these can be practiced without students overtly knowing the terms of grammar. These activities focus the attention of students on the style and arrangement of language. Teachers select as material sentences from professional writers, particularly those whose flair for language they appreciate, and present this material to students in altered forms for the students to manipulate and then eventually imitate. Descriptions of the latter three activities are given below.

Sentence Unscrambling

In sentence unscrambling, the teacher takes a lively sentence from a printed source and scrambles its parts. For example, a sentence portion from Willa Cather's *Neighbour Rosicky*, "Over yonder on the hill he could see his own house, crouching low, with the clump of orchard behind and the windmill before," might be divided into the following parts:

> could see his own house
> over yonder on the hill
> crouching low
> with the clump of orchard and the windmill before
> he

Students are then asked to rearrange the parts into a well-formed sentence. In addition to the original arrangement, students might come up with other alternatives as well, such as

> Crouching low, with the clump of orchard and the windmill before, he could see his own house over yonder on the hill.

This exercise accomplishes a number of things. First, it gives students a sense of how phrases can occupy different positions within the sentence, particularly those interesting adverbial phrases that add spice and heft to writing. Second, in many cases the placement of these phrases leads to different rhetorical effects and these can be discussed in the class. This gets students thinking about the effect that language has on the whole composition and encourages them to think through their own prose and the possibilities it has.

After students have reassembled the sentences, they can be asked to write their own sentences that imitate those they have reassembled. In doing this, they can practice these structures for themselves in a creative way. What they do is strengthen their facility to manipulate language without concerning themselves about what the parts are called.

Sentence Combining

Sentence combining gives students a chance to take short sentences and make them into a single sentence that has greater texture and complexity. Again, teachers can base their sentence combination exercises on published sentences or they can make up their own. For example, a teacher might take the following sentence from William Faulkner's *A Rose for Emily*, "When we saw her again, her hair was cut short, making her look like a girl, with a vague resemblance to those angels in colored church windows—sort of tragic and serene," and turn it into the following short clauses.

> We saw her again.
> Her hair was cut short.
> Her haircut made her look like a girl.
> She resembled an angel in a colored church window.
> She was sort of tragic and serene.

Students then reassemble these short clauses into a single sentence. They might come up with any number of possibilities, such as the following:

> We saw her again, looking sort of tragic and serene, her short haircut making her look like a girl, her face resembling an angel in a colored church window.

This activity works better after students have had practice with sentence-combining exercises and have gained a feel for the placement possibilities of sentence-modifying expressions. Interesting class discussions can ensue as students discuss the different rhetorical effects that are generated by varying the placement of the modifiers.

Sentence Expanding

Finally, sentence expanding presents a stripped-down version of a published sentence to students with places in the sentence marked for insertion with the students' own creative phrasing. A sentence like the following from Saul Bellow's *Seize the Day*, "Patiently, in the window of the fruit store, a man with a scoop spread crushed ice between his rows of vegetables," is presented to students in the following form:

> * A man * spread crushed ice between his rows of vegetables.

The asterisks mark places for inserted material. This gives students a chance to think about content and structure and again provides classroom opportunities to discuss how placement of material leads to different rhetorical effects.

The preceding suggestions present a handful of ways that teachers can address stylistic issues without overtly teaching or mentioning grammar or grammatical terms. For those who dislike grammar and are uncomfortable with an overt presentation of this subject, and also who have the freedom to do so, I encourage them to adopt a kind of no-grammar approach as outlined here and to do so with a spirit of investigation and an eye toward monitoring the progress of their students who are schooled with this conscious approach, both in their own class and in the years ahead. At present, I know of no research that measures over an extended period of time the effects of this approach on English language teaching. Thus, it is an open question what this approach may mean in the long run. But the methods given here have been tested and used profitably in a number of classrooms.

The Grammar-Appreciation Approach

The grammar appreciation approach is in essence a language-appreciation approach, and it is crucial to understand its overall goal. Its aim is not to make students proficient in grammar drills or even simply to embed a few techniques in their heads relating to the conventions of written English. Rather, it aims to make students fall in love with language and to pique their natural curiosity and intellectual hunger so that they might understand language and see its fascinating brilliance. In aiming for a different goal, the approach will also strengthen the sentence-level competence of students.

Thus, the overt presentation of grammar in the classroom does not start with rote memorization of terminology, but is conducted as a discovery procedure by asking the students on their own to take apart language and reassemble it in any way they please. Terminology is introduced later in the process after students have discovered parts and pieces of language and they themselves feel the need to have names by which they can refer to the discoveries they have made. This approach recognizes that most people take language for granted and often fail to notice the intricacies of language and its rhetorical possibilities, even though they exploit many intricacies and rhetorical possibilities every day, at least in their speech.

This grammar-appreciation approach highlights the fact that grammar instruction is often presented to students (like most academic subjects) before they realize the importance of what they are learning. Especially as students get older, it becomes increasingly harder to teach subject matter that they don't value. Hence, teachers must create the need for the material or, in this case awaken the need. Every student needs language, and every student has a need to understand what he or she values. The grammar-appreciation approach, then, seeks to lead students to value what they need. Language is one of the most personal and emotive possessions that any person has. Attitudes toward language are one of the biggest social determinants in society. It pays to teach children from very early on about language to increase their appreciation of their own and others' language, to give them as clear an understanding of language as possible so that their attitudes toward varieties of language are based on knowledge rather than ignorance, and to give them an appreciation of their own intelligence and ingenuity.

Just as a number of factors support the no-grammar approach, there are also factors that support the grammar-appreciation approach. A number of readers may have been distinctly uncomfortable with the no-grammar approach outlined previously; for them, we need to evaluate the research a little more thoroughly.

For the most part, the little research that has been done on grammar instruction suggests that teaching grammar by drill and rote in the context of one semester as one segment of teaching writing is not beneficial. There are many reasons why this is not surprising. Chief among these is that grammar instruction in this context adds to a content overload for students. Are we teaching all the following in one semester: how to craft thesis statements, how to pay attention to audience and voice, how to read critically, how to incorporate outside material in students' writing, etc., etc.? This list alone shows the great intellectual demands we are placing on students every semester we teach writing. Now we add another complex topic, grammar instruction, to the list. Something is bound to lose out, and often as not it will be understanding the grammar instruction. This scenario is like teaching a class on quantum physics and devoting some hours of instruction to multiplication and division. Then students are tested to see how proficient they are in quantum physics at the end of the class. Undoubtedly, the students' ability in quantum physics would not be improved, but that does not mean that multiplication and division are unnecessary to quantum physics. Instead, the more complicated procedures of quantum physics research depend on being able to do basic mathematics automatically, without thinking about it.

What this points to is that grammar should be taught not first and foremost as a form of remediation in the midst of teaching other aspects of writing, but over a period of years during which teachers and students have some time to consider the system of grammar apart from the demand of grammatical performance in writing. In this context, one has the leisure to play around with grammar and explore its rationale and systematic nature. The student can then understand grammar, rather than be pressured to perform grammatically when their hold on the concepts is tentative. This does not mean that grammar should be taught apart from its application to good style in writing. Rather, it means that time can be taken to help students understand English grammar. Then they will be able to apply it to their writing.

Some research studies have criticized grammar instruction because improvement was not detected at the end of the semester. Yet we should not be surprised at this, because language throughout the school years is a developing skill, and learning about language (grammar) is a developing skill as well. Thus, measurable improvement may not come in neat increments at the end of every lesson and semester. Rather, improvement takes time, and some kinds of improvement are constrained by age-based stages of development. If teachers do directly teach grammar, they need to have a long-range view that they are adding to a student's overall understanding and feel for language. The hope is that the student who receives good grammar instruction over a number of years will be better able to apply that knowledge to the increasingly sophisticated writing he or she is called on to do than the student who does not have this grammatical understanding.

Hence, the research does not give us a conclusive verdict on the merits of grammar instruction.

There are a number of positive reasons for incorporating direct grammar instruction in the classroom. One reason why a grammar-appreciation approach is plausible is because direct grammar instruction can work. Many teachers (and students) have told me of successes they have experienced in the classroom when grammar knowledge was transferred to writing. Jack Sofield, a radiologist from Tennessee, relates from a bygone era how his mother would not answer him if he ended a sentence with a preposition. If he asked his mother, "Where's my hat at?" the room stayed quiet. Today, most people don't care too much if we speak this way, but Sofield makes the point that his mother's strictness made him pay attention to language and gave him a heightened awareness of its characteristics. Individual success stories like these suggest that it is possible to learn about the grammatical properties of language, and so we need to beware of being too pessimistic about the effectiveness of grammatical instruction.

Another reason for teaching grammar is that we equip students with a vocabulary for talking about language and thereby give them the means to enter an educated community that discusses language. Every academic discipline has a way of talking about its subject matter, and writing and language need one, too. Knowing grammatical terms allows students to enter into a conversation about language with the widest possible audience. If students learn terminology when they are younger, they can understand these terms when they are used by teachers in higher grades, from high school to college. Knowing the terms will also allow students to understand and use grammar handbooks when they get to college, an important skill, because it means that students will be able to diagnose and solve their own structure difficulties instead of relying solely on the instructor.

Another reason we can cite for teaching grammar is that we otherwise run the risk of setting the ultimate level of student achievement too low. As teachers, we don't know in advance how much writing knowledge each student will need. It is better to equip as many as possible with as much as possible.

Writing is a complex task, and a successful writer must do a number of things well. The writer must match the purpose of his composition to the needs of his audience. The writer must organize his composition. The writer must have control of his content. The writer must write in a cohesive way so that paragraphs are both internally unified and linked to one another. Finally, the writer must write prose that is free of grammatical errors, that has punctuation that serves the purposes of his composition, and that is socially appropriate for the intended audience. There is a general consensus among teachers that issues of grammar and usage are the least important of all the aspects that good writing requires. But labeling grammar as least important obscures the fact that it is still necessary not only for academic writing and for writing that will be published, but also for the kind of writing required for getting a good job. Too often, a negative attitude toward grammar has become a reason for not addressing student difficulties with grammatical concerns, and the outcome is that after twelve or more years of school students may still have serious problems in putting together sentences free of grammatical and punctuation errors.

A more helpful approach for the students would be for teachers to have the mind-set that twelve years is enough time for students to be trained to do all of the things listed above—good organization, good content, good grammar, etc.—so that by the time a student is ready to enroll in college, she will be competent in the basics of writing and ready to tackle the more challenging task of academic writing at the college level. A teacher's goal for all students then should be for them to write consistently grammatical sentences by the time they get to college, a goal that is reasonable if the appropriate instruction is spread out over twelve years.

Another reason for direct grammar instruction is that students need grammatical competence so that they can be freed to concentrate on higher-order concerns. In other words, grammar in writing is similar to exercise in sports. For example, the goal of a basketball player is not to be proficient in running laps but to be skilled in making lay-ups. Furthermore, a basketball player needs to be able to make lay-ups and other harder kinds of shots throughout an entire game, which is tiring because of the extensive running up and down the court. Now imagine an athlete who perfected his ability to shoot lay-ups, but whose physical conditioning was poor. His shooting ability would be severely limited in an actual game after fatigue set in. Even more telling, his shooting form would likely deteriorate as his body compensated for tired muscles. If his physical conditioning were good, then the athletic ability and skill in shooting and dribbling and all the other facets of the game could be displayed throughout the entire contest.

This is exactly what our students encounter in writing. Control over the grammatical and stylistic elements of writing frees up a writer to concentrate on and perfect her ability in her finer points of writing, the points that teachers usually prefer to teach and focus on. Students who lack ability and confidence in the stylistic aspects of writing tend to be dragged down by these deficits. They are not able to give as much of their attention to higher-order concerns like content and organization and audience because they know that the words are not right. We don't want our students to be like a basketball player who has mastered the skill to make a flawless lay-up, but who does not have the muscle strength to lift his arms over his head.

Another reason for teaching grammar directly to students is that the no-grammar approach may not work for all students. For students who read and write a lot and who come from language backgrounds in which their variety of speech is closer to the kind of written English used in academic settings, the hands-off approach to grammar often works fine. These students "know" the kind of language they need to use in school, and they will need little direct intervention in their prose. However, as students diverge from this norm because they come from less academically prepared backgrounds or because they speak varieties of English that diverge more sharply from the standards of the classroom, a strictly hands-off approach just doesn't work in many cases. Delpit has written of this for black English speakers and Reyes for Hispanic students. But the same things hold for any student whose background does not encourage written literacy. These students don't "know" in advance the language they need for academic writing, and assigning lots of reading by itself is not the magic cure-all for their grammar problems. As Christensen long ago observed, "If reading literature" was the key to writing success, "English teachers would be our best writers and PMLA would year by year take all the prizes for nonfiction."

Finally, teaching grammar directly encourages students to pay attention to language, to think about the medium, to think about words and their orders and patterns. Students are more likely to notice what is going on in a written text because learning about grammar focuses them on the words and their structure. The method that we all would prefer for making students think about written language is reading, but reading draws students' attention primarily to meaning on a global level. That is, reading alone does not tend to draw students' attention to how we got to that meaning. Grammar draws students' attention to the technical aspects of written language, which *is* how the writer gets to the global meaning of the text.

Let's give a list of some specific content that all graduates of twelve years of education should master: parts of speech, grammatical roles, and identification of phrases within a sentence. Again, teachers should not stop at this level of content. What about infinitives and gerunds, participles, and the like? Teachers might be tempted to stop before they reach this point on the grounds that such esoteric knowledge is not necessary, but remember that we are viewing grammar as a part of this holistic thing called language. These further grammatical categories become issues in areas of consequence to writing, such as passive sentences or parallelism breakdowns, as in the following ill-formed sentence: *Jane wants to go to Florida on Spring Break, swimming in the ocean, and that she might get a tan.* With further grammatical training, a teacher can talk about the specific units in the sentence with her students and pinpoint in detail what is wrong. Without grammatical training, a teacher is reduced to handwaving: the sentence is wrong, fix it.

How to Teach Grammar Appreciation

If you are teaching grammar to middle school and high school students, especially students who may be turned off to grammar, one of your goals should be to introduce the subject in a way that stimulates their intellectual curiosity and that suggests starting out with an inductive approach by which students are exposed to language and allowed to play with it and to find for themselves the patterns in it, rather than starting from a top-down approach that spoonfeeds all the insights to students without getting them involved.

Let's picture how this might work for teaching the basic division of the sentence into its subject part and predicate part. One possibility is to write a number of sentences on construction paper and then cut the paper into two pieces at the boundary between the subject and predicate. Then the pieces are mixed in a hat and students are asked to extract pieces and make sentences out of any two pieces that can be fixed together. The exercise becomes more enjoyable if the teacher chooses sentences whose parts might lead to humorous or colorful new sentences when mixed. The following sentences provide an example of what this might look like. At an early stage, the teacher will want to be sure to control for subject–verb agreement so that all the sentence subjects and predicates can fit together grammatically.

> Principal Smith / respects Central Middle School.
> Baby Joy / has a dirty diaper.
> The funny dog / chased the neighbor's cat.
> Our class / loves to study.
> The hardworking student / asked the teacher for more homework.

When given the freedom, students will construct not only the ordinary sentences but also new ones that can add a chuckle to the activity, such as "Principal Smith has a dirty diaper."

Once students have had some fun making a number of sentences, the teacher can select one at random and ask students to find all the other pieces of paper that have parts that can substitute for the subject. She does the same for the predicate part of the sentence so that all the sentence parts are divided into two groups. At this point, she can talk to the students about the structurelike character of English. Sentences are like a puzzle that has various pieces that fit together. She can also introduce the terms *subject* and *predicate* to talk about these newly identified parts of the sentence.

This exercise can be followed up in a number of ways. Students could be asked to make up their own novel subjects or predicates and add them to the mix. (Teachers will need to control for subject–verb agreement again.) Teachers could talk about other sentence types, such as imperatives, in which the subject is usually left unstated (*Go to your room!*) or questions, in which the subject appears in the middle of the predicate (*Did you go to the concert last night?*). A teacher could also immediately link this activity to a writing exercise by asking each student to form all the sentence parts into complete sentences and then having them write a narrative or essay that uses these sentences. However the activity is continued, starting your grammar class as a discovery procedure is more likely to set a positive tone and make the concepts come alive to the students.

Parts of Speech

Parts of speech refer to those basic categories that are named noun, verb, adjective, and so on. A student with the inability to identify parts of speech is severely limited in talking about language—in understanding both what might be wrong with a sentence and how to fix it. Thus, they are limited in their ability to diagnose their own sentence construction problems.

Again, it is more interesting to start this section off by allowing the students to make grammatical discoveries on their own. One way to do this is to give students a series of sentences that all have a word missing that belongs to the same category. Again, the activity becomes interesting as the sentences are varied enough so that humorous and colorful sentences are made depending on the choice of word. In the examples given next, a slot for nouns is left blank.

The _____ has four legs.
A _____ makes a good pet.
My _____ talks to me every morning.
I ate a _____ for breakfast.
Kim gave a present to her _____.

Students then supply possible words to fit the blanks and are encouraged to be creative as possible. Thus, the word *dog* supplied for the first two sentences can also be inserted to make "My dog talks to me every morning" for a smile, "I ate a dog for breakfast" for a grimace, and "Kim gave a present to her dog" for a look of satisfaction from all the dog lovers in the class. The word *teacher* supplied for the last sentence can also lead to gems like "A teacher makes a good pet."

Once students have assembled a large group of nouns, the teacher can impress on students that they have identified pieces of their language that have similar properties, and of course we need some name for this type of piece, so the teacher supplies the term *noun*. This kind of discovery exercise can be applied to all the word classes of English.

Once students have discovered and played with the basic categories, they can be introduced to more challenging work, because eventually we want them to be comfortable with identifying the parts of language in a real-world text, such as their reading and their own writing. In particular, we can give students practical tests for identifying parts of speech on their own. At this point, it's useful for us to remember and for us to point out to students that we are teaching them something that they already know, but that this knowledge is unconscious. The fact that we all understand others and that when we speak others understand us shows us that our brains handle these properties of words just fine.

These tests or rules that we can teach students have the benefit of making grammar as concrete as possible. The value of the rules is that students will now look for something specific in the language, rather than try to understand language without any categories in place. This gives students a vocabulary and system for understanding their errors and difficulties with style. For the student who never makes a mistake in her prose, knowing about the structure of language may be unnecessary. For the rest of us, an understanding of grammar turns an abstract thing like the English language into a more concrete object so that we can see what is going on in a text.

Traditionally, students were taught to identify parts of speech by tests of meaning, for example, a noun is a person, place, or thing. These tests were popular because they were easy to apply. They drew on a speaker's implicit knowledge of words. They also were roundly criticized for shortcomings. For instance, in example 1, the noun *destruction* seems to be an action, rather than a person, place, or thing.

1. The destruction of the city frightened me.

The thing to do is not simply to eliminate the traditional test, but to add other tests to it to provide a fuller picture of these parts of speech and a sounder basis for determining the category for individual words.

Therefore, we will be talking about *meaning* tests and *structure* tests for determining parts of speech. As students master the application of both kinds of tests, they will be better equipped to diagnose what is going on in a sentence. Structure tests identify parts of speech on the basis of their structural properties, in particular, where they occur in the sentence relative to other words or categories of words. Generally, structure tests are more accurate tests in determining grammatical categories, and this should be emphasized to the students; but it need not be a reason for eliminating meaning tests as well from your students repertoire of grammatical tools. Linguistic textbooks today have sections that provide structure tests, and teachers are well advised to consult these works to make themselves more knowledgeable about the structural properties of English words. The following sections show that we can apply meaning tests and structure tests to identify nouns and adjectives.

Nouns

Meaning Test: A noun is a person, place, or thing.

Structure Test: A noun can occur in the following positions:

> the _____
> the (adjective) _____

The meaning test is the test that probably first comes to the attention of speakers when they deliberately consider a particular sentence they have encountered. It allows speakers to intuitively access the implicit knowledge of the meaning of the word that is stored in their head. Also, in the great majority of cases, it will give the right results for grammatical analysis, although we have already shown that there are important exceptions to the meaning test in the case of nouns that have a verblike meaning. This test will also be of limited help when a truly novel noun is encountered for the first time, as in example 2.

2. The scientist could not calculate the syzygy of that distant moon without more information.

The *American Heritage Dictionary* defines *syzygy* as "either of two points in the orbit of a celestial body where the body is in opposition to or in conjunction with the sun," but chances are your students don't know the meaning of the word or even have a reasonable guess if it was given in an opaque context. This is where structure tests become useful.

The structure tests identify that nouns follow determiners (or articles) like *the* _____ or determiners plus adjectives like *the big* _____. Other parts of speech are excluded from such positions, which makes this a good test for one of the two most important parts of speech.

Someone might object that the second structure test is flawed because it depends on a category, adjective, that has not been defined yet. This is a reasonable objection, but not a fatal one, because these tests are being used pedagogically rather than in a strict system of logic. And they are being used to teach something in the sense of making explicit the implicit knowledge that the students already have in their heads. Hence, if these tests are being taught to young students who have truly never learned the category of adjective, then specific examples of adjectives should be used, and adjectives can be varied to fit the noun that follows. If the tests are being taught to older students who have previously been exposed to the category of adjectives, they may already have enough working knowledge of the category to apply the test correctly.

Teachers must also be aware of how to apply the test correctly. As the tests were written, they would also allow adjectives to be inserted in the specified positions in examples 3 and 4.

3. the *big* dog
4. the big *red* dog

These examples show that it is always possible to add an adjective, in fact an unlimited number of adjectives, before a common noun. If a student suggests this answer, the teacher can encourage students to access their innate knowledge by having them apply both the structure and meaning tests, because only the word *dog* satisfies both kinds of tests in examples 3 and 4. Using these tests as pointers to a student's innate knowledge makes them useful, even when there are exceptions to them.

Adjectives

Meaning Test: An adjective describes, modifies, or qualifies a noun.

Structure Test: An adjective occurs in the following positions:

the _____ (noun)
very _____

These tests show that what is really useful is to present the tests for nouns and adjectives together because their structure tests depend on one another. As always, teachers should start with clear cases to define the categories before they move to more difficult ones. Students should be taught all the tests and asked to apply them to each example as they learn them. This way they will be able to see the full range of structures that a given part of speech can occur in. Applying all the tests at one time will allow students to make more precise assessments of the words in a sentence. For example, suppose students are asked to determine the part of speech of the word *school* in the following phrase (5).

5. the school president

It is important to apply all three tests to this case. Does the word *school* describe or modify the president? The answer would be yes. The word *school* also appears in the position *the* _____ (noun), which allows it to confirm one of the structure tests. But the word *school* fails the last structure, as shown by the impossibility of example 6. (Note that the * at the beginning is a convention that signals an ill-formed sequence of words.)

6. *the very school president

The tests then serve a useful purpose in pointing to another structure, that of the compound noun, a construction made of two nouns. At this point, a teacher might be tempted to ask what difference it makes to writing whether one has a noun–noun combination or an adjective–noun combination. But there are important differences between the two as regards the way language works. For example, the noun–noun compound cannot have an intervening adjective (example 7), whereas the adjective–noun compound can always have another adjective inserted inside it (example 8).

7. the school president   *the school big president
8. the tall president   the tall, handsome president

Likewise, the teacher should be aware of those classes of adjectives that do not occur in the structure tests given previously, in particular those adjectives that occur after nouns, such as *asleep* in example 9.

9. the writer asleep at her desk

The adjective *asleep*, though, does not occur between the determiner and noun (example 10) or after *very* (example 11).

10. *the asleep writer
11. *very asleep

These examples are best handled after introducing more canonical adjectives to students.

Finally, we can point out to students that nouns and adjectives seem to have a fair amount in common when it comes to their language properties. The structure tests have already shown that both can be used to modify other nouns. There are also common positions in which they both occur, such as following *be* verbs, as in examples 12 through 14.

12. Kim is president.
13. Kim is happy.
14. Kim is asleep.

These three examples show how this position takes nouns and both kinds of adjectives, but also that nouns and adjectives are related categories.

Teaching students these kinds of tests is especially useful for identifying the open classes of English—nouns, adjectives, verbs, and adverbs. Tests can also be given for identifying the closed classes, such as prepositions and conjunctions. What we are doing here it equipping students to understand the structure of sentences on their own, apart from books and their teachers, so that they can become experts on their own language and writing.

Phrases

Phrases are adjacent sets of words that have a strong connection to each other. Once parts of speech are mastered, students should become proficient at identifying phrases, that is, how words chunk together in a sentence. Again, the unconscious grammar in their heads allows them to do this naturally in speech. Teaching students about grammar allows them to consciously identify which words go together in a sentence. Here, as in other places, teachers depend on the innate linguistic ability of students. Given a random sentence in English, speakers will bring intuitions about which words are especially closely linked in terms of meaning. Students should be asked to identify which words have closer meaning relationships with other words in the sentence. For example, in example 15,

15. Marty chased the cat.

teachers can ask students about the determiner *the.* In particular, they can elicit whether *the* has a closer relationship to the word before it, *chased*, or the word which follows, *cat.* The teacher should expect that the majority of students will intuitively identify *the* as having a closer meaning relationship to *cat* than to *chased.* Looking at unambiguous examples like these helps to develop in students a functional understanding of phrases.

Phrases have both a structural and a meaning aspect. For this, too, it is useful to teach students specific rules for determining phrase boundaries. At least three rules can be given to students for identifying phrases.

The first rule is that phrases can be replaced by pro-forms. Pro-forms are words that "stand in" for a phrase, of which pronouns are the best-known example. Pronouns like *it* and *they* can take the place of a phrase that has previously been mentioned in the discourse. But there are also pro-verbs such as *do*,

16. Yesterday, Cory raked the yard.
17. Yesterday, Cory did.

and pro-adjectives like *such*, to name a few.

18. Candy likes very scary movies.
19. Candy likes such movies.

Pro-forms do not pick out unconnected words in a sentence. Thus, in example 20,

20. Fay went to the store.

replacement by a pro-form shows that the sequence *went to the* is not a phrase by itself, because the following sentence is ill-formed.

21. *Fay did store.

However, the pronoun *it* could replace the words *the store*, the pronoun *she* could replace *Fay*, the pro-form *there* could replace *to the store*, and the pro-form *did* could replace *went to the store*, showing that all these sequences are phrases.

22. Fay went to it.
23. She went to the store.
24. Fay went there.
25. Fay did.

The tests also show that a phrase can consist of a single word in the case of *Fay*.

The second test is that a phrase can be moved around in a sentence; that is, it may show up in different positions inside a sentence. As an example, consider example 26.

26. Teenagers enjoy very scary movies.

The sequence *very scary movies* is a phrase, and this is demonstrated by its ability to appear in other places in the sentence.

27. Very scary movies is what teenagers enjoy.
28. Very scary movies are enjoyed by teenagers.

If we try to move less than the entire phrase, we get an ill-formed sentence.

29. *Scary movies is what teenagers enjoy very.
30. *Very scary is what teenagers enjoy movies.

Teachers should note that many sentences in English have alternate word orders, but these less common orders often need the addition of certain words and phrases to make them sound more natural. Sometimes, for example, a phrase following the verb can be directly moved to the front of the sentence with no other change in the structure. Thus,

31. I hate peas.

would become

32. Peas, I hate.

However, in isolation, *Peas, I hate* may sound unnatural to some students, in which case the sentence can be improved by adding intensifiers like *really*.

33. Peas, I really, really hate.

The third test is that phrases can stand alone as the answer to a question, but nonphrases cannot. For example, a number of questions can be connected to the previous sentence, *Fay went to the store.* Teachers can state the questions and then elicit or give the typical answer to them.

34. Who went to the store? Fay.
35. Where did Fay go to? The store.
36. Where did Fay go? To the store.
37. What did Fay do yesterday? (She) went to the store.

However, there is no question that can elicit an answer like

38. *Went to.

Once the concept of phrases is instilled in students, the teacher can plunge ahead to talk about different kinds of phrases. Phrases can be identified by what linguists call their head, the core or kernel word of the phrase, the central word that gives the phrase its character. Our phrasal analysis of the Fay sentence identified the following phrases: *Fay, the store, to the store, went to the store.*

Let's take the phrase *the store*. If we sought to reduce this phrase to its most central element, we would say it was the word *store*. Identifying the part of speech that *store* belongs to in this sentence identifies the kind of phrase it inhabits. In this case, *store* is a noun, and so *the store* must be a noun phrase. Moving up to one more phrase, the word that is central to the phrase *to the store* is *to*. Because *to* is a preposition, *to the store* must be a prepositional phrase. Likewise, the kernel word of *went to the store* is *went*, the verb, and thus students will have identified a verb phrase.

Once students have become comfortable with identifying the beginnings and ends of phrases, they can be introduced to some of the difficulties of establishing phrase boundaries in a sentence. A good case to begin with is when a prepositional phrase follows a noun phrase in the predicate, as in examples 39 and 40.

39. Mick sent the package to the store.
40. Mick followed the road to the store.

Applying our phrasal tests will identify *to the store* as a prepositional phrase, but this is where the fun begins. The phrase *to the store* functions differently in each sentence. In the first, *to the store* is not part of the noun phrase that precedes it. This can be shown by applying our tests. For example, the pro-form test reveals that we can't insert a pronoun that will take the place of the sequence *the package to the store*. That is, the sentence

41. Mick sent it.

is not an equivalent for

42. Mick sent a package to the store.

One could say

43. Mick sent it to the store.

or

44. Mick sent the package there.

but, in these cases, the pro-form is standing in for the phrase *the package* or *to the store*, respectively.

However, in the following sentence, a pronoun could take the place of the entire sequence *the road to the store*. Thus, the sentence

45. Mick followed it.

could stand in for *Mick followed the road to the store*.

The other tests give the same results. If *a package to the store* were a phrase in example 42, we should be able to move it as a unit elsewhere in the sentence; but a couple of sentences show that this sequence does not move as a unit.

46. *The package to the store Mick sent.
47. *It was the package to the store that Mick sent.

However, the phrase in the other sentence can be moved.

48. It was the road to the store that Mick followed.

Finally, treating the sequence as a stand-alone answer to a question shows the same thing.

49. What did Mick send?
50. *The package to the store.
51. What did Mick follow?
52. The road to the store.

Hence, all these tests give students a direct way of determining phrase boundaries.

The case we have given here of a prepositional phrase following a noun phrase and of trying to decide whether the two combine as a phrase together by themselves is exactly the kind of case that makes for fruitful learning about grammar in the classroom, because the ability to consciously determine how words chunk together in a sentence is central to applying rules of punctuation and style and central for making conscious decisions about how to write and alter the sentences of our written discourse. Making this process explicit and conscious in the minds of students has the benefit of adding more information and skills to the students' ability to diagnose and analyze their writing.

Conclusion

This chapter has presented two divergent methods for approaching grammar: the no-grammar approach, which attempts to stay away from the explicit mention of grammar, and the grammar-appreciation approach, which invests some time and effort into immersing students in a knowledge of language. We can imagine any number of methods in between these two opposites in which teachers will present more or less explicit instruction in language and grammar.

Ironically, though, both approaches have at least two important similarities. First, they both require teachers to be knowledgeable about grammar. All writing teachers need a solid grounding in grammar so that they can consciously distinguish among the kinds of problems students have in writing. They need to know when a student's problems are related to confusion over words, perhaps due to the difference between speaking and writing, such as writing *could of* for *could have.* They need to know what's at stake when a student writes correct English, but uses limited sentence variety, such as always writing with the usual subject–verb–direct object order. And these difficulties need to be distinguished from problems like vague pronoun reference, which is usually connected to the writer writing to himself rather than keeping his audience in mind. Without a solid foundation in grammar, the teacher may blur all these problems together and so won't necessarily prescribe the kinds of language exercises that address them.

A second similarity is that both approaches take a long-range view of improvement. Neither focuses on grammar firefighting, putting out every grammar blaze that erupts in student writing. If grammar instruction is limited to simply teaching students grammar dos and don'ts in the midst of all the other complicated things they are learning about the writing task, students are less likely to really understand the grammar they are being taught. The no-grammar approach takes a conscious hands-off policy when it comes to student error. The grammar-appreciation approach is also not predicated on the teacher being the grammar police. For the latter, red inking mistakes works best when it can be connected to previous grammar instruction. Otherwise, it is prudent to ignore student errors for the sake of keeping the student's attention on fewer writing issues at a time.

These approaches can be illustrated by going back to the scenario with Jamie and his teacher Ms. Denton given at the beginning of this chapter. The first problem we come to in Jamie's excerpt is the sentence fragment *Going down the highway.* If Julia Denton practices the no-grammar approach, she will not red ink Jamie's paper here but will look to see if she finds this pattern of error in his writing. Assuming that she does, she will then use a writing activity that addresses the problem. One possibility is to give the class a sentence-combining exercise that uses gerund clauses like *going down the highway* as one of the parts to be joined. Julia knows that these exercises won't necessarily result in instant perfection, but she will be monitoring Jamie's later writings to see if he begins to use this more sophisticated sentence pattern correctly.

If Julia Denton practices the grammar-appreciation approach, she will have been laying a foundation of grammar all the way along. If her students know subjects and predicates and phrases and parts of speech, then she can ask Jamie to identify these things in that first fragment. Where is the subject? Where is the predicate? And if Jamie discovers that "going down the highway" lacks a subject and lacks the kind of verb that can make up a predicate by itself, then Jamie has begun to develop the ability to diagnose his own grammatical problems.

REFERENCES AND RESOURCES

Christensen, Francis. *Notes Toward a New Rhetoric.* New York: Harper & Row, 1967.

Delpit, Lisa. "Skills and Other Dilemmas of a Progressive Black Educator." *Harvard Educational Review* 56.4 (1986): 379–385.

———. "The Silenced Dialogue: Power and Pedagogy in Educating Other People's Children." *Harvard Educational Review* 58.3 (1988): 280–298.

Hunter, Susan, and Ray Wallace, eds. *The Place of Grammar in Writing Instruction: Past, Present, Future.* Portsmouth, NH: Heinemann, 1995.

Jannedy, Stefanie, Robert Poletto, and Tracey L. Weldon, eds. *Language Files: Materials for an Introduction to Language and Linguistics,* 6th ed. Columbus: Ohio State Press, 1994.

Killgallon, Don. "Sentence Composing: Notes on a New Rhetoric." In *Lessons to Share: On Teaching Grammar in Context*, ed. by Constance Weaver. Portsmouth, NH: Boynton/Cook, 1998; pp. 169–183.

Kolln, Martha. "Closing the Books on Alchemy." *College Composition and Communication* 32 (1981): 139–151.

————. *Rhetorical Grammar: Grammatical Choices, Rhetorical Effects*. Boston: Allyn and Bacon, 1999.

Levinson, Stephen C. *Pragmatics*. New York: Cambridge University Press, 1987.

Moran, Michael G., and Ronald F. Lunsford. *Research in Composition and Rhetoric: A Bibliographic Sourcebook*. Westport, CT: Greenwood Press, 1984.

Murdick, William. "What English Teachers Need to Know about Grammar." *English Journal* 85.7 (1996): 38–45.

Nagy, William E., Patricia Herman, and Richard Anderson. "Learning Words From Context." *Reading Research Quarterly* 20 (1985): 233–253.

Noguchi, Rei. *Grammar and the Teaching of Writing: Limits and Possibilities*. Urbana, IL: National Council of Teachers of English, 1991.

Reyes, Maria De La Luz. "Challenging Venerable Assumptions: Literacy Instruction for Linguistically Different Students." *Harvard Educational Review* 62.4 (1992): 427–446.

Vavra, Ed. "On Not Teaching Grammar." *English Journal* 85.7 (1996): 32–37.

Weaver, Constance. "Teaching Grammar in the Context of Writing." *English Journal* 85.7 (1996): 15–24.

5 Technology: Power Tools for Writers

NANCY ZUERCHER

Writing, indeed learning on any level, is not inextricably tied to technology. But writing coaches for the twenty-first century must know as much as possible about technology's potential to enhance learning and, specifically, to enhance writing. Nancy Zuercher opens this chapter with a description of high school students using technology in a historiography class, an interdisciplinary course in which they can earn credit in English, history, or business. This vignette demonstrates Zuercher's overall premise: technology is not an end in itself, but rather a set of power tools for various writing tasks. Everything she explores in this chapter addresses a central question: How can we best integrate technology into our classrooms to foster good writing?

Certainly, with the constant evolution of these power tools, no written document can keep pace with every change. Still, the strengths of Zuercher's chapter are her clarity of explanation regarding a range of technological tools, as well as her candor about her own experiences in the implementation of technology. Specifically, from her position as director of South Dakota's Writing Project, she offers concrete examples of practitioners in grades 6–12; the strategies of these teachers are applicable for any English and language arts context.

Zuercher leads us through each step of the writing process, giving practical applications of technology for each stage. Next, she devotes a major section of the chapter to Internet writing possibilities and provides resources for teachers who need to implement technology based on these resources (or lack thereof) in their own teaching environments. Finally, Zuercher offers readers an extensive list of resources for integrating the best and most useful technologies, always in the service of writing.

Technology Integration in a High School Historiography Course

"Break a cow to milk"? This expression interrupted my reading of Erika's engaging story about a South Dakota cowboy.

"Everybody knows that," she said. "Don't they, Levi?"

"Yeah," said Levi, glancing up from editing his story.

"It's a mystery to me, though," I said, noticing that both Erika and Levi proudly wore belts with rodeo prize buckles. "I'm a guest editor from East River who loves your story and wants to know. I didn't grow up on a ranch like you did."

"Well," she said, "It's training a cow to get used to being milked. They have to learn to stand still and some other stuff."

This conversation took place in the historiography class at Belle Fourche (South Dakota) High School (1996–1997) as students edited their writing for their publication *On the Banks.* Their teachers, Jean Helmer and Bev Crabill, had invited me to work with the students.

The historiography class focuses on researching and writing local history. The community of Belle Fourche is the classroom for this cross-disciplinary course in which students may earn credit in English, history, or business. Jean Helmer, the English teacher who created the course, describes its effects: "It's great—it works. I think the best thing about it is that it changes students' perceptions of adults, the community, and themselves. They learn they can do all sorts of things. They discover they can do things they never dreamt would be possible." Students succeed because their teachers organize the class for their success. "We demand greatness, not obedience," says Jean. "The most important things they learn are to access, synthesize, and evaluate information."

From the first day of class, writing is the primary instructional tool. Students begin as historiographers by responding to these prompts:

- What is your name, and how did you come to be called by that name?
- What is history?
- Describe your community.
- Identify three of your attitudes toward life.
- What are the roots of these attitudes?

Discussion surrounding these questions builds these students into a community. After their discussion, their teachers name them "researchers" and then "writers."

Historiography students use technology throughout the semester as they research and write. After they identify their favorite niches in the community's history, they seek the expertise of local residents and design interview questions. Then, using tape recorders, they interview at least three local residents and later transcribe their interviews. Next, they verify the accuracy of their transcribed information with their interviewees. Once students compile several interviews, they double-check the contexts of their stories in old newspapers and courthouse records and with artifacts in local museums. Then, using their interviews and background research, they compose on the computer three different articles: an oral history piece (a Studs Terkel style narrative), a feature story based on compiled research, and a piece of creative nonfiction. Then comes the hard work of revising, more revising, editing, and practicing with different readers. "Students learn that 'research' means 're-search' with an emphasis on 're,' " Jean notes. When their articles are ready to publish, students lay them out in a desktop publishing program. They also learn hypertext mark-up language (HTML) so that they can publish *On the Banks* on the World Wide Web. Copies of *On the Banks* sell at local businesses, and its Web edition led Gateway (the computer manufacturer) to inquire about purchasing several articles directly from the writers. The class also celebrates the publication of *On the Banks* with a gift to the community, an evening of storytelling.

Technology was integrated into the class throughout the semester from initial interviews to Internet publication. Students used tape recorders, transcribers, word processing programs, digital cameras, and the Internet as writing tools. They learned this technology as they needed it. As Bev Crabill, the history teacher, said, "We never limited them. For example, *On the Banks* was a print magazine until the day that a student said, 'Why couldn't we publish on the Internet, too?' We asked them what will it take? What tech do you need? Their knowledge of technology is driven by their curiosity. That's how the project makes everyone, regardless of ability, succeed."

The historiography class provides an excellent model not only for teaching writing using an authentic task, but also for teaching writing with technology in grades 6–12. In historiography, technology is not an end in itself, but rather a set of power tools for various writing tasks. The classroom is also a community of writers where the teachers are literally "guides on the side," rather than "sages on the stage." Although the teachers provide clear expectations, a firm structure, and a timeline, students have many choices within this framework. These choices empower them as writers and as persons in an environment that promotes active learning. At one time or another, each person in historiography is a teacher, and each person is a learner.

Technology Integration in a Sixth Grade Writing Classroom

Like the Belle Fourche historiography class, Ann Haggerty's sixth grade English classes at the Vermillion (South Dakota) Middle School use computers as tools for writing. Her classroom bulletin board's published poems and stories show that students write often in this classroom, though not exclusively with computers. Haggerty explains: "I have one computer in my classroom with full Internet hook-up. Mostly students use this during study hall to do research and word processing." Although Ann's classes can use the school's state-of-the-art computer lab of twenty-five computers, all of which are online, she notes that she has to reserve it, sometimes months ahead. She anticipates inheriting additional computers from the keyboarding classroom when it is updated. This pattern of computer accessibility is common in middle and secondary English classrooms.

Like many teachers and school administrators, those in Ann's school are concerned about students keeping their focus on educational purposes when they use computers. Her school district has its own *Computer, Network, & Internet Procedure Handbook.* School personnel enforce it with a monitoring system that allows one adult to monitor four screens from his or her computer and to speak by microphone to a student in another room. Ann comments, "We've had a few problems this year, but the policy is strict, so students lose privileges immediately, and they can lose computer privileges for good if they violate the rule more than twice." Her comments illustrate the general principle that, when a school implements a sensible computer policy consistently, students come to understand that they must observe it or face logical consequences. A sound policy not only frees teachers from being technology police, but also allows them to focus on using technology as a tool for teaching and learning.

Considering school policies, accessibility of computers, and our purposes for using them, how can we best integrate technology into our classrooms to foster good writing? This is the central question for the rest of this chapter, which explores teacher-tested strategies that encourage good writing with word processing, e-mail, and the Internet.

Word Processing

A good word-processing program like WordPerfect, ClarisWorks, or Microsoft Word will suffice for writing on a computer. Word-processing programs can be used throughout the writing process, from generating ideas through publishing. Many of these programs also build in desktop publishing and web page design, and most offer macros, or templates, for memos and letters that can be especially helpful for business and technical writing.

No additional software is needed, although software sales claims may tempt teachers and administrators. Before they succumb, both groups need to ask important questions: How does the software foster good writing? Is the software's pedagogy compatible with course objectives? Was it designed by experienced classroom teachers? And the most important question, as Pam Childers, a veteran Tennessee high school teacher, notes, is "How will it improve writing, thinking, and learning?" (Hobson and Fitzjerrells 209).

After all, the computer is a tool. How we use it in the context of classrooms determines its value. It can't replace or even substitute for a teacher, but in a teacher's hands it can be a powerful tool. Word processing provides options for writing. Students can try a variety of strategies and incorporate the ones that work best for their writing process if teachers introduce them throughout the writing process and invite students to experiment with them. The writing strategies that follow can be adapted to all kinds of writing, including expository, imaginative, business and technical.

Prewriting, write before writing, invention, and creating. Many students discover that composing at the computer helps their writing process. After experimenting, a few generally prefer to prewrite with pencil and paper; most prefer a mix of pencil and computer techniques. Jean Helmer observes "a tactile connection between a topic and the physical writing." Choices belong to the student, because the purpose of prewriting is to generate writing, not to use a particular technique as an end in itself.

Most writing classes use journals for private writing. Journals may be handwritten or computer generated. (If the j-word is an issue, "journal" can be replaced with notebook, daybook, reflections, learning log, uncollected works, daily writing, mindsprings, or a name created by the writer that has a positive personal connotation. Writing in it then can become a joy instead of a chore.) Writing a journal on computer, also called an electronic journal or e-journal, is similar to writing a journal on paper; only the tools differ. An e-journal may begin with a single file that dates each entry. When the file becomes too long, the writer can organize it into files of months or weeks. The advantage of e-journals is that writers can then copy and paste gems from them into their public writing without recopying.

A teacher can respond to e-journals in several ways: hand writing responses on paper, writing in the student's journal file at the end with a font different from the original, writing in the journal's text in ALL CAPS, or composing and sending responses in e-mail.

Other workable strategies for prewriting include invisible writing, listing, journalist's questions, free writing, cubing, and guided imagery. All except the first work equally well on paper or on computer. For *invisible writing*, the writer turns off the monitor to make the screen blank and writes. This strategy works well for writers who interrupt their prewriting to correct and revise. The other prewriting strategies can work as invisible or visible writing. *Listing*, also called *brainstorming*, is simply jotting a list quickly without judging. *Journalist's questions* are the familiar "who, what, where, why, how, and when." *Free writing* is writing nonstop on whatever comes to mind for a set time, about 5 or 10 minutes. With *cubing*, a writer examines a topic quickly from six different perspectives (the six sides of a cube), each for two to three minutes.

1. Describe it. What does it looks like, sound like, feel like, taste like, smell like?
2. Compare and contrast it. What's it similar to and different from?
3. Analyze it. Describe its parts.
4. Apply it. Write about how it can be used.
5. Argue for it or against it.
6. Evaluate it. Write about its worth and value.

Responses can be both rational and imaginative. The important thing is to generate ideas quickly without judging or self-editing.

Guided imagery is imaginary time travel with an initial long prompt. It works well for generating sensory details for narration and description. The teacher guides students' imaginations, first by inviting them to relax in a comfortable position, close their eyes, and concentrate on a predetermined place or scene, which may differ for each student. The teacher then slowly says something like "You are about to travel in time and in your imagination. Just relax and let the scene play on the movie screens of your minds." No writing or discussion takes place at this phase of guided imagery. Instead, the teacher gently speaks to engage students with open-ended remarks, such as "Look around you (pause). Ahead (pause). To the left (pause). To the right (pause). Behind you (pause). Up (pause). What do you see? (pause). Hear? (pause). Smell? (pause). Taste? (pause). Walk around a little. What do your feet touch and how does that feel? (pause). Are you by yourself or are other people with you? Take a few moments to experience all of this place (long pause). Soon it will be time to leave this place and return to our class (pause). When you're ready, open your eyes slowly." After a moment, the teacher invites students to free write about their imaginary time travel, making sure to capture as many details as possible. To ensure that, a teacher usually plans 10 to 20 minutes of writing time, depending on the students' engagement.

The teacher's voice and questions are crucial to guided imagery, because they influence a student's engagement. Questions need to be sense-specific to include all the senses, yet otherwise general, to allow for diverse places, both indoors and outdoors. For example, "You notice color and light and feel the air on your cheek as you look up" instead of "as you look at the ceiling (or sky)." The tone of the teacher's voice is likewise crucial. It needs to be calm, warm, and encouraging.

Writers often use several of these prewriting strategies for one project. A computer allows writers to see the results all at once as they can open several windows and move and size them. Then, using copy and paste functions to move their text, writers can map, design a flow chart, or even outline their papers to give themselves a sense of direction for drafting. Some word-processing programs include graphics programs that are useful for such maps, although designing elaborate maps and diagrams may pull some students away from the purpose of organizing their ideas for drafting.

Drafting with a computer is easy, especially for those who know typing or keyboarding. Words seem to flow from the fingers onto the screen. I recommend turning off the function that supposedly corrects spelling and grammar as words appear on the screen, because these instant warnings interrupt drafting and its primary aim of generating text. (For example, as I drafted this section, I turned on Word's Spelling and Grammar checker, and it flagged "corrects" in the previous sentence. To discover why, I had to interrupt my writing, pull down the Tools menu, only to find that it incorrectly recommended "correct" as a substitute!) Spelling and grammar checkers are better used later in the composing process, during editing. When a computer-generated draft is completed and printed, many students view the printed copy as finished text. Clare LePell, a California high school teacher, observes that as "an illusion of perfection in which the mere neatness of the print often stops students well before they've entered the gutsy work of revision and editing." Usually, drafts will benefit from revising.

Revising means literally "seeing again." Revising is different from editing; revising is seeing the forest; editing is seeing single trees, even leaves. Revising is generative; editing is polishing for publication (in the sense of going public). Revising involves higher-order thinking and the global concerns of context, organization, and development. Editing involves lower-order thinking, the smaller parts of writing—generally, details of grammar, usage, and mechanics. Sentences may be considered in either group.

Word-processing writers usually revise continually on the same copy, although some may print many drafts. The number of drafts, however, is no indication of the quality or extent of revising. On a computer, drafts are snapshots in time, if they're saved as separate documents; if they're not saved separately, there can be no drafts, just a final product. Word processing makes teachers rethink the value of requiring several separate drafts, as Jane Zeni, editor of *WritingLands* did. She also recommends that teachers and students talk about real revision, as opposed to merely moving blocks of text and making other changes just for the appearance of change (50–53).

As revision is global and generative, a teacher needs to structure revising to guide students. Otherwise, as Nancy Sommers points out in her classic article, inexperienced writers attend to words and punctuation marks first; in other words, they skip revising as they gravitate immediately to editing unless a teacher intervenes. To help students move to global revision, we can teach them how to move chunks of text by cutting and pasting, saving several alternative versions for discussion. We can show them how to experiment by adding, subtracting, rearranging, and substituting chunks of text larger than words or phrases. Word processing allows writers to do that with ease. Furthermore, most revising strategies adapt well to word processing. I also like my students to keep their contexts in mind as they revise and to read as if they were their intended readers. When writers become so familiar with their own texts that they can't see opportunities for revision, they can get a fresh view merely by changing their text to a different font, an easy change on a computer. Students can also work collaboratively. Reading others' texts, on screen or off, helps writers become more perceptive about their own writing.

Before working with revising strategies, students should make a copy of their draft just for revising and save it and the original on disk. The original could be named "Paper 1" and the copy "Paper 1—copy." I find that uniform naming helps when I look at students' disks. If students' work is saved to a file server, the original could be named with the writer's initials, for example "Paper 1—NZ."

With just one computer in the classroom and a projector, a teacher or student can put a draft on the screen for modeling revising strategies. It is helpful to have a rubric for the assignment or some guiding questions. If everyone has a paper copy of the projected text, reading becomes easier. The alternative to providing paper copies is to enlarge the font size of the projected text. After the teacher models the strategy for the whole class, students are ready to work with it in pairs or groups. Some of my students prefer to work with paper copies, and others prefer to work on the computer. I do make sure that they have tried both ways several times, though, before I let them choose whether to work on paper or on computer.

If everyone has a computer, students can trade computers and write comments in ALL CAPS in the text. Additional readers could use symbols, such as ^^^ or ***, to enclose their comments. If the word-processing program has color capacity, each reader can put comments in a distinctive color on the screen. However, only a color printer can reproduce the effects on paper. Although some books suggest writing comments in different and distinctive fonts, I find that pulling down an often lengthy menu to change a font for each comment is inefficient and, more important, detracts from my concentration on the text.

For making global coherence—or the need for it—easily visible, Steve Krause, who teaches at Eastern Michigan University, suggests a technique that works to check overall organization and coherence. Students copy the first sentence of each paragraph and then paste it into a new document. The result is a working abstract of the paper that readily shows connections or nonconnections between sentences. This technique works particularly well for students who resist outlining.

James Strickland, who teaches at Slippery Rock (Pennsylvania) University and conducts summer workshops in writing with computers for middle and high school teachers, suggests several collaborative strategies for revising, which students do in pairs—always with a copy of their draft. To use these strategies, writers begin by mixing up the original order of the text in some way, and the reader is challenged to rearrange the text. The results show how one reader interprets the text, and the writer may choose whether to incorporate them into a revision, for the writer owns the text. In Strickland's first strategy, the writer mixes up the original paragraph order on a copy of the draft for the partner to place in sequence. Ideally, the partner will be able to reproduce the original order; if not, the two can discuss possible revisions and transitions. Strickland's second strategy, paragraphing, should be used with a different partner or text. On a copy of the draft the writer omits all paragraph breaks, and the partner's challenge is to paragraph the text. His third strategy, sentence separation, breaks the paper into one long, randomly ordered list of sentences, each beginning on a new line. This exercise is also excellent practice of copy and paste commands! The reader then reorders the sentences and supplies indentations (48). Discussion between partners after each of these activities provides valuable insights for both. When more than one student works with the same text, writers often face conflicting choices and gain more insights into ways that their writing affects different readers.

As Ann Haggerty observes, "Students are more willing to make changes and to take risks as writers when they don't have to rewrite the entire piece by hand. Once a rough copy is word-processed, students are more willing to revise, revise, revise. That improves the quality of writing."

Editing may include spelling and grammar checkers, but these are neither teachers nor panaceas. Although they highlight problems and suggest changes, these changes need a human being to decide whether to approve them, ignore them, or seek alternatives. Often suggestions by spelling and grammar checkers appear inscrutable to the point of frustrating students. Sometimes the choices provided reveal more about the limits of the technology than they do about editing and spelling savvy. I usually demonstrate these limits by adapting a strategy advocated by middle school teachers Linda Rief and Nancie Atwell. I put some of my writing in progress on the large screen and discuss what Word offers as "corrections," explaining how I decide which comments to ignore, which to follow, and where to find more information when I need it.

Teachers can also demonstrate other functions of word processing that can help writers edit. Selecting a common problem from recent papers, a teacher can do a minilesson, which also models how to use the Find command to search for the problem. For example, if a paper suffers from lifeless verbs, searching for forms of "to be," "to have," and "to get" will locate the verbs, although each verb form will have to be a separate search. The replacement may come from the original sentence, especially from nominalizations, and may result in strengthening the whole sentence. The Find command can also help to locate homonyms, such as there/their/they're, sight/site/cite, to/two/too. It can identify possible problems with the indefinite "you." It can target punctuation, especially commas, with potential problems including comma splices, items in a series, and compound or complex sentences. When students locate a potentially troublesome word or punctuation mark, however, they will have to decide what to change and what to leave in place. In the tradition of Atwell and Rief, many middle and high school teachers offer minilessons for writing strategies and problems throughout the semester. They or their students could develop minilessons in a PowerPoint format and save them to an accessible file. The whole class, small groups, or individuals could then use them when needed.

Students can also use the Find command to check for their individual problems. To help track their progress, they can keep writing improvement logs on their disks. The logs list their problems and progress toward solving them.

James Strickland's students play editing games to help strengthen their writing. In his version of the Great Punctuation Game, students remove all punctuation marks on a copy of their text by using the Find/Replace function. They also remove all capital letters by selecting the entire text and choosing lowercase. Another student then works to reconstruct the text. Each correct mark earns one point, and new punctuation that the writer accepts gets two points. In Replace the Verb, a student works with another's copy of text from beginning to end, finding each verb and, if possible, substituting a more active and descriptive verb. Each replaced "to be" verb is worth two points; the others, one. As Strickland notes, it's the conversation, not the points, that makes the games worthwhile (82–83).

No matter how many editing strategies and games, how many times a piece is spell-checked, read backward and forward, more glitches seem to appear. Sometimes editing is like peeling an onion. Students can become discouraged, even when they learn that professional writers and their teachers have had similar experiences. It helps to talk about this in class; it's a way to relieve tensions and the loneliness of the process and also to laugh and to learn.

Publication may be anything from posting a print copy on a bulletin board to publishing in a magazine or book, on an e-mail listserv, or on a web site. Students can include graphics available in newer word-processing programs to attract readers and illustrate the text. They can also use desktop publishing programs to turn papers into a variety of formats that look professionally designed. With Power-Point, teachers and students can enhance their oral presentations and also provide handouts for their audiences. Some word-processing programs even include the option of saving a paper in HTML ready to upload to a web page. An excellent annotated directory of web sites aimed at writers under age 25 is Sites for Young Adults Who Love to Write (and Ones to Inspire Those Who Don't!), sponsored by the Philadelphia Education Fund. Katherine Cantrill's class, Creative Writing on the Web, at Philadelphia's University of the Arts scrutinized many possibilities for their list before releasing it.

Word processing can be a versatile tool throughout the writing process. By using it, teachers and students may discover even more ways that it can promote good writing. When they discover them, they may want to discuss them further with other students and teachers. E-mail offers an easy and quick means for doing that.

Internet: E-mail

At a recent professional meeting, a high school teacher complained, "Students always want to check their e-mail. It cuts into class time." Why did she complain instead of rejoice that her classroom had e-mail access and that her students wanted to read and write? Her tone of voice suggested that she was worried about her lack of control. E-mail *is* engaging. It is also writing. A wise teacher can guide students to use it for promoting communication within a class or even around the world, as Ted Nellen has done with his telementoring program. Sometimes, for our students to benefit, we have to give some control.

E-mail is asynchronous communication available 24 hours a day. For writers, this means convenience and more. For teachers, it means teachable moments and connections to other teachers beyond their schools. For students, it means enhanced opportunities to learn. The availability of free e-mail accounts on the Internet at Netscape, Yahoo!, and other suppliers makes e-mail accessible even to those who don't own computers. Community libraries and public schools often provide such access.

Excellent basic instruction and "netiquette" for e-mail can be found in *Writing Online: A Student's Guide to the Internet and World Wide Web* (14–22) by two experienced and talented writing teachers, Eric Crump and Nick Carbone. Eric Crump is the webmaster for National Council of Teachers of English, and Nick Carbone directs the writing center at Colorado State University's writing center. They also emphasize the importance of e-mail: "Familiarity with e-mail will be an expected skill in many of the employment markets, including the academic market. Knowing how to use e-mail will become as necessary as knowing how to use the telephone" (14).

E-mail has its counterpart for bulk mail, *listservs,* on almost every topic imaginable. Listservs multiply opportunities to ask authentic questions and receive almost instant answers. Among educational listservs, NCTE maintains several, accessible through its web site, for communication among teachers. Teachers interested in teaching imaginative writing will enjoy the Teachers and Writers Collaborative listserv, and those interested in writing with technology can join the Alliance for Computers and Writing (ACW) listserv; the authors of *Writing Online* are both active members. For subscription information, use the web sites for these organizations listed at the end of this chapter. Teachers can also set up private listservs for their classes in cooperation with their local e-mail provider.

Students can use e-mail to communicate with students outside class, to ask the teacher questions, to send drafts for response, and to respond to others' drafts. They can relay information that relates to others' research projects. E-mail promotes collaboration, from gathering ideas for group projects to arranging a time and place for group meetings, and e-mail exchanges can substitute for face-to-face meetings when weather or schedule conflicts prevent them.

E-mail helped to connect a mentoring project between my English methods students and high school seniors 60 miles apart. Sue Morrell, an English teacher at Bon Homme (South Dakota) High School and I created the project to give my students authentic experience in designing and teaching writing assignments and to give Sue's students real audiences beyond the classroom for their writing. The project also provided us with opportunities for classroom research.

We organized so that each of my students had a miniclass of three or four of Sue's students to mentor. My students posted their draft assignments, including rubrics they designed, on our class listserv, for other class members to review and revise them before e-mailing them to their miniclasses. One assignment was to write a new vignette for *The House on Mango Street* from the point of view of a newcomer to the neighborhood. Students e-mailed their drafts to their mentors for coaching and then, using their mentor's comments, revised their drafts. They e-mailed their revisions to their mentors, who graded them, based on the rubrics. When the e-mail connections went down for a week, we resorted to U.S. mail. As Sue and I had students copy messages to us, we could monitor our classes' progress daily and provide individual help when students needed it.

How did high school students evaluate this authentic experience enabled by technology? At the end of the semester one high school student wrote

> Speaking for myself, I have been kept interested in these projects. They call for the use of imagination and that I do not have the time to use very often. I think writing about past experiences and childhood events is fun, because it enables me to relive what happened. . . . Also, when I read through the three options for the assignment, I had ideas for them all. That doesn't happen very often. Usually I hate all of the options and the assignment seems completely unappealing. I liked this assignment.

Although e-mail enabled this project, this student's response took it for granted, emphasizing writing.

How did we evaluate the mentor project? Despite technological glitches, both mentors and high school students were not only motivated to write, but also improved their thinking and communicating skills. Their communication went beyond getting acquainted because, as Sue explained, "We deliberately sought to do more than just chat on line. We wanted to think together." Creating a project like this one means that teachers need to structure the plan for purposeful communication, take risks, and have alternative plans ready to use when the technology fails.

E-mail is but one learning and writing opportunity that the Internet provides. Much more than text is just a few clicks away.

Internet: Beyond E-mail

The Internet extends the classroom to the world and brings the world to the classroom. Students can virtually travel around the world, get up-to-the-minute news, visit museums and libraries, hear music, and view videos. There are so many opportunities for research, learning, and making meaning that a teacher needs to structure and focus classroom uses of the Internet carefully. Larry Lewin, who teaches at Monroe Middle School in Eugene, Oregon, shows how he did that. He chose web sites for his sixth grade literature and writing students to learn about a Mexican holiday, Dia de los Muertos, as background for a novel the class was reading, and he developed his own guiding questions for their learning. He also found web sites for his eighth grade language arts and American history students to compare with their textbook's treatment of the Boston massacre. He chose the best material for his instructional objectives, while challenging his students and taking care that they could manage the information without feeling overwhelmed.

Martha Rekrut, English Department Chair at Warwick (Rhode Island) High School, would agree that careful planning is a key: "My recommendation to teachers who want to incorporate the Internet into their regular curriculum is to do what you expect students to do. Then you will know what they will experience, you can anticipate many of the difficulties they will encounter and you will be able to create a manageable lesson in terms of time and content" (553).

If the reader feels overwhelmed by the previous paragraphs, he or she can get acquainted with the Internet at the National Writing Project's "Getting Started Using the Internet" (http://www-gse.berkeley.edu/Research/NWP/start.html). Here a novice will find a glossary of Internet terminology and a step-by-step process to begin exploring. Other web sites offering abundant links to information about writing with technology include the following:

- National Council of Teachers of English (NCTE)
  <http://www.ncte.org>
- National Writing Centers Association
  <http://departments.colgate.edu/diw/NWCA.html>
- Kathy Schrock's Guide for Educators
  <http://discoveryschool.com/schrockguide/>
- Teachers and Writers Collaborative
  <http://www.twc.org>

Exploring them is a good way to combine learning the technology with gathering information.

Information is not knowledge. Using information—any information, but especially what's on the Internet—demands critical thinking and evaluation. There is no central Internet administration or gate keeper. Anyone can set up a web site on the Internet; it is very democratic. Because it is, students must develop workable strategies and questions for evaluating information that they find on the Internet. Among the many guidelines available on the Internet, I especially recommend two: those by Kathy Schrock for high school and middle school and those by Widener University librarians Jan Alexander and Marsha Ann Tate. The latter nutshells evaluation into five words, "accuracy, authority, objectivity, currency, and coverage," and also provides an explanation for each. This web site also provides different checklists for personal pages, information pages, persuasive pages, and others.

Recognizing the end tag of an Internet address, known as a Uniform Resource Locator (URL), can cue questions about the purpose of a web site and its bias. Sites with ".com," commercial sites, raise questions of what's the business and what's for sale. Those with ".org" represent nonprofit organizations and lead to questions of purpose. The tilde (~) followed by a name indicates a personal page, which is a flag to check the author's credentials. Sites with ".gov" in their URLs are government agencies and may contain only the agency's position on issues. Sites including ".edu" are educational institutions. Frequently, emphasizing and practicing evaluation strategies and raising questions will help students to internalize them and will also improve their chances of choosing the best resources, not just accepting the first few search results.

Knowing the differences among facts, inferences, and value judgments will also help students to assess the quality of information. They also need to be able to spot the difference between advertising and information. Blinking ads with enticing messages can kidnap unsuspecting Internet users away from their original tasks.

Most important, and unfortunately often the least emphasized, students also need to know about the ethical uses of the Internet. Using someone else's words and ideas without proper credit is wrong no matter what the writing tool. As Crump and Carbone said, "Technology does not determine integrity" (103).

Internet technology makes it possible to assemble an entire paper quickly by cutting and pasting from several Internet sources. This is stealing or plagiarism. Although clever students can often disguise their sources, Internet technology also makes it possible to detect plagiarism. I have had good luck finding plagiarism by tying an entire suspected sentence (enclosed in quotation marks) into a search engine. But this is after the fact. I prefer to be proactive, teaching and reinforcing students to be honest writers first.

For me, such teaching begins with guidelines for evaluating sources and students posing research questions that genuinely interest them, preferably questions that they're passionate about pursuing. This promotes ownership and self-motivation. However, this alone is not enough for most students; they need the added motivation of deadlines and products required at least once a week, if not more. Searching for a variety of the best sources—primary, secondary, online, print, people, onsite, film, video—is next. I specify a minimum number of sources and due dates for collecting sources. The process continues with the students' abundantly documented research logs, which contain dates, resources, annotations, and evaluation. Students need to show that all their sources are of high quality. I look at their logs about once a week, because I know how students (and I, too) tend to procrastinate. In this assignment, where the journey is more important than the destination, my students write two papers. The first is an I-Search paper to inform next year's students about their search processes.

As they draft their papers, they follow Crump and Carbone's suggestions to use contrasting fonts to differentiate their own words from the words of their sources, for example, typing words in Geneva 12 and copying material from their sources in **Chicago 14** (104). This technique has the added advantage of making the amount of quoted material obvious. Only after editing their final copy do students make their fonts uniform. Next, my students use their research materials to write subject-centered papers, this time as experts writing to audiences they designate who will benefit in some way from the material. Although it takes time, teaching students to use the Internet responsibly and ethically for educational purposes is a challenge worth meeting.

Most high school and middle school students have more experience than their teachers using the Internet, and they can often help beginners. For beginners, whether teachers or students, getting started can feel overwhelming, starting with the browser's screen. Its array of buttons, icons, pull-down menus, links, and changing cursor can discourage a novice initially. With use, the browser's screen becomes familiar. In the Dakota Writing Project, we model teaching the Internet so that participating teachers can then adapt our strategies in their middle and high school classrooms. We like to have new users actually using the Internet, rather than hearing a lecture about it, so we guide their introduction, briefly explaining the icons and buttons in the top row, as they move the cursor on their screens, pull down menus, and click on icons. Those who are experienced Internet users offer immediate help to beginners working near them.

Next we play a search game. After a demonstration of a search engine, we divide into groups and use it to search for answers to questions such as these:

- When is Albert Einstein's birthday?
- How fast do a hummingbird's wings flap in a second?
- Who wrote the novel *The God of Small Things*?
- How did Vermillion get its name?
- What were the underlying causes of the Civil War?

When we find an answer, we print the page containing it. When everyone has finished, we discuss how we found our answers and evaluate the quality of the web sites where they appeared.

Adapting his experience in the Dakota Writing Project, Matthew Okerlund, a Dakota Writing Project teacher at Sioux Falls (South Dakota) Roosevelt High School, created a research assignment for his students using a single database, SearchBank, because it is comprehensive, well organized, up to date, and easy for students to use. Knowing well the power of the Internet to distract his students from the assignment, Matt works hard to keep students on task and does not permit them to leave SearchBank. If they wander into other parts of the Internet, they lose privileges and get an instant *F* for the entire assignment, a major one that lasts 6 weeks.

Matt begins by asking students to think of a topic and five questions that a reader might ask about it. Then pairs of students exchange topics and questions; their discussion adds to the writers' perceptions of what their readers might like to know. It also helps to make the writer's research authentic. These reader questions then help to frame the writers' search for information. Next, Matt teaches students how to work with several sources that address the same question, stressing that students need to apply critical thinking to all information, for it is not of uniform quality, even in SearchBank. Matt's students write the results of their research in traditional research paper form.

His careful approach to a research assignment may avoid the pitfalls of Internet research, such as the copy-and-paste papers made from a search engine's first few hits, that discourage many English teachers. When students have clear expectations and guided processes, they are more likely to select quality information and write responsibly.

The Internet also offers opportunities for writing and publishing. Students of Al Doyle, Technology Coordinator at Polytechnic Preparatory Country Day School in Brooklyn, New York, wrote news stories for publication on the PBS Olympic Cyberschool web site. The opportunity energized students to write and gave them school-wide recognition; these benefits convinced Doyle to make Web publishing part of many subsequent writing assignments. Some schools, such as Belle Fourche High School, encourage students to publish on their web sites. Students can also submit their work individually to e-zines, online magazines, or anthologies. They may also create their own, as Scott Christian, an Alaska middle school teacher, and his students did (Edgar).

To help writers, many schools have added an online component to their writing centers. Accessible 24 hours a day, these online writing labs (OWLs) offer assistance ranging from online handbooks to responding to papers submitted for commentary. Some will accept queries and papers from outsiders and usually respond in 2 to 3 days. While I invite students to explore these OWLs, including sending queries, I leave the decision to them. Many prefer the alternatives of face-to-face conversation, with their writing groups or with me, or of referring to a familiar handbook as they revise and edit. The web site for the "grandparent" of OWLs, Purdue University's OWL, includes a directory of OWLs on many campuses, as does the web site of the National Writing Center Association (NWCA).

Three high school teachers active in NWCA, Pamela Childers, Jeanette Jordan, and James Upton, have created writing centers in their schools. Although all three teachers value computers for teaching writing, they agree that students should have choices of writing tools throughout the writing process. The teachers stress that, while OWLs extend access to help with writing to time beyond the school day, they can't replace their face-to-face interactions with students, which are important to students of high school age. More important, their writing centers' priority is writing; technology is a tool that supports writers to improve. Sensing competition between writing and technology for prominence, they want to "foreground writing and background technology in their writing centers." The solution in Jeanette Jordan's writing center (at Glenbrook North High School, Glenbrook, Illinois) is deliberate exclusion of Internet access; students can access Internet in computer labs elsewhere in the school. Although Pam Childers' writing center (at the McCallie School, Chattanooga, Tennessee) has its own OWL (http://blue.mccallie.org/wrt_ctr/), she is adamant that the center's face-to-face workshops with students and faculty and individual conversations between tutors and students take priority over technology (Childers, Jordan, and Upton).

One Web resource that offers engaging and imaginative strategies for writing improvement is Traci's Lists of Ten (http://www.daedalus.com/teach/tens.html). The collection, always in lists of ten items, includes "Prewriting Exercises for Personal Narratives," "Ways to Respond to Student Drafts," "Unusual Sources for Research Papers," "Ways to Work on Grammar Collaboratively," "Audience Analysis Exercises," and "Creative Writing Activities." Vistors are invited to comment on the web site and to request a future list of tens.

The Internet also empowers teachers and writers who pursue its opportunities for interaction and making meaning. These opportunities usually begin as ideas, not as packaged programs; then technology becomes a means to transform the ideas into reality. *The Nearness of You* tells two such stories. In the Kentucky Authors Project, students and published authors connected online, first to get acquainted as persons and then as writers. Authors' comments to individual students about their writing then helped the students polish work for their portfolios. In Canada's Writers in Electronic Residence program, students and published authors exchanged their writing and responses. The program deemed their interactions more important than the other information (Edgar). Reading these stories may suggest ways of adapting them to other classrooms or of gaining confidence from their risk-taking spirit to construct our own interactive projects.

MOOs offer more opportunities for interaction and making meaning. They are virtual communities, constructed imaginatively through language and accessible through the Internet. MOO stands for MUD Object Oriented, and MUD stands for Multi-User Domain. In a MOO, users become a community. Everyone in the community can participate in real-time discussions by "typetalking." A teacher can facilitate discussion by providing a focus before MOOing. This might range from a question to reading a story or article. Once on a MOO, so much discussion usually occurs that it becomes difficult to read every comment as it's typed, just as it's not easy to hear everything at a party. At first, this effect can be daunting for beginners. However, after a MOO discussion, those in the conversation can read every comment on a printed transcript and reflect on the discussion.

As participants express ideas in their own language, they learn actively and construct meaning as they discuss.

Although MOOs sound similar to chatrooms, they differ. MOOs let teachers and students build their own virtual spaces. For example, I created The Write Place at Diversity University for small- and large-group conversation. Figure 5.1 is a snapshot of its screen.

At the Write Place, we can sit on the virtual chenille sofa or in the virtual hammock for conversation. We can sip virtual coffee, available on the virtual table. The virtual recorder will record our virtual conversations. When we finish, we can evaluate these conversations by doing EVAL and later by reflecting on the transcript of our conversation that comes to us in e-mail. All activity in a MOO is language activity, and writing is the means. Its potential is as boundless as the imagination. Better than reading about a MOO, however, is experiencing one.

To get started MOOing, a teacher can explore "A Gentle Introduction to MOOing" by my colleague Michelle Rogge Gannon and visit a MOO as a guest. After learning some MOO basics, a teacher can arrange to take a class on a MOO. Such classes are often available.

Technology provides powerful tools that, if used appropriately, can foster good writing. To make the best use of them in our classrooms, we need to use them for writing, too, and to be open to learning more about them through teacher research and from our students. We need to be continually observing how students

---

*** Autoconnecting . . . ***

*** Connected ***

The Write Place

Welcome to the Write Place for talking, writing, and thinking. The room smells like fresh spring air, and you feel relaxed and eager to participate.

You see chenille sofa, hammock, table, and fireplace.

You see Nancy's Recorder, NanS, and EVAL.

Last connected Tue Apr 20 13:23:05 1999 EDT from sunburst.usd.edu

There is new activity on the following lists:

Builders (#9806)   396 new messages

FIGURE 5.1

work with technology, assessing how it fosters their learning and making meaning, nurturing what is working, and changing what is not working. In the process we may change ourselves and our teaching. This is our ongoing challenge. In the process, remember that the challenge *is* ongoing. Some parting advice: Give yourself time for learning and expect glitches. They are a few of your teachers.

REFERENCES AND RESOURCES

Paper Publications and Authors' Conversations

Atwell, Nancie. *In the Middle: New Understandings about Writing, Reading, and Learning,* 2nd ed. Portsmouth, NH: Heinemann, 1998. This edition includes many of Atwell's minilessons.

Childers, Pamela B., Jeannette Jordan, and James K. Upton. "Virtual High School Writing Centers: A Spectrum of Possibilities." *Wiring the Writing Center.* Ed. Eric H. Hobson. Logan, UT: Utah State University Press (1998), pp. 137–150. Three classroom teachers explain their diverse experiences with their respective schools' writing centers.

Crabill, Bev. Telephone interview, February 21, 1999.

Crump, Eric, and Nick Carbone. *Writing Online: A Student's Guide to the Internet and World Wide Web,* 2nd ed. Boston: Houghton Mifflin, 1998.

Doyle, Al. "A Practitioner's Guide to Snaring the Net." *Educational Leadership* 56.5 (February 1999): 12–15.

Edgar, Christopher, ed. *The Nearness of You: Students & Teachers Writing On-Line.* New York: Teachers and Writers Collaborative, 1996 (also published as ERIC ED413869). Writing with technology in this collection focuses on writers, both student and professional, and using technology to enhance learning and making meaning.

Haggerty, Ann. E-mail to the author, February 17, 1999.

Helmer, Jean. E-mail to the author, November 1998–February 1999.

———. Personal interview, March 13, 1999.

Hobson, Eric H., and Michelle Fitzjerrells. "An Interview with Pam Childers: English on Disk and On-Line: Process, Possibilities, Perils." *Clearing House* 71:4 (March/April 1998): 208–213.

LePell, Clare. Note to the author, July 25, 1999.

Lewin, Larry. " 'Site Reading' the World Wide Web." *Educational Leadership* 56.5 (February 1999): 16–20.

Morrell, Sue. E-mail to the author, November 1998–March 1999.

Okerlund, Matthew. "Research with SearchBank." Teacher Demonstration. Dakota Writing Project, Vermillion, SD, June 25, 1999.

Rekrut, Martha. "Using the Internet in Classroom Instruction: A Primer for Teachers." *Journal of Adolescent and Adult Literacy* 42:7 (April 1999): 546–557. This helpful article also includes her school's technology use policy.

Rief, Linda. *Seeking Diversity: Language Arts with Adolescents.* Portsmouth, NH: Heinemann, 1992.

Sommers, Nancy. "Revision Strategies of Student Writers and Experienced Adult Writers." *College Composition and Communication* 31.4 (December 1980): 378–388. A classic article challenges teachers to develop revision strategies that lead students toward adult writers' mind-sets.

Strickland, James. *From Disk to Hard Copy: Teaching Writing with Computers.* Portsmouth, NH: Boynton/Cook Heinemann, 1997. Viable strategies for writing with computers from prewriting through publishing.

Vermillion Public Schools. *Computer, Network, & Internet Procedure Handbook. Adopted 3/10/97.* Vermillion, SD: Vermillion Public Schools, 1997. One school district's locally published policies.

Zeni, Jane. *WritingLands: Composing with Old and New Writing Tools.* Urbana, IL: National Council of Teachers of English, 1990. Stories of Gateway Writing Project (Missouri) teachers who integrated computers into their teaching of writing as told by their director. The book also details how to construct a *WritingLand,* a technological and collaborative environment for writing.

Internet Resources

Because the Internet is a living database, it constantly changes. What is active one day may disappear the next. The resources listed here were active at the time I wrote this chapter. Most of the sites listed are well established and reliable. Many contain abundant links to other valuable online resources for teaching writing.

Alexander, Jan, and Marsha Ann Tate. Evaluating Web Resources. Wolfgram Memorial Library, Widener University. http://www2.widener.edu/Wolfgram-Memorial-Library/webeval. htm   (September 22, 1999). Its checklists for specific types of Web pages are particularly useful.

Alliance for Computers and Writing (ACW). http://english.ttu.edu/acw   (September 22, 1999). This organization for all who teach writing with computers is actively seeking to include K–12 teachers.

Assembly for Computers in English (ACE). ACE Home Page. http://www.dsu.edu/ACE/ (September 22, 1999). This NCTE assembly encourages online conversation and contributions to its journal.

Belle Fourche High School. Historiography Class. *On the Banks.* 1996–1997. http://belle.tie.net/ school/bfhs/historio/histmenu.html   (September 22, 1999).

———. 1997–1998. Student Pages. http://belle.tie.net/school/bfhs/   (September 22, 1999).

Childers, Pamela B. Caldwell Writing Center. http://blue.mccallie.org/wrt_ctr/   (September 22, 1999). A high school OWL.

Diversity University. Main Campus. http://www.marshall.edu/commdis/moo/dumoo4load. htm   (September 22, 1999). An educational MOO with a virtual campus that includes a student union, classroom buildings, an aquarium, an AIDS quilt, and more. You can log in as a guest and take a tour.

———. DU Rainbow MOO. http://rainbow.uwp.edu/rainbow/   (September 22, 1999). A special MOO for K–12 teachers and students with a great list of links. Teachers may bring classes here after filling out a special application.

Easson, Roger. Evaluating Web Sites. http://www.cbu.edu/~reasson/eval1.html   (September 22, 1999). A comprehensive list of links.

Gannon, Michelle Rogge. A Gentle Introduction to MOOing. http://www.usd.edu/~mrogge/ MOO.html   (September 22, 1999). A humorous and informative story with links to MOOing guides, MOOs, and MOO design.

Gardner, Traci. Traci's Lists of Ten. http://www.daedalus.com/teach/tens.html   (September 22, 1999) or http://www.ncte.org/traci/tens/   Innovative writing prompts throughout the process.

Krause, Steve. Word Processing Ideas. http://www.emunix.emich.edu/~krause/Tips/word. html   (September 22, 1999).

National Council of Teachers of English (NCTE). http://www.ncte.org   (September 22, 1999). Learn about NCTE, find teaching ideas, subscribe to NCTE-Talk ("a global teacher's lounge," in Ted Nellen's words), look for a job, and more.

National Writing Centers Association. http://departments.colgate.edu/diw/NWCA.html (September 22, 1999). This NCTE Assembly provides abundant resources for writing; also an index of OWLs.

National Writing Project. http://nwp.berkeley.edu/   (September 22, 1999). Link to the writing project in your state; find ways that the Internet supports writing, learning, and more.
———. Getting Started Using the Internet. http://www-gse.berkeley.edu/Research/NWP/start.html   (September 22, 1999).
Nellen, Ted. Cyber English. http://199.233.193.1/cybereng/   (September 22, 1999). A New York City high school teacher, students, and mentors function as a community on the cutting edge of writing with computers.
———. Student Writers on the Web. http://www.tnellen.com/ted/horizon.html   (September 22, 1999). How the author's writing classes transform from word processing in 1983 to Cybercomp in the late Nineties.
Philadelphia Education Fund. Sites for Young Adults Who Love to Write (and Ones to Inspire Those Who Don't!).   http://www.philaedfund.org/wedweb/html/yawriting.html/ (September 22, 1999).
Purdue University. Online Writing Lab. http://owl.english.purdue.edu/   (September 22, 1999). One of the best maintained and earliest OWLs.
Schrock, Kathy. Kathy Schrock's Guide for Educators. http://discoveryschool.com/schrockguide/ (September 22, 1999). A comprehensive web site for educators in all disciplines. Links to "Literature and Language Arts" and "Critical Evaluation Tools" relate to this chapter.
Teachers and Writers Collaborative. http://www.twc.org/   (September 22, 1999). Resources for teaching writing, especially imaginative writing.

6 ESL and Dialects in the Writing Classroom

MARK HONEGGER

Just as technology is an inevitable reality for the writing classroom, students from diverse cultures who may be learning English as another language are another significant reality for English teachers, particularly in the United States, a nation of choice for immigrants worldwide. The challenge of language diversity and of addressing the needs of writers meeting English as a new and most often additional language is another area where writing teachers struggle. Mark Honegger brings to this chapter his extensive background in working with English as a second language students and his own experience of living in another culture.

This chapter deals primarily with two related but different topics—ESL/EFL students (English as a Second and English as a Foreign Language) and students whose dialect or variety of English is markedly different from the academic form of English used for speaking and writing in the classroom. The chapter is also divided along these lines. The ESL section is primarily for the teacher who has only a few such students in his or her classroom, not for someone who is teaching an entire ESL class. Many good publications are available for straight ESL teaching, but it is another challenge for teachers who are teaching straight writing classes but have only a few ESL students in their class.

Doug Kelly was surprised when three weeks into the fall quarter he found out that he would get three new students in his class, a brother, a sister and a cousin, recent immigrants from Eastern Europe, and that they knew very little English. After the first sigh, he assessed his plans for the quarter. Doug had put together a great syllabus, one that would require more preparation ar.d work on his part, but that would also be more challenging for his students. Now these plans looked to be in disarray. Back in his university days, Doug's training for ESL students consisted of one week in a methods class—a lot of discussions about student diversity—but little practical knowledge about how to teach another language. He was afraid that the burden of attending to ESL concerns would be a drag on the whole class.

As the weeks wore on, Doug's worries did not abate. The three students were quiet and reserved, probably because the couple of hundred words in their English vocabulary ran out very quickly in most conversations. Twice a week, they were given ESL lessons by the district language specialist. On the one hand, Doug was grateful for this more direct language training that they surely needed. On the other hand, their twice-a-week absence was disruptive and interfered with the continuity of their writing lessons as much as their limited English. Doug wished now that he had taken that TESOL seminar in his undergraduate days. His county was expecting a rapid increase in the population of ESL students, and he knew he wasn't really prepared for that.

English as a Second Language

A number of terms have been proposed for the academic discipline that deals with this kind of English teaching (Prator 19–21). TEFL (Teaching English as a Foreign Language) first gained prominence, but the term was not considered accurate for learners in countries where English was already prominent, such as Malaysia and Nigeria. TESL (Teaching English as a Second Language) was coined as a more inclusive description, but many students were learning English as a third or fourth language. TEAL (Teaching English as an Additional Language) caught on in Canada, but the term of choice today for the profession is TESOL (Teaching English to Speakers of Other Languages). However, I will use the term ESL broadly to refer to the many different academic settings where nonnative speakers learn English.

It would be easy for a teacher to dread the addition of a small number of ESL students to her classroom as just one more burden to juggle on top of everything else. Yet there are reasons to view the addition of ESL students to a composition class as something beneficial, an opportunity that will enrich the class, rather than detract from it. ESL students can add a richer cultural environment to the class. A teacher can use the opportunity to celebrate the diverse cultures of the world. If a student from a non-American culture is comfortable in the class, the teacher can encourage this student to share her own unique cultural traditions. A teacher might invite the parents or other relatives of ESL students to the class to share with American students for a multicultural lesson. This has the dual purpose of teaching students about other cultures and making the family comfortable with an English-speaking classroom, so that the student feels that the school is on her side as she learns English.

The presence of an ESL student also gives the class an opportunity to learn about linguistic diversity. American students, sadly, have been sheltered from the linguistic diversity of the world, much to their disadvantage. Keeping students locked in an English-only atmosphere narrows their cultural horizons and weakens our society's ability to relate wisely in the global community. Exposure in the classroom to other languages promotes a positive attitude toward language learning. Research for the past 20 years has pointed out that bilingualism confers intellectual benefits on students and enhances their cognitive processes. Likewise, in an increasingly global marketplace, the United States will need more, not less, citizens who speak other languages. As your ESL students practice their English, there may be an opportunity for them to teach some of their native language to the rest of the class in a relaxed and free setting. This may just be the boost some American students need to enhance their own language learning down the road.

What Are ESL Students Like?

Teachers must be careful not to stereotype ESL students with regard to their abilities or attitudes. Much harm can come from putting these students in a box. Every student, no matter where he is from, comes to us a unique person. Teachers do a great disservice when they culturally stereotype their students on the basis of cultural or ethnic background. For example, Asian cultures are described in many types of literature as societies that prize harmony above individual freedom. This may be true in some cases, but there are two dangers when a teacher applies this to her Asian students. First, there is, strictly speaking, no such thing as Asian culture. Stereotypes are always oversimplifications. Many diverse cultures originate from within the Asian continent, all of which have their own characteristics. Each culture may or may not hold to the maxim of "prize social harmony above individual freedom," and the degree to which this maxim determines behavior will vary across cultures. Second, even if a student does come from a specific Asian culture that is considered to be harmony loving, this does not mean that the individual student necessarily prizes social harmony above individual freedom. Every one of us is a complex being who is shaped not solely by culture, but also by family upbringing, experience, and the unique aspects of our personality that come from within ourselves. As teachers, then, we must give space to allow our ESL students to disconfirm the cultural stereotypes we may have.

We must also allow our ESL students to have diverse attitudes toward the classroom and toward our approaches to teaching composition. This chapter will later suggest a number of ways in which we can address the learning needs of ESL students, but, at the outset, we must not assume that every approach can be applied to every student. Some students will like a more directed approach to identifying errors. Some will appreciate an indirect, Socratic approach by which teachers give hints and try to lead students to discover their errors themselves. The best thing teachers can do is to be knowledgeable about as many diverse approaches as possible so that they can apply the most appropriate one for the student and learning situation involved.

Background

Without getting too far afield, it will be useful to present some background on the development of ESL, not for its intrinsic historic interest, but to illustrate some of the issues teachers must consider in their approach to ESL students.

Celce-Murcia (6–8) identifies nine approaches used in the twentieth century for teaching language. I will describe these next because they show what teachers have emphasized in foreign language classrooms. These approaches will give us some context for comparing the strengths and weaknesses of different ways of teaching language. Before reading the following paragraphs, readers are invited to jot down the three considerations they would deem most important when teaching writing to an ESL student. The following questions might be useful as you think about these issues: What should be emphasized the most in composition for ESL students? How do the needs of ESL students and native speakers differ with regard to composition? What unique needs do ESL writers have? What is a good place to begin with ESL writers?

The first approach Celce-Murcia mentions is the *grammar-translation approach,* which was adopted from the teaching of classical languages. A typical exercise was to translate languages from the target language into the speaker's native tongue. The emphasis was on grammatical accuracy, and students were not taught how to communicate in the target language.

A second approach, known as the *direct approach,* was a reaction to the grammar-translation approach and called for students to be able to communicate in the target language. All instruction took place in the target language rather than in the students' native language. Natural conversation was emphasized through dialog and anecdotes. Physical props such as actions and pictures were used when the meaning was unclear. Reading was done for pleasure rather than as a means of grammatical analysis, so grammar was learned inductively.

The direct approach required teachers who were fluent in the target language, but the United States lacked enough fluent speakers for the foreign languages that were taught; so the pendulum of language teaching swung again, and the *reading approach* became dominant until World War II. As its name suggests, reading was the language skill that was emphasized. Vocabulary was controlled and grammar that was deemed useful for reading was taught. Translation was again a prominent classroom activity.

Two approaches arose in reaction to the reading approach, *audiolingualism* and the *situational approach.* Both emphasized listening and speaking skills. In fact, spoken language was seen as the key to all language learning and preceded reading and writing. In audiolingualism, lessons were organized around dialogs that students memorized, based on the view that language was basically a form of habit formation. In the situational approach, language was introduced as it was appropriate to a specific situation, like ordering a meal at a restaurant.

The *cognitive approach,* like many of the previous approaches, rose as a reaction to the teaching that was in vogue at the time, in this case audiolingualism. It again treated reading and writing as of equal importance with listening and speaking. Language learning was viewed as the acquisition of rules, rather than the formation of habits by students. Teaching grammar and vocabulary was acceptable. Crucially, this approach viewed student errors differently, as something that was normal during the learning process, and so the quest for perfection was abandoned. Not surprisingly, pronunciation was de-emphasized.

The *affective–humanistic approach* arose to address the lack of emotional factors in the second language classroom. The relationships in the classroom between teacher and student or between student and student took center stage. Artificial or contrived language exercises were out. Communication needed to be meaningful to be effective. Concern for the feelings of all persons in the classroom was promoted, and acquiring a second language was seen as a means of self-realization for the student.

The *comprehension-based approach* viewed the ability to understand language as central to developing the skills of speaking, reading, and writing. Not surprisingly, listening with nonverbal responses is what kicked off the language learning process. Language ability progressed by continuing to increase the difficulty of material to be understood. Students were not forced to speak before they were ready, and the correction of errors was de-emphasized because it could interfere with comprehension.

The last approach was the *communicative approach.* This approach viewed language primarily as a means for communication. The syllabus would be organized around the social situations of language, rather than around linguistic structures. Cooperative work among students was encouraged. Authentic materials were used to give language its real-life quality. The various skills—speaking, listening, reading, and writing—were integrated from early on.

Each of these approaches was based on a specific view of language and emphasized different things in the classroom. This historical overview does more than show the fashions and fads in pedagogy and the classroom. It also highlights a number of issues that teachers of ESL students face. Some of the variables mentioned cannot be altered in your classroom. In the majority of cases, writing teachers will not speak the native language of their ESL students and so will be forced to give explanations in the target language—English. Hence, there is always the possibility that the student won't understand what you said simply because of the language barrier. However, most of the variables illustrated by the nine approaches can be modified in your classroom, and they give writing teachers a number of different ways to approach ESL composition.

Language as Communication versus Language as Language

A teacher with ESL students is forced to grapple with tough questions concerning this marvelous possession we call language. Unfortunately for the practically minded pedagogue, there is no consensus as to what language is, in and of itself. Language is so big and ubiquitous, so abstract, that it resists reductive and simplistic definitions.

One view of language is that it is a grammatical system; it contains rules for organizing its sounds, it has a certain structure, and it produces meaning. Another view of language is that it is primarily communication, the things we do with language. One can see that both of these definitions have truth to them, but each of these views also leads to much different practice in the classroom. Viewing language as a grammatical system tends to favor an approach to education in which the class focuses on grammar and learns rules that reveal how the system of the language is structured. Viewing language as communication favors an approach in which students are put in situations where they can practice and learn how to produce language that works in these situations.

Both approaches have their strengths and weaknesses. The communicative approach is currently in favor in TESOL circles. It tends to elicit more language from learners and frees them up to worry less about mistakes. Nonetheless, for certain aspects of learning English, focusing on communicative aspects doesn't help. An example would be the determiner system in English, a particularly difficult portion of the English language for speakers of other languages to learn. In the first pair of sentences, the use of *a* sounds natural but *the* sounds strange. It is just the reverse in the second pair of sentences.

1. I need a college education.
2. ?I need the college education.
3. ?I need a help.
4. I need the help.

Teaching these sentences in a particular context, perhaps a conversation in which a high school senior is talking to her parents, doesn't make clear what is going on here, because the subtleties of the English determiner system have to do with language as a grammatical system. Context is not sufficient to explain when you use *a/an* and when you use *the*.

On the other hand, the approach in which language is viewed as an object in and of itself easily leads to a situation where students can pass paper and pencil language tests, but are unable to carry on a spontaneous conversation in the target language. Nonetheless, if we avoid trying to mention grammar, we are left to handwaving when certain kinds of errors are encountered, like the determiner facts just listed. Keeping both these aspects of language in mind can lead to a balance. We don't want the teaching of grammar to bog down students so that they are unable to get a word out of the end of the pencil, but we do, as teachers, want to be able to diagnose their grammatical and structural problems, and we want to talk with them as intelligibly as we can about those problems. Therefore, the teacher needs to know more grammar than the student so that he can accurately assess the language problems that will arise in the prose of his ESL students. The more he understands grammar, the better informed he will also be as to when to intervene with a grammatical explanation and when to concentrate on the communicative issues in the writing. This leads to a scenario for the student in which communication is emphasized, especially at the beginning of the language learning process, and direct teaching of grammar is added as the student gains confidence and fluency and as more sophisticated writing is required.

Fluency versus Accuracy

This championing of the communicative approach in TESOL also carries with it a prioritizing of fluency over accuracy. Students are encouraged to talk and talk and talk (or write and write and write) with little or no error correction given by the teacher. The assumption is that students can learn another language in the way they learned their first language. Parents rarely correct the grammar or syntax of their children. Instead, they communicate, and children use language and develop their abilities because they need to carry out some task. Requiring accuracy is seen as counterproductive to language learning.

As always though, there are advantages as well as disadvantages. Although fixation on accuracy at early stages can be deadly to developing both fluency and confidence on the part of the student, ignoring issues of accuracy can also lead to a pernicious problem for ESL students: they become frozen in certain patterns of error, or they fail to develop certain syntactic patterns through neglect. Once unwanted habits are solidified in a second language, they are particularly difficult to dislodge. It is an open question in the TESOL field what the right balance between fluency and accuracy should be; nonetheless, teachers must develop for themselves a feel for encouraging robust fluency, especially at the beginning of the process, while looking for timely intervention to develop accuracy before frozen error patterns occur.

Error Correction

The aforementioned considerations raise a challenge for teachers to have a global strategy for error correction. Some approaches try to virtually eliminate any type of error correction. Other approaches thrive on it. Again, there is reason to believe that extremes in either direction are counterproductive to learning. Teachers should develop an overall pedagogical strategy: this means that they have decided in advance of any writing task what the purpose of that task is for the ESL student. When a task is for the purpose of developing writing fluency, teachers should refrain from error correction. They should encourage the student to write as much as possible and should praise the writing where the prose communicates. When a task is geared for accuracy, knowledgeable error correction is appropriate, and the student's attention can be directed to the finer points of English usage and style.

Teachers also need to develop their ability to explain errors. In particular, they need to know when they can give a communicative explanation to a writing problem and when they will need to give a grammatical explanation. Problems with determiners, as mentioned earlier, or issues such as subject–verb agreement are not well addressed by communicative explanations. However, many aspects of English style do lend themselves to a communicative explanation. For example, many ESL students struggle with socially appropriate forms for making requests. Consider which one of the following sentences would be appropriate for an undergraduate seeking to make an appointment with her professor.

> Could I meet you at 3:00?
> I'd like to meet you at 3:00.
> Please let me meet you at 3:00.
> I want to meet you at 3:00.
> I will meet you at 3:00.

English speakers know that the first choice is most appropriate for the social situation, but it may not be similar to the form ESL students use in their native language. Teachers, though, can address these problems by pairing up language with communicative situations.

How Much Understanding Is Required to Learn?

The comprehension-based approach (cf. Krashen 1983) demands that the understanding of a language precede growth in that language. This is a commonsense approach to language learning. In the majority of cases, it does seem that language progress depends on understanding. However, this may not always be the case. If you consider the development of understanding in your native language, you realize that your use of words does not follow an even increase in understanding. Both in youth and adulthood, we use words when we have a partial or maybe even no understanding of what they really mean.

If we apply this to ESL students, it raises interesting questions about the kind of language learning that each student thrives on. One concern of Krashen and others was to get rid of the stifling attention to accuracy that inhibited language learners at the initial stages of the process. Some students rarely opened their mouths because they were too afraid of making a mistake. For our purposes, the teacher will need to determine what each individual is comfortable with, particularly an individual's comfort with ambiguity. Some people have little tolerance for ambiguity and uncertainty, and these students will need a larger dose of understanding before they can move to the next step. Others will be able to tolerate more uncertainty, and they will be able to experiment with language, even when their knowledge of the meaning of words and structures is less secure. Likewise, teachers should monitor their error correction to see if it is inhibiting their students' fluency.

Cultural Base for Knowledge

One opportunity that would enrich every person's life is if he or she lived abroad for a year or more in another culture. This not only teaches you about another culture, but it also helps you to see your own culture in a new light and to realize how deeply embedded a number of your activities are in the cultural fabric of your life. For example, do you brush your teeth before or after breakfast? When you visit friends, do you call them in advance or just show up at the door? In both cases, your culture determines in advance which is polite and acceptable, but not every culture answers these questions the same way. Culture affects the schooling system and the approach to organized knowledge as well. In particular, teachers may find that students who have been schooled in another culture may have different values for what constitutes good writing style. In the United States, academic writing tends to prize directness and a linear development of ideas. Other cultures may prefer a more subtle and indirect development of ideas. Both approaches have their own strengths and weaknesses, but teachers need to keep in mind that they may be introducing ESL students, especially those who have substantial schooling abroad, to a form of writing that they have not previously valued or used.

Emotional Considerations in the Classroom

The affective–humanistic approach pays considerable attention to the emotional climate of the classroom. Teachers of ESL students need to be aware of emotional issues that may arise with ESL students. These may include either strong identification with the host country or perhaps the opposite, strong antipathy for the host country. Recent arrivals could be experiencing culture shock. ESL students may have been used to a very relaxed classroom or an especially regimented form of schooling. This calls for special sensitivity on the part of the teacher. The knowledgeable teacher will be able to distinguish these affective difficulties from the intellectual challenges that arise in learning to write in English.

Relation of Writing to Other Language Skills

Finally, the teacher of ESL students needs to think about how the development of writing skills relates to other language skills. Writing problems may be encountered that can best be solved by focusing on an activity outside writing. For example, a common ESL problem is the failure to realize the morphological endings of words, such as the *-s* plural or the *-ed* past tense ending. While the problem is especially noticeable in writing, it might be due to difficulties in listening and speaking. Many languages favor syllables that end in vowels; hence their words usually end in vowels. Students may not hear the plural marker or the past tense marker on words and may fail to utter them consistently as well. In such a situation, the writing teacher may need an oral approach to the writing problem, engaging students in conversations that require plural nouns and past tense verbs. This will help ESL students to practice listening for the suffixes of words and uttering them. In general, the writing teacher may need to incorporate more listening, speaking, and reading activities to enhance the composition processes of their ESL students.

Practical Considerations

Having considered some of the theoretical questions that apply to ESL composition, we can turn to some practical issues for ESL students in a classroom of native speakers. As mentioned before, teachers should keep in mind the individuality of their ESL students and anticipate that some factors may not apply equally to every student; but teachers who prepare for these issues in advance can have an informed flexibility that will allow them to map out the most effective path for a given student as they become acquainted with his or her writing needs.

Placement Concerns

When teachers receive one or more ESL students into a class of native speakers, one thing that must be done early on in the semester is an evaluation of whether the students in question are correctly placed or not. Do these students have enough proficiency to participate in the general syllabus for the rest of the class? Teachers may need to administer an in-class writing assignment early on to assess the language and writing abilities of their ESL students. If the teacher decides that the students will be able to keep up with the rest of the class, things can proceed in a normal fashion. If it is obvious that the ESL students are lacking the proficiency to participate in the class syllabus, alternative arrangements should be made. In the latter case, the students should be placed in another class where they would receive appropriate challenges for their level of proficiency if the resources are available. Perhaps the school district might have tutors available to work individually with a small number of ESL students. On the other hand, if there is no possibility of moving the students to a more appropriate class, the teacher is advised to put the ESL students on a syllabus that is geared to their level of English. Research suggests that the acquisition of a second language follows much the same course as the acquisition of our first language: we acquire and internalize various rules of English in a specific order. Later stages of the process cannot be mastered before earlier stages. Applying this to the writing classroom, it is counterproductive to give difficult assignments to ESL students when they need to cut their teeth on simpler tasks that address whatever stage they are at in the writing process.

Teachers must be careful though when making this initial evaluation. ESL students as a group, even as they become especially proficient in English, may be prone to make specific ESL errors that are persistent and hard to dislodge. Teachers must take these kinds of errors into consideration when making their initial assessment. They should evaluate the general communicative competence of the written work when they decide whether the student can maintain the pace of the class.

With an early evaluation, teachers can also make more precise assessments of their ESL students, much along the lines they make for native speakers. Students can be evaluated for their ability to communicate in English (rhetorical ability) and their grammatical competence (syntactic ability). A handy criterion is to place them into one of the four following categories: (1) plus rhetoric/plus syntax, (2) plus rhetoric/minus syntax, (3) minus rhetoric/plus syntax, and (4) minus rhetoric/minus syntax (Kroll, *Second Language* 44). This categorization gives some direction as to how ESL students may fit with the rest of the class. Those in category 1 should be able to participate in the class syllabus. Those in category 4 are prime candidates to be put on their own syllabus applicable to their English ability. Those in category 2 may possibly be able to keep up with the class if they receive special help with the mechanics of their writing. The other possibility is to begin the semester with category 2 students involved in their own writing tasks that are simple enough to allow the students to sharpen their mechanical prowess, and then perhaps allow the students to catch up with the class syllabus later in the term. A similar approach may be useful for those in category 3, with students being given transparent assignments with simpler rhetorical challenges.

Timed Writing

ESL students are likely to have greater difficulty with timed writing because of their lower proficiency in English, and even students with good verbal skills in English may have great difficulty with timed writing. Depending on when a student began to acquire her ability in English, she may not be able to rely on the intuitive knowledge that native speakers use as they compose, but may have to rely exclusively on patterns learned at a later age. Composition is such an open-ended process that, when a person brings fewer language resources to this task, she may need more time to find something to say. She will also need more time to proofread and correct errors than a native speaker.

Teachers should be aware of this limitation for ESL students, and as far as possible teachers should be encouraged not to weight much of an ESL student's grade on timed writing. Instead, allow an ESL student to concentrate on writing for which there is time for proofreading and revising and for which the teacher can intervene in the writing process as language challenges arise.

Shared Writing Problems

We have already mentioned that ESL students may need a different syllabus than the rest of the class. Nonetheless, much of what ESL students struggle with in composition are the same problems that native speakers struggle with. They, too, will need help formulating thesis statements, writing with strong details, and organizing their essays. In this regard, the communicative approach is helpful in focusing the student's attention on the written conversation she is having with her audience. Teachers must not let their attention get so wrapped up with the ESL-specific difficulties that they lose sight of the bigger picture. Furthermore, even if assignments need to be altered to fit the specific needs of ESL students, ESL writers and native speakers can still benefit from being taught together the same common instruction about composition.

Curriculum Issues

It is perhaps more important in ESL writing than in teaching writing for native speakers for teachers to give careful consideration to what each assignment on their syllabus is intended to accomplish. We have already noted the need to develop both fluency and accuracy in the ESL student. Bearing this in mind, the teacher needs to choose assignments that develop both, and she needs to be clear when she is working on each aspect of writing. If her ESL students are struggling with the production of written text, she would be well advised to fill the beginning of her syllabus with assignments that favor fluency: these might include journals and short narratives. In general, the early stages should include more controlled writing: tasks in which ESL writers attend to one variable in the composition process. Today, in composition circles, a high premium is set on open-ended, student-centered learning, yet ESL students need to be given do-able tasks that can accommodate a limited vocabulary and knowledge of structure. These might include something as simple as dictation, an exercise that gives students the practice of writing a well-formed text. This can then lead to imitation; a partial text can be dictated to students, who then complete the passage following the content and style of the original (Kroll, *Teaching* 250). Assignments that are designated as fluency enhancing should not be evaluated for errors, but for the amount of output and their communicative value. The teacher may also want to include assignments that call for accuracy and precision, in which case more specific error correction may be called for. If the teacher wants to give an open-ended assignment to the entire class, she needs to be aware of how controlling all the aspects of composition at one time may overload some ESL writers.

A Note on Reading

The relationship of reading to writing for ESL students has produced its own share of controversy in the field. When an emphasis on process in writing took hold of the field of composition, the reading of texts was downplayed in favor of concentrating on what the students themselves produced. This reflected the maxim that one learns to write by writing. Whatever value this approach has for native speakers, it probably is of less utility for ESL writers. For the ESL student, reading does more than provide content for thought and discussion; it also provides a model for what an English text looks like. Reading is necessary to expand the vocabulary of ESL students. It can also be used to show the effect of different grammatical structures and elements of style.

However, readings must be chosen very carefully to be of maximum benefit for ESL writers. What is of paramount importance is that the teacher choose readings that have a controlled vocabulary. When an ESL student encounters a text filled with unknown words, the value of the reading for his language ability breaks down rapidly. Many teachers are of the opinion that reading a text with a challenging set of words is an excellent way of expanding a student's vocabulary. However, there is reason to believe that this is not an efficient way of learning the meanings of new words (Miller and Gildea 583–585). The problem is that reading a word in a single passage does not usually narrow down the range of possible meanings. This forces the reader to choose from among too many possibilities, making it likely that he will guess wrongly much of the time.

Using a good dictionary may appear to be a solution to this problem, and while it is worthwhile to teach students how to use a dictionary, it is not an effective tool for expanding vocabulary through reading. First, a student will typically encounter a number of definitions for most words, and she must choose the appropriate one for the word as it is used in the context she has encountered. This is no easy task; normally many of the definitions will fit the context in question, and so the student is back to the problem of disambiguating meaning without enough help. Second, consulting a dictionary, especially repeatedly while reading the same text, is obtrusive. As she reads, a student builds up a representation of the text's meaning, a complex activity, and repeatedly modifies it. Then she must interrupt this complex process and put the text's meaning on hold while starting another complex task, trying to compute or guess which definition from the dictionary matches the use of the word. Then she returns to building up the meaning representation of the text again. This is a laborious process that is likely to interfere with both learning the meanings of words and understanding the text.

This is why ESL students should be given texts with a controlled vocabulary, in which most of the word choice is already in the vocabulary of the student. New words need to be introduced to the student, but ideally these will be defined for their context immediately in the margins or at the bottom of the page. The other possibility is for the teacher to give a list of contextually appropriate definitions in advance of the reading so that the ESL student can read the text efficiently and gain the maximum benefit from the exercise. As time is available, putting ESL texts online in a hyperlinked format is an extremely attractive option for lessons in vocabulary building.

Activities for ESL Students

Here is a list of a few suggested activities for ESL writers. They favor physical and concrete activities as a means of developing confidence and proficiency in English. You can view the list as a way of stimulating your own creativity or as encouragement to see how much fun it can be to teach ESL writers in a mainstream classroom.

- Depending on the age and background of the student, one worthwhile activity would be to do a unit on the home country or culture of the student. This allows the student to become the teacher and feel a certain competence because he is the expert in this regard. Previously, the student may have felt like he was the pupil of both the teacher and the rest of the class, because his English skills were behind those of the people around him. So it is good to reverse roles so that he too can contribute to the learning environment. Having ESL students is a wonderful opportunity for a teacher to develop an appreciation of diverse cultures and peoples.

- Watch a sitcom in class that epitomizes American culture. Have your students write a letter back home describing what Americans find funny.

- Take a field trip to a local-color café. Students can write an account of their experience there, the customers, the decor and draw or find pictures that capture the atmosphere of the place.

- Organize a class featuring a favorite sport of the student's home culture: perhaps soccer, or badminton, or skiing. Students can write about their favorite athlete or describe a memorable match, game, or race they saw.

- Give your class a chain story. Each person writes one line of the story at a time. The next person writes a line and then folds down the paper to cover the line they had just read, so the next student can read only the immediately preceding sentence. Then read the story and enjoy the humor. This task gives ESL students a very specific, very limited piece of writing, but allows them to work together with the other writers in the class.

■ Take the class to an art gallery and ask each student to write a paragraph describing his or her favorite work of art.

■ Have your students each write the words for a song. You can supply a standard melody for the class like "Yankee Doodle Dandy," but the students compose the verses. Other types of formulaic writing (chants and certain types of poetry) can be used effectively as well. These kinds of tasks provide ESL students with a ready-made genre so that they can concentrate on word choice and on the intonation and melody of the language.

■ Finally, enjoy your ESL students. Your attitude will be contagious for the entire class.

Dialects

Before we get into our discussion of dialects, a few terms need to be defined. The word *dialect* itself is sometimes objected to because it carries pejorative connotations for some people. I will use the term in a purely objective sense to refer to a variety, in this case, of English. In addition, I will use the term *Standard English* to refer to that variety (or more accurately those varieties) of speech and writing that is used in the classroom and other formal settings. Strictly speaking, I should write the term Standard English in scare quotes to signal to the reader that I am talking about a mythological beast. As *The Story of English* so aptly points out, there is no such thing as "Standard English." There are varieties of speech that are perceived as more standard or less marked than others; however, everyone speaks a dialect or variety of speech. Correspondingly, I will use the term *nonstandard dialect* or *nonstandard variety* to talk about those varieties of English that are perceived to be different than the mythical Standard English. Hence, the reader needs to know that *standard* refers to the perceptions of speakers, not to any intrinsic characteristic of the language variety itself. Some of these dialects have become familiar to the general population. Black English (BE), also known in the literature as African American Vernacular English or by the more highly charged term Ebonics, has become popularized through film and music. Hispanic English or Spanglish is also entering the mainstream in areas with large numbers of Latino speakers. But nonstandard dialects are not restricted to ethnic groups; we find them among the white population as well, for example, Appalachian English. As our country becomes more racially diverse, we find that race and ethnicity are less predictors of language.

In addition to students whose native language is not English, there are an increasing number of students who speak a variety or dialect of English that is noticeably different from what we call Standard English. There are very strong attitudes toward nonstandard varieties of English in the United States right now, but before we can profitably deal with them, we must first lay the groundwork for understanding the nature of and linguistic relationships between these dialects.

Our society is filled with many negative reactions toward nonstandard dialects that are based on fundamental misunderstandings of the nature of language. Many people assume that nonstandard dialects are defective languages that represent a deficit in thinking or logic or an impoverished upbringing. We know now, thanks to linguistic research, that these opinions are not true. All dialects are complex, rule-governed systems. All varieties of English are acquired in a systematic fashion. Each dialect has a different set of rules, but none of them is deficient as a system of language, and all are capable of communicating complex and novel ideas. Thus, speaking a nonstandard dialect is not an indication of intellectual deficit or logical error any more than speaking Standard English is.

This means that attitudes toward nonstandard dialects are socially constructed. They have no basis in linguistic reality and no justification. People form their attitudes based on how they view the speakers of that dialect. Groups that have more power and wealth have a form of speech that is seen as more desirable. Typically, negative attitudes correlate with racial and cultural prejudice, rather than being a reflection of some true deficit in the language.

It is important for teachers to grasp the linguistic facts behind this story, because it should also inform their practice in the classroom and their motivation. Why should we teach a standard dialect to minority language students? It cannot be because there is something wrong with their native dialect. It can only be because we are trying to enrich their language abilities and empower them to work and participate in the wider American community. Teaching a second standard variety of English to minority language students will help them succeed in school. It will help minority speakers communicate with the widest range of people in society. But it will not make them better people or thinkers, because these factors have nothing to do with the variety of speech that is most natural to each individual.

It is useful to examine how dialects differ from one another. They differ in phonology, meaning, and structure. Phonology refers to the sound system of language. One of the most obvious things speakers notice about dialects is their differences in the pronunciation of words. What is crucial for our purposes is that a difference in pronunciation is not something that degrades a person. No one pronunciation is superior or inferior to another pronunciation. They are simply different and reflect different phonological systems. One well-known phonological difference is that in Black English (BE), a hard *th-* sound as is heard in words like *them* is often pronounced as a /d/ so that *them* comes out as *dem*. The rule for this in

BE is regular, and the fact that it is regular shows that BE speakers are not making random mistakes. Rather, their speech reflects a different underlying system.

In addition to sound changes, there are differences in the semantics or meaning of words. Another example from BE is the use of the word *bad* to mean *good* or to make a positive judgment. Again, this is not a deficit in BE. BE speakers have no problem understanding one another.

Finally, there are differences in the syntactic system, the structure of words among different dialects. This is perhaps the hardest difference for teachers to deal with. With practice, we can become used to and compensate for pronunciation differences. We can learn individually the meaning of words used in nonstandard dialects. But syntax is a harder system to comprehend. Many teachers are not well versed in the structure of their own dialect, let alone the structure of other dialects; yet this is one of the most crucial areas for writing teachers to understand, as differences in syntax will always intrude on the writing process.

The danger is that when teachers do not understand the differences between, for example, BE syntax and the syntax of more standard varieties they are likely to make mistakes in helping their students' writing, because they will misunderstand what students are saying in the first place.

Let's give an example. One of the syntactic distinctives of BE is the use of *be* to convey a habitual action or state of affairs (Smitherman 331). Most English dialects do not have a verb form that conveys habituality; they are forced to add a word or phrase to the sentence to communicate this idea; but BE, like many other languages, has its own verb form for this. Thus, sentence 5,

5. He be lookin good.

means that the person in question habitually dresses well, whereas the very similar sentence 6,

6. He lookin good.

means that the person in question looks good only at present.

The teacher needs to understand this pattern. Without some understanding of the syntactic patterns of BE, the teacher might mistakenly correct sentence 5 with sentence 7.

7. He looks good.

This leads to confusion on the part of the student. The sentence in (7) is synonymous with (6) but not with (5). And a student who receives the wrong corrected form is likely to respond with, "No, he always be lookin good," rather than understanding the correction the teacher has given him.

Another example from BE that pains teachers is the occurrence of multiple negation. BE has a form by which negation is attracted to the first element in the sentence that can take a negative. Labov cites the following examples (314):

BE	*Standard*
He don't know nothing.	He doesn't know anything.
Nobody don't like him.	Nobody likes him.
Nobody hardly goes there.	Hardly anybody goes there.
Can't nobody do it.	Nobody can do it.

Again, when teachers are ignorant of the syntax of BE, they will be unable to offer the kind of correction that can help students. It is easy to ignorantly treat these examples as simple lessons in logic: two negatives make a positive. Therefore, *he don't know nothing* must mean *he knows something;* but far from being insightful, such an approach betrays fundamental misunderstanding about how language works. Many languages of the world, including English at earlier stages of its existence, used two negative words in a sentence, not to cancel each other out but to reinforce one another and sometimes to strengthen the assertion. There is nothing illogical or strange about the BE expression, and what the teacher needs to do is to understand the pattern that BE uses so that BE expressions can be paired up with their corresponding Standard English examples, which tend to avoid double negatives in formal discourse. Teachers can point out the explicit rule to BE speakers: the first word in the sentence that can take a negative form in addition to the negative word in the sentence triggers the rule. This can have the effect of impressing the speaker with the logic of the system, giving him confidence about the complexity and genius of his own variety of speech, and teaching him that the Standard English expression is not better than his sentence, only different.

Teachers are advised to consult materials that document the syntactic patterns of the dialects they are working with and to make it a goal to continually learn more about the nonstandard dialects of their students so that they can provide the right kind of correction for their students.

Strategies

Teachers can employ a number of strategies to encourage the development of bi-dialectalism, fluency in two dialects of English. First, teachers must remember that their students whose proficiency is in nonstandard dialects can usually understand standard English, as evidenced by their ability to use national television and radio. This can be used as a springboard to introduce students to standard dialects. One can encourage students to imitate or mimic the style they hear or television, like a game of sorts.

Second, students can be taught that the varieties of speech that are most acceptable to the majority of society today have a prestige that is due to historical accident and not to any superiority in the language itself. There are many negative attitudes for teachers to overcome on both sides of the fence—among speakers of standard and nonstandard dialects. We don't want to stigmatize minority language speakers or demonize their nonstandard dialects, but we also don't want to feed the negative attitudes of minority language speakers toward the dialect we are promoting in the classroom. It is common for students to be teased by their peers when they speak with a standard dialect. Demythologizing standard dialects puts varieties of speech on the same plane, which is where they belong, so that students are not climbing upward but are moving laterally among equals.

Third, teachers can construct exercises where students translate back and forth between dialects. For example, BE speakers can be asked to translate standardized sentences into BE and BE sentences into standard dialects. This sharpens students' awareness of the systematic difference in structures and enhances their confidence in knowing how to write the same thing in two different forms of speech.

Fourth, there is evidence that early instruction in the student's native dialect leads to greater academic success, rather than thrusting the student immediately into a situation where the only acceptable medium is a standard English that the student has not mastered. At the beginning stages of writing, it may be useful to encourage fluency rather than accuracy for minority language speakers by allowing them to write in their dialect.

Fifth, students can be taught how to code switch between standard English and their own dialect. This can take a number of forms. Role play and drama can give students a chance to hear the difference in dialects. Likewise, students can be asked to write stories or plays in which characters of different dialects speak to one another, and students can be encouraged to make their material as realistic as possible.

REFERENCES AND RESOURCES

Celce-Murcia, Marianne, "Language Teaching Approaches: An Overview." In *Teaching English as a Second or Foreign Language,* 2nd ed. Ed. Marianne Celce-Murcia. Boston: Heinle and Heinle, 1991, pp. 3–11.

Krashen, Stephen. *The Natural Approach: Language Acquisition in the Classroom.* New York: Pergamon, 1983.

Kroll, Barbara, ed. *Second Language Writing: Research Insights for the Classroom.* New York: Cambridge University Press, 1990.

———. "Teaching Writing in the ESL Context." In *Teaching English as a Second or Foreign Language,* 2nd ed. Ed. Marianne Celce-Murcia. Boston: Heinle and Heinle, 1991, pp. 245–263.

Labov, William. "The Study of Nonstandard English." In *Language: Readings in Language and Culture,* 6th ed. Eds. Virginia P. Clark, Paul A. Eschholz, and Alfred F. Rosa. New York: St. Martin's Press, 1998, pp. 313–320.

McCrum, Robert, William Cran, and Robert MacNeil. *The Story of English.* New York: Viking, 1986.

Miller, George A., and Patricia M. Gildea. "How Children Learn Words." In *Language: Readings in Language and Culture,* 6th ed. Eds. Virginia P. Clark, Paul A. Eschholz, and Alfred F. Rosa. New York: St. Martin's Press, 1998, pp. 580–587.

Prator, Clifford H. "Cornerstones of Methods and Names for the Profession." In *Teaching English as a Second or Foreign Language,* 2nd ed. Ed. Marianne Celce-Murcia. Boston: Heinle and Heinle, 1991, pp. 11–22.

Smitherman, Geneva. " 'It Bees Dat Way Sometime': Sounds and Structures of Present-day Black English." In *Language: Readings in Language and Culture,* 6th ed. Eds. Virginia P. Clark, Paul A. Eschholz, and Alfred F. Rosa. New York: St. Martin's Press, 1998, pp. 328–343.

7 Attention Deficiency in the Writing Classroom

ELLEN SHANNON

Some students face challenges in the writing classroom with English as a second language; teachers of writing can see these difficulties and more easily work to address student needs. Some students, however, and an increasing number, have "invisible" difficulties to overcome. Writers with attention deficiency are another of the groups that writing coaches need to guide toward success. Ellen Shannon, herself a person with attention deficiency, first makes this invisible condition more visible as she discusses some of the characteristics of learners with attention deficiency. Since, as Shannon acknowledges, many of the issues and behaviors that accompany ADD/ADHD (attention-deficit disorder and attention-deficit/hyperactivity disorder) may have greater impact in the writing classroom than elsewhere, she devotes her discussion to a series of positive strategies.

A major focus of Shannon's chapter is to identify alternative strategies to accommodate the particular learning styles of students with ADD/ADHD. While Shannon draws on the Six Thinking Hats' work of Edward deBono, Howard Gardner's multiple intelligences, and David Lazear's implementation of the multiple intelligences, she provides the Theme Park of the Writer's Mind to maximize the gifts of students often seen as problematic. A particular strength of Shannon's chapter is her list of resources and references. Frequently, teachers simply need more information to help them understand and tap students' abilities. The resources on ADD/ADHD are current and timely for the present educational climate in which too many students still lose out and drop out when they are perceived as learning disabled.

I was a student with undiagnosed attention-deficit disorder throughout my education. For me, classroom problems included an inability to focus on single tasks, poor pacing with the teachers and other students, flooding of multiple ideas and concepts in my mind at the same time, significant levels of anxiety most of the time, oppositional actions, ororverbalizing, difficulty thinking and expressing myself in linear thought patterns, forgetfulness, distractibility, and much frustration for both my teachers and me. These concerns were described by some of my teachers as being due to immaturity, aggressiveness, lack of discipline, inability to take responsibility, disorganization, sloppiness, and the like. I was also a fat child, so my situation was complicated by a body image problem.

I believed many of the negative descriptors of myself. After I was diagnosed, I learned a lot more about ADD/ADHD (attention-deficit disorder and attention-deficit/hyperactivity disorder), and I'll offer more positive descriptors for the same behaviors. One simple success strategy is to rename the qualities observed in students with ADD/ADHD in more positive terms so that students can believe their successes are part of the learning game.

Although many of these behaviors and issues present themselves across the curriculum, their impact can be much greater for the student with ADD/ADHD in the writing classroom. Because the writing classroom deals with both the sensitive area of communication and the use of critical thought processes, the writing classroom is the foundation of academic and interpersonal success for our students. Classroom strategies that enhance students with disabilities' success potential in writing classes will also have positive outcomes in other classes, because students will acquire the tools to identify and articulate problem areas. Alternative strategies create a means for students with disabilities to be proactive in creating successful learning paths for themselves. These same strategies will also have positive outcomes for our more mainstream students.

My own experiences in the classroom as a student ranged from wonderful to disastrous. Wonderful was when I had educators who could help me pace myself and who would allow me to tap into my creative energy. For example, in the eighth grade our English class studied satire. Our teacher assigned a paper to get us to describe and analyze satire. Instead, I wrote a fairly lengthy satire of my own, incorporating the structure of the piece of literature assigned, and updated it as a humorous piece of rock and roll rebellion. Although I could have been chastised for not following the outline of the assignment, the graded paper I received back was filled with accolades about my brilliance and creativity. This educator's comments also included suggestions for improvement and corrected the standard issues of mechanics and grammar. I was thrilled and also very motivated to please this educator. I had previously been a disruptive behavior problem in her classroom. Success in the classroom caused improvement in behavior; I was transformed into a student who craved her feedback and wisdom.

When events like this occurred, most educator–student interactions for me were extremely positive. I have very fond memories of educators who had the ability to help me maximize my strengths and minimize my weaknesses. Educators who can give these kinds of responses to students with ADD/ADHD can provide that same kind of support.

Since I was prone to challenging authority (and I still am), disaster occurred when I was unable to be a teammate with my teacher. Then I was at my absolute worst and probably contributed to the burnout of more than one frustrated teacher. The teachers' belief system saw me as monstrous. Sadly, they did not know that much of my aggression grew out of fear of their disapproval. How could they? I couldn't tell them in linear thought patterns nor with the appropriate effect to the situation.

I am consciously using the term *educator* to refer to successful interactions and the term *teacher* to refer to frustrating interactions for all parties involved in an attempted learning experience. Those I refer to as educators were all different in personality and approach. What they shared was a commitment to their craft, a passion for teaching, and an emotionally engaging way of interacting with me as their student. They validated my attempts at developing a positive self-image and my learning style. They saw me as I wanted to see myself.

I was introduced to journal writing as a learning strategy when I was a high school sophomore. My instructor would give me a few trigger phrases like "if I could change things in the world, I would . . . " or "I am most stimulated and motivated when. . . ." These journal assignments were so wonderful to me because, when the feedback was given, it felt like I was having a conversation with someone I really respected and admired. The journals allowed me the opportunity to use humor, to express feelings, to express my resistance to authority, and to feel creative and free. I continued to ask him for topic areas to expand my journal for the remaining years of my high school education. He also assigned us our first big paper, and we worked in groups. His classroom was a cooperative learning classroom that was full of constructive noise and energy; there was a lot of laughing. As a learner whose dominant styles included the kinesthetic and interpersonal, my learning access channels were thrown wide open. I couldn't wait to get to that class and bask in the glow of learning and information. I feel a sense of joy and stimulation in recounting the memories of those experiences. My vocabulary grew, my writing skills advanced to a significantly higher level, and my interest in learning about things from Bible stories to linguistics to sports has grown for life.

By using coaching techniques and validating me, these educator–coaches handed me a set of keys for learning and a passion for knowing. They did not ask less of me; in fact, they asked more. They introduced me to a higher standard of learning and achieving by expecting the use of expanded vocabulary, with significantly more complexity in the reading and writing assignments. Although much of this would not be fully realized until I was well into my twenties, their positive actions helped me build a foundation that would later lead to more traditionally measured academic success in college and in life. As my educational coaches, they sensed when I was getting bored and challenged me. Although some teachers wrote me off, these educators believed in me (even at times when I gave them little reason to) and helped me to believe in myself. It is the meeting of my experience as a student writer and as an educator fulfilling the role of writing facilitator that led me to understand what those educator coaches were doing so well. Among other things, they made an emotional connection with me. They also gave me immediate feedback and created an environment in which I felt safe to take risks and grow.

In their book, *Performance Breakthroughs for Adolescents with Learning Disabilities or ADD*, Geraldine Markel and Judith Greenbaum include a chart (see Table 7.1) that contrasts the characteristics of unproductive classroom systems with the

TABLE 7.1 The Classroom System

Unproductive, Chaotic System	Example
The focus is on a "quick fix" for classroom problems and for remediating student deficits.	Immediate student referral to special education.
The teacher, the student, the system, and/or the family is blamed.	All actors feel blamed by each other. Strategies take a back seat to attempts to escape or identify guilty parties.
Instruction emphasizes rote and recall learning.	Extensive use of auditory strategies and memorization without opportunities to analyze and discuss.
Curriculum is lockstep and test driven.	Standardized testing and achieving higher scores drives classroom planning, interactions, and teacher evaluations.
Assessment relies on teacher-made or standardized tests.	Assessment of student performance is based on single-learning-style response testing. Application of learned material and ability to demonstrate skills is de-emphasized.
Teaching techniques and classroom organization are based on a single philosophy or theoretical approach.	Curriculum and teaching strategies set by administrators and political forces. Limited opportunities for teacher, student, or parents to operate as a team.
The teacher rewards only achievement, individual initiative, and competition.	Only "the best students" are rewarded. Single, rigid definition of "the best students" based on outcomes of standardized testing and compliant classroom behavior.
Teaching is based on a single (verbal) view of intelligence. The teacher does not consider different learning styles.	Lecture format and emphasis on verbal transmission of information governs classroom management.
The teacher controls all aspects of classroom life.	Teacher style and interest are the dominant forces governing classroom activity.

Productive, Continually Improving System	Learning Strategies
The focus is on preventing problems while addressing deficits and maximizing student strengths and interests.	Ask students to identify their perceptions of their strengths and deficits. Create a project that allows students to explore prior experiences with success in the classroom and create a mechanism for them to share these with the group.
Personal responsibility and commitment ("I am the system") are stressed.	Encourage student to work with others in identifying deficits and strengths. Create time for discussion about blaming and explore problem-solving models to engage students.
Instruction emphasizes authentic learning, critical thinking, learning of skills.	Use discussion, interactive games, the arts to give students opportunities to apply their learning. Use journals and the Theme Park of the Writer's Mind.
Curriculum decisions utilize feedback on student performance.	Teachers create opportunities to apply their experiences with students to drive better curriculum decisions based on student needs and interests.
Assessment vehicles include portfolios, observations, projects, and criterion or mastery tests.	Use of diverse opportunities for assessment will show strengths and allow students to show their interests and skills while identifying areas of needed improvement with the teacher as coach and team member.
Teaching techniques and classroom organization reflect thoughtful integration of philosophies and research.	Teachers are encouraged to participate in meaningful professional development opportunities. Teachers are rewarded for risk taking and sharing with one another and their students.
The teacher rewards effort, improvement, and group accomplishment.	Emphasis on shared learning, the strength of many talents to make stronger and more interesting learning opportunities and outcomes. Use of six thinking hats and multiple intelligences to engage students in the observation of diverse student gifts and talents.
Teaching takes account of multiple intelligences.	Lesson plans are developed with emphasis on reaching students by the use of multiple intelligences, such as writing on the board, using pictures, having students quantify things.
Students are active, self-managed learners involved in setting educational goals.	Students are encouraged to set goals, identify interests and needs, and create their own learning environments.

productive systems that serve our students well in achieving their potential. The chart identifies several key areas consistent with using the Six Thinking Hats of Edward deBono and the multiple intelligences first articulated by Howard Gardner and implemented by David Lazear to create a productive and continually improving system. These areas include instruction that emphasizes authentic learning, critical thinking, and learning of skills, instead of instruction based on rote and recall learning. These authors also cite the incorporation of a variety of strategies based on students' learning styles and on encouraging students to be self-managed learners involved in setting educational goals, as opposed to basing the learning on a single verbal view of intelligence and teacher control of all aspects of classroom life. Because the Lazear strategies and my model are open ended and allow students to have freedom and choice in the direction of their experiences, students have the opportunity to create emotional bonds with their learning, their peers, their writing coaches, and their writing.

As a writing coach, I want to keep both myself and my students stimulated and engaged while using learning strategies for strengthening the quality of student writing in the classroom setting. I want my students to get to know themselves and to see me as invested in their success as writers and communicators. The strategies in this chapter are drawn from the work of Edward deBono's *Six Thinking Hats,* Howard Gardner's work on multiple intelligences, and my own experiences with reframing behaviors that may be perceived as negative into positive forces for the writing coach–student interactions.

Students with disabilities like mine can be among the most challenging because they are often bright, confusing, impulsive, chaotic, disruptive, and time consuming in an environment where so many other students and concerns compete for educator time and attention. These students also have enormous potential. Even though I graduated near the bottom half of my high school class, I have since earned a master's degree and taught writing at the University of Michigan. I wasn't lazy; I was just unable to tap my resources in a consistent way that would lead to success in my junior high and high school classes. By utilizing tactile, visual, rhythmic, kinesthetic, and auditory strategies in partnership with our student writers, we can encourage our writing students to tap into their personal resources earlier in the game. As educators, we want to create an inclusive classroom. These strategies can be used in classrooms consisting entirely of students with learning disabilities, or with a mixture of students, or with groups of all mainstream students (although I suspect that there are few groups of students without some students with learning disabilities).

American education strategies are designed to follow a linear, logical thought process. Students are presented with a set of facts, each lesson builds in a structured progression on the next, and students are expected to follow the path because it is clearly presented in a step by step fashion. This structured progression serves most of the population well. However, large groups of students fail to reach their potential because this system eludes them if the way they process information does not match a linear plan. They fail because they relate to information in a variety of ways, including seeing a bigger picture without its component building blocks, learning kinesthetically through their physical sensation of the experience, or seeing patterns that relate to feelings, interpersonal dynamics, or rhythms.

David Lazear's *Seven Ways of Knowing: Teaching for Multiple Intelligences* makes use of Howard Gardner's theory of multiple intelligences. In the book's foreword, Howard Gardner identifies his goal "to convince readers of the plurality of intelligence . . . " and to make the point that "intelligences work in combination . . . I'd like to think any topic worth mastering—from Newton's laws of mathematics to perspectival drawing to an understanding of political revolutions—can be presented more effectively if the theory of multiple intelligences can be drawn upon pedagogically." In saying this, Gardner draws us into the practical uses of Lazear's handbook for identifying and tapping our multiple intelligences in the writing classroom (Lazear vi).

Keeping in mind that many students with ADD/ADHD share some characteristics that are, in fact, advantages and strengths, our approach to working with students with ADD/ADHD should take a different and more positive approach. These shared gifts (although not always developed to the same degree in each person) may include the following:

1. They can utilize the brain's ability to alter and create perceptions.
2. Some are highly aware of the environment.
3. They are more curious than average.
4. They think mainly in pictures instead of words (this may vary with different disabilities).
5. They are highly intuitive and insightful.
6. They think and perceive multidimensionally (using all the senses; hence, one of the values of using Lazear's and my model's thinking tools).
7. Some can experience thought as reality.
8. They have vivid imaginations (R. Davis 5).

As you can see, these gifts or talents, along with the assets the students with these gifts bring to any group, also have the potential to provide strong challenges in the classroom setting. These gifts can be maximized by using Lazear's methods for helping students identify their dominant learning styles while explaining them to your students as multiple intelligences. Just the use of the term *intelligences* to describe a student's approach to learning and information access sets a more positive tone.

The multiple intelligences include the following:

- Verbal/linguistic (production of language, memory and recall)
- Logical/mathematical (scientific thinking, abstract pattern recognition, ability to handle long chains of reasoning)
- Visual/spatial (forming mental images, perceiving from different angles)
- Body/kinesthetic (learning by doing, mind–body connection)
- Musical/rhythmic (recognition and use of rhythmic and tonal patterns, sensitivity to sounds)

- Interpersonal (working cooperatively in a group, sensing perspectives of others)
- Intrapersonal (metacognition and intuition)

By using the multiple intelligences with our students, we are expanding our repertoire exponentially, since our current teaching methods are focused almost exclusively on the use of two of these intelligences: the verbal/linguistic and the logical/mathematical (Perzanowski handout, Adult Attention Deficit Disorder Conference, Ann Arbor, MI, 1999). The important point is that lesson plans or even strategies based on the learning and expansion of our ability to access information through the rhythmic learning path, the kinesthetic paths, and the interpersonal path are not actively used beyond the primary grades. Eliminating the use of these paths after the early elementary years erases much of the pleasure of learning for students with dominant learning styles that are not grounded in the mathematical/logical and linguistic areas.

Attached to each multiple intelligence are the information entrances that make the most sense to the learner with that particular gift or combination of gifts. These are only a beginning, and it must be stressed with our students that they have a responsibility to expand their own repertoire of information entrances. They can do this by observation of other students, by dialoguing with other students, and by partnering with other learners of similar and differing talents in classroom settings and for homework assignments.

A sample idea for observation of other students includes creating a small group of learners with varying learning styles who work on solving a problem together, with the rest of the class sitting around the group of problem solvers. The external group of students makes notes about their observations of uses of the multiple intelligences, the strengths the problem solvers bring to the process, and how the varying learning styles observed work together and complement each other. At the end, the entire class discusses its experience during the learning exercise. A part of each lesson should include an emphasis on respect for the varying multiple intelligences and strengths and with what each may bring to enhancing a community of successful students. This activity also presents an opportunity to encourage students in expanding their skills and interests into learning styles different from their own. Have them consistently partner with one or two other students with different learning styles so that they get frequent exposure to relying on different strengths and different students in the class.

Using the Theme Park of the Writer's Mind
for Successful Writing Exercises

Many students struggle with understanding the various components of successful and complete writing, such as narrowing topics, organizing their thoughts for various audiences, and bringing depth and interest to their writing. Their dominant style of information processing takes over their work and limits their ability to speak to a broader audience and to cover a topic completely. Our students are often baffled by the comments we make about their writing and respond by shutting down. They shut down because, as teachers, we rely on our own dominant and preferred learning styles and communicate through our own information entrance filters. So if a student is an auditory learner and we don't ever mention something in a "sounds" format, at some level the student can't "hear" what we are saying; or if a student is a visual learner and we don't allow the student the benefit of some visual stimulation or images in our feedback, the student thinks that she or he has been overlooked or devalued.

Using my Theme Park of the Writer's Mind in the writing classroom provides us with a nonthreatening, visual and experiential approach to addressing the various components of well-integrated thinking processes that are the foundation for excellent writing as well. I think writers and thinkers enjoy the whimsy of the idea of using eight theme or amusement park images. A similar model developed by Edward deBono uses six "thinking hat" components in corporate settings to develop creative ideas.

The Theme Park of the Writer's Mind model is based on getting students to see the importance of using multiple thought modes to create a complete writing package rather than a two point back and forth argument. Students go on an imaginary trip to a theme park that will take them through a process of planning steps and thought modes for developing and organizing their writing. The components of thinking in the Theme Park of the Writer's Mind model follow.

Kiosks and Brochures Thinking

When entering the theme park, the student must gather information about the various components of the theme park. A small kiosk and a brochure created by the teacher can be the symbols for gathering information and can also be a model source providing some basic information about the Theme Park of the Writer's Mind to get the student started. The questions asked in this mode are

What information do I have?
What information do I need?
How is the information presented?
Where will I get the information?
What information is missing?
What questions should I be asking?

Balloons, Colors, Light, Smells, and Sounds Thinking

These symbols represent engagement with the project. In a theme park, the balloons, the colors, the lights, the smells, and the sounds draw the visitor into the experience. Without the smells, sights, and sounds of the amusement park, the experience would be very different and far less stimulating. The questions the student should ask are

> What interests me about my topic?
> What might interest others about my topic?
> What might I include to make my topic stimulating to others?
> What will stimulate me and hold my interest in this topic?
> What emotions, feelings, and intuitions do I have about my topic?

Midway Games Thinking

The midway games thinking mode is based on identifying and using resources. To win at the midway games, one needs to understand the various rules, skills, or resources to break balloons with a dart, to successfully toss a ping pong ball into a fish bowl, or to land a skee ball into the highest scoring ring. The questions asked in this mode are

> What resources do I have?
> What skills will I be using?
> What rules will I be following?

Carousel Thinking

A carousel is a simple theme park attraction. Carousels are predictable. We can count on them to have the same consistent features: horses that go up and down, a circular support that always goes around and around, and the happy music that always pumps away in the background. Carousel music is one of the most traditional sounds of a theme park and represents the idea of basic premise. In this thinking mode, the carousel represents the writer's assumptions and premises. The questions asked in this mode are

> What is my basic premise?
> What am I assuming and may need to define or explain for my reader?
> What is predictable in my ideas?
> What do most people already know about my topic?

Roller Coaster Thinking

The roller coaster is a staple of major theme park attractions, but it is the ride that has constantly been improved, modified, or changed over the years. "Higher, faster, bigger, wilder" has been the motto of roller coaster engineers striving to make their roller coaster the biggest thrill for their riders. Roller coasters have gone from wood to steel. The coaster engineers have created steeper hills, tighter turns and loops, more speed, new seating configurations including standing passenger configurations, and other exciting changes of direction. Roller coaster thinking focuses on new ideas, modifications, and variations. The questions asked in this mode are

What new ideas do I have?
What alternatives to my initial approach have I discovered?
How could I go about this differently?

Water Slide Thinking

The water slide and splash rides at a theme park are designed to give an exciting and refreshing cool down to the park's guests. This is a major benefit to hot and tired amusement park travelers. The water slide thinking mode represents benefits, positive thinking, and what is good about the student's idea. The questions asked in this mode are

What is the value or benefit of my ideas and thoughts?
What is good about this idea or point?
What is my vision? What is my dream?

Haunted House Thinking

The haunted house in a theme park poses many frightening and unworkable alternatives to its visitors. A visitor to a haunted house must frequently modify thinking because of the exposure to alarming events, sudden changes, and the need to identify danger. Thinking is constantly in a state of arousal and one needs to decide the risks and choices that won't work. The questions asked in this mode are

What is wrong with the idea?
What is wrong with the thinking?
What might cause the communication to be unsuccessful or misunderstood?
What errors exist?
What is risky thought?

Monorail Thinking

The monorail or park train in a theme park allows visitors to get a complete overview of all the park's attractions. Visitors can ride the park train and make decisions about the order and location of each attraction so that they can plan their visit for maximum interest and fun. Like riding a monorail or park train, this mode of thinking allows writers to put things in order and to structure the components of their thinking and their writing. It provides the opportunity to control the thinking and writing processes. The questions asked in this mode are

What is my focus?

Where are various focus points?

What steps have I completed so far?

What do I need to do next?

How can the order of my writing about my thinking add to my reader's interest and understanding?

As an assessment tool, the Theme Park of the Writer's Mind can be divided into skill development areas. The instructor can comment on students' writing using the theme park attractions to point out where the writing may break down.

Is it a lack of proper information? *brochure, kiosks*

Was the premise predictable? Did the writer assume information the reader may not have? *carousel*

Could the student have placed ideas in a more readable format or sequence? *monorail, park train*

Did the student do an excellent job with or fail to include other viewpoints counter to his or her own? *haunted house*

Did the writer put forth new proposals and ideas? *roller coaster*

Did the writer establish the value and benefit of his or her position? *water slide*

Did the writer utilize multiple resources effectively? Could the writer have used better or different resources? *midway games*

Did the writer confuse emotion and intuition with facts? *balloons, colors, lights, smells, sounds*

As the writing coach comments in the language of the theme park, students get a visual and less threatening critique of their writing.

Homework assignments and group projects can be set up that require students to work in a single feature area to identify the strengths and limitations of that thought mode. The writers can form groups of varying sizes to explore the strengths and limitations of working with two or three of the attractions. And, of course, eight students can be assigned to work together as a team to write a group paper or create a presentation for the class using all eight attraction thinking modes, with each person taking responsibility for the correct use of one of the thinking modes. The class then critiques the work of the teams of eight in a large group setting.

Other assignments of interest to students using the Theme Park of the Writer's Mind may be to analyze the use of the eight theme attractions in writing found in newspapers and periodicals. Students can explore different styles of periodicals and discuss why some writing requires more emphasis on one theme park attraction mode than on another.

Additional Ideas for Writing Exercises

Getting to Know Me: Writing Environment

Create a class chart by covering all the walls of the classroom with a continuous piece of newsprint to symbolize the total classroom use of student contributions to the writing process. Each student picks a space to write within and draws a border around his or her area, leaving an opening in the border to connect with others. The initial focus is on individual student self-defining. The students choose markers to express the color of their writing personas, write their names as they want to be known to the writing classroom members, and answer questions that include the following:

> Before I attended school, my favorite toys and activities were . . .
> My favorite school activities are . . .
> In my free time, my favorite activities are . . .
> I like to listen to . . .
> My favorite idea is . . .
> I learn things most quickly when . . .
> I get my best ideas when . . .

First the students work individually on their areas of the paper, and then they travel around the classroom when others are finished to observe writing that interests them. This is a foundation for a discussion about their strengths and how they like to get information. It can also be the foundation for a discussion of audience if a next step is taken and students are assigned someone else's block and asked to describe what information they were able to gain from the other student's area. The students can also be asked to find the person—based on the paper environment—most different from themselves, and to partner with the other student for one-to-one discussions. In these discussions they should be encouraged to discuss both similarities and differences. At the end of the interactive piece, the students are assigned to write one or two pages on their observations and the possible uses of the information gained.

Under the Big Top or the Writing Umbrella

A circus tent or umbrella with eight different colored panels can be used to create a colorful thinking mode depiction in front of the classroom to represent the eight thinking modes. The big top or umbrella symbolizes complete thinking. If one panel is missing, its ability to serve as a functioning tool will be undermined. Student writing partners analyze each other's writing to see if the fabric of thought adequately covers the writing.

The Principal Principle

Ask students to identify a problem they would like to change at their school. First, students work individually using their dominant natural intelligence mode or theme park attraction mode to write a letter to the school principal about the problem and to create an idea for a solution. Have the students edit their work and add to it by using their second favorite information path. The students then share their letters with another person who has a different style. Have the students help each other make their writing more clear by identifying strengths and weaknesses. Ask a few student pairs to share their progress.

If possible, invite the principal to come to hear the finished products. The writing coach might have the principal complete a block on the classroom writing profile surrounding the classroom. The principal's block will help students gain a better understanding of their principal's problem-solving approach. Having the students comment on this information should be insightful.

Theme Park Meets Multiple Intelligences

Identify a concern that many students have, for example, teasing and harassment at school. Have students answer the following questions in small discussion groups of four or five students:

- What have you heard about this problem?
- What have you seen happen that makes you think this is an important issue?
- What emotions does this problem bring forth?
- Draw the shape of the problem for the rest of the group.
- If the problem were in a movie, what type of music would be playing?
- What would the rhythm of the music be?
- How does your body feel when you are teased or harassed?
- What space do you want to separate you from the harasser?
- What steps would you take to stop the person doing the teasing?
- What body cues might you get from the other person about their intentions? Reactions? How do they differ for the person doing the teasing and for the person being teased?

Have the group use the Theme Park of the Writer's Mind approach to create a piece of writing they think will help students to deal with this problem.

The more actively we engage our writers in the planning process through discussion and interaction, the more confident they may feel as they put their thoughts on paper. Their ideas have been both validated and challenged in discussion. The students have the opportunity to see that a wider range of modes exists and that their ability to communicate their written thoughts to a broad audience is strengthened by observation, discussion, and experimentation. The writing process becomes both a public forum for exchange of ideas and a private exercise for them to draft their thoughts. Giving the students the opportunity to identify who they are and to see the linkages with others allows students to see how their strengths make a stronger product when linked with others of different strengths and talents. They also gain practice in all the modes via their interactions with others.

The student with ADD/ADHD will thrive in a classroom that provides stimulation for all students. Exuberance, when it is not restricted and caused to become a distraction, can be guided into a positive force of enthusiasm. Instead of fighting forces over which students feel limited control, empower students to identify areas such as emotion and kinesthetic motion as strengths rather than demons to be controlled at all costs. Using this approach of empowering students takes pressure off the educator/coach to be controlling most of the time and behavior in the classroom. By thinking of shaping and following the natural motivators, the blend of educator knowledge and experience will flow more comfortably with educator/coaches' attempts at guiding students to more effective paths to the acquisition of writing skills.

Finally, it is important in working with students with ADD/ADHD to create rubrics that they will understand and be able to use in assessing their writing. These rubrics should include the Theme Park of the Writer's Mind and the Multiple Intelligences so students can understand that they will be rewarded for using their natural or dominant styles and will also be rewarded for growth steps in using multiple styles and critical thinking approaches.

REFERENCES AND RESOURCES

Bender, William N. *Understanding ADHD: A Practical Guide for Teachers and Parents*. Upper Saddle River, NJ: Prentice Hall, 1997. Basic guide on working with students with ADHD.

Boyles, Nancy S., and Darlene Contadino. *The Learning Differences Sourcebook*. Los Angeles: Lowell House, 1997. Comprehensive introduction to a wide range of ability issues that provides thorough, basic information on the impact on learning. Includes information on beginning to identify areas of concern for students, parents, and teachers, with chapters on acceptance, accommodations, and various success strategies and support organizations.

Campbell, Linda, et al. *Teaching and Learning through Multiple Intelligences*. Needham, MA: Allyn and Bacon, 1999. Excellent, up-to-date resource on applying multiple intelligences with students and teachers.

Davis, Barbara G. *Tools for Teaching*. San Francisco: Jossey-Bass, 1993.

Davis, Ronald. *The Gift of Dyslexia*. San Juan Capistrano, CA: Ability Workshop Publishing, 1995. Ronald Davis is dyslexic himself and, after being labeled retarded in school, went on to eventually become an engineer, businessman, and sculptor. His book offers clear and simple assistance for overcoming dyslexia. Recommended for teachers, parents, therapists, and dyslexics. Typeset in "dyslexic-friendly" larger typesize with few hyphens.

deBono, Edward. *Edward deBono's Mind Pack: An Interactive Guide to Expanding Your Thinking with Games, Puzzles, and Exercises*. New York: Dorling Kindersley Publishing, 1995. A Six Thinking Hats kit is included with this set. Includes other games and strategies for learning and critical thinking in a fun way.

———. *Edward deBono's Super Mind Pack: Expand Your Thinking Powers with Strategic Games and Mental Exercises*. New York: Dorling Kindersley Publishing, 1998. Updated version with new games and thinking strategies.

———. *Six Thinking Hats*. Boston: Little, Brown and Co., 1985. Book describes in detail the Six Thinking Hats strategies, with discussion of uses for different settings.

———. *Teaching Thinking*. New York: Penguin, 1976. More Edward deBono for advanced reading on lateral thinking strategies for the truly interested.

Dowdy, Carol A., et al. *Attention Deficit/Hyperactivity Disorder in the Classroom: A Practical Guide for Teachers*. Austin, TX: PRO-ED, Inc., 1998.

Frank, Marjorie. *If You're Trying to Teach Kids How to Write . . . You've Gotta Have This Book!* Nashville, TN: Incentive Publications, 1995. Teacher- and student-friendly resource book with many practical ideas for classroom use. Written in an upbeat and affirming style.

Gardner, Howard. *Frames of Mind: The Theory of Multiple Intelligences.* New York: Basic Books, 1985. Original writing by Howard Gardner about multiple intelligences.

Hartmann, Thom. *ADD Success Stories: A Guide to Fulfillment for Families with Attention Deficit Disorder.* Grass Valley, CA: Underwood Books, 1995.

———. *Attention Deficit Disorder: A Different Perception.* Grass Valley, CA: Underwood Books, 1997.

———. *Beyond ADD: Hunting for Reasons in the Past and Present.* Grass Valley, CA: Underwood Books, 1996.

———. *Healing ADD: Simple Exercises That Will Change Your Daily Life.* Grass Valley, CA: Underwood Books, 1998.

———. *Think Fast: The ADD Experience.* Grass Valley, CA: Underwood Books, 1996. All these books by Thom Hartmann contain firsthand experience and practical ideas for addressing a variety of concerns with ADD.

Kennedy, Patricia, et al. *The Hyperactive Child Book.* New York: St. Martin's Press, 1993.

Lazear, David. *Seven Ways of Knowing: Teaching for Multiple Intelligences.* Palatine, IL: Skylight Publishing, 1991. Contains exercises for working with multiple intelligences, including identifying preferred learning styles and expanding skills by working in areas of strength and deficit. Written in a layout easy to use and reproduce for use in the classroom.

Macbeth, Fiona, and Nic Fine. *Playing with Fire: Creative Conflict Resolution for Young Adults.* British Colombia: New Society Publishers, 1995. Contains exercises on conflict resolution that work well with Six Thinking Hats and multiple intelligences for teachers who want to have interesting and safe classroom conflict and group problem solving.

Markel, Geraldine, and Judith Greenbaum. *Performance Breakthroughs for Adolescents with Learning Disabilities or ADD.* Champaign, IL: Research Press, 1996. Solid, practical information from working practitioners for bringing out the best in students with learning disabilities. Good information on utilizing various professional resources and personnel both inside and outside school systems.

Markova, Dawna, and Anne R. Powell. *Learning Unlimited: Using Homework to Engage Your Child's Natural Style of Intelligence.* Berkeley, CA: Conari Press, 1998. Includes some good exercises that students, teachers, and parents can easily use to identify students' natural style of intelligence. Source of quick and fun ways for students to gain insight into their natural styles of intelligence.

Myers, Isabel B., with Myers, Peter B. *Gifts Differing: Understanding Personality Type.* Palo Alto, CA: Davies-Black Publishing, 1995. Use of the Myers–Briggs indicator for exploring teacher-preferred styles and ways to work with students whose approach to information processing and problem solving may differ from the teacher's.

Neuville, Maureen B. *Sometimes I Get All Scribbly: Living with Attention Deficit/Hyperactivity Disorder.* Austin, TX: PRO-ED, Inc., 1996. Contains information written from the perspective of students with ADHD.

Perzanowski, Jan. Local, state, and national educational consultant and speaker for ADD, scotopic sensitivity syndrome, early intervention, and multiple intelligences. Coordinator of the Section 504 and Chapter 1 programs (K–12) for the Wawasee Community School Corp., Syracuse, Indiana.

Rief, Sandra. *The ADD/ADHD Checklist: An Easy Reference for Parents and Teachers.* Upper Saddle River, NJ: Prentice Hall, 1998.

———. *How to Reach and Teach ADD/ADHD Children: Practical Techniques, Strategies and Interventions for Helping Children with Attention Problems and Hyperactivity.* New York: The Center for Applied Research in Education, 1993. Both of the Sandra Rief books contain a wealth of practical information on proactive problem solving about attention deficit, written for both parents and teachers.

Smith, Joan. *Learning Victories: Conquering Dyslexic, Attention Deficit and Learning Challenges.* Sacramento, CA: Learning Time Products, 1998. Contains practical information in a quick-study format with case studies teachers should find interesting and useful. Contains exercises for use in the classroom and with individual students.

Turner, Diane, and Thelma Greco. *The Personality Compass: A New Way to Understand People.* Boston: Element Books, 1998. Fun book for use with teachers and students to help them understand their dominant and preferred approaches to problem solving. Affirms the necessity of using many types of strengths to create effective teams. May help students understand how their strengths can be used with others to achieve higher goals.

Weiss, Lynn. *ADD and Creativity: Tapping Your Inner Muse.* Dallas, TX: Taylor Publishing, 1997. Written primarily for adults, but may be great for older teens seeking a successful role model. Focus is on the use of creative abilities, overcoming confidence issues, previous failures, and identifying particular talents and abilities.

8 Working and Writing with Nontraditional Ninth Graders

DAN MADIGAN AND DEBORAH ALVAREZ

Chapters 6 and 7 addressed groups of students who, for particular reasons, call for special awareness and variation in strategies for coaching writing. In Chapter 8, Dan Madigan and Deborah Alvarez discuss a much broader group: ninth graders. These students who are in the transition area, often the oldest students in a middle school setting or the youngest in the grades 9 to 12 context, may be the ones who vary most in motivation. Frequently, ninth graders may be unable to conceive of a career path or to seriously think about college. Some may not elect a college education. Thus, many of the traditional ways of teaching English and language arts, with a heavy emphasis on writing, which seems more connected to the college bound, are not effective.

Despite the challenges both teachers and students face in a language arts class for nontraditional ninth grade students, such as students who openly resist the reading and writing of the academic essay, this chapter explores ways in which both the teacher and student can enjoy successful writing and reading experiences. Over time and upon reflection, we have learned what it means to teach nontraditional ninth graders within a framework of concepts and philosophies that support learning as a social construct, as lived and authentic experiences for ninth graders. (For further reading in this area, we offer the following list of authors: Bissex, Dewey, Madigan & Rybicki, Taylor & Dorsey-Gaines, Vygotsky.)

Although Madigan and Alvarez are the principal narrators of this chapter, Jane's voice and those of her students, particularly one student they have named Michael Jay, occupy a prominent place. The voices of the students presented provide a representation of the nontraditional student. The voices of Jane, Deb, and Dan describe the learning activities that have proved successful for them. They offer a series of vignettes of their students as points of discussion about process and pedagogy for teaching writing and as examples for the critical examination of appropriate writing tasks for a specific group of students.

For my first 13 years of teaching high school English, I was sure that I had accumulated enough experience and expertise with English to handle any learning situation with any student. That was before I met my first class of nontraditional ninth
graders. At first, I was frustrated with their movements, their immaturity, their
naivete, and value system regarding writing and reading that was much different
from my own, but in the next two years of teaching, my ninth graders taught me
how to teach reading and writing to them.

—Deb

Most of my 14-year teaching career in secondary school was spent teaching language arts. During that time, it seemed that no one wanted to teach the nontraditional students in our rural school. Gradually a colleague and I drifted toward these
nontraditional language arts students and classes. From the first day we met our
ninth graders, we felt we were in over our heads. Yet those experiences are the most
memorable of my 24-year teaching career.

—Dan

Jane has taught freshmen for 25 years, both in private and public schools. Each new
year, she faces her students with enthusiasm, energy, and a sense of hope. Because
of her seniority, Jane can teach any level language arts class in her high school. Yet
year after year, she chooses to teach only nontraditional ninth graders. She loves
them; she understands them; and she is often frustrated with them.

—Jane

Upon entering high school, ninth graders enter a new phase of their education that
challenges them in many ways. This challenge is even more apparent for students
who enter into a nontraditional curriculum: students who choose such educational
paths as vocational–technical programs; students who are uncertain of their goals
after high school; students whose reading and writing abilities are minimal according to state standards; students who do not want more academically oriented
course offerings; and students who may not have been encouraged to pursue a college education. These students often pose the most difficult challenge for teachers
new to teaching and teachers who are newly experiencing the teaching of nontraditional ninth graders.

Attempts to reach, as we define them, nontraditional freshman writers have
often brought us to the brink of rejecting every teaching method and theoretical
position that we have tried to incorporate into our teaching practice. Like Jane and
many other teachers of nontraditional freshmen, we have been frustrated, anxious,
and confused when our teaching methods and strategies don't work across the
board, despite our best efforts to incorporate into our curricula and classroom
practices the theories and philosophies that support effective literacy activities,
such as writing workshops, reading circles, and new ways of enhancing learning
with technology. (For example, writer's and reader's workshops are included
in texts by Atwell, O'Conner, Romano, Zemelman & Daniels). Too often, we find
that our language arts classrooms for nontraditional ninth grade language arts

freshmen don't seem to sponsor literacy for our students as we had once thought, as Brandt suggests (1998).

The Learning Environment: A Glimpse of Jane's Classroom

Jamie, Robert, and Ryan sat at a table, talking. Once again, Jane advised the boys to get busy and read. She then turned to help Melissa working at a computer. Jamie hurled barbs. Robert's voice rose. Ryan encouraged the melee. Returning to their group, Jane pulled Ryan aside, spoke to him very quietly, and then walked him away from his friends. Over her shoulder, she shot a furtive look at Jamie,
"Read your book."
"I don't want to read."
"He can't read," said another student with a snicker.
Laughter followed from others in the class until Jane put her forefinger to her lips, signaling a quieting.
"SHHHHHH."
Don, conspiring with Ryan, tried to distract Linda as she worked tirelessly on her writing. Exasperated, Linda pleaded,
"Don, if you don't want to learn, then don't. Don't interfere with me or somebody else who's trying to learn."
Across the room, Jamie opened his book and began reading. Almost immediately, Don asked to go to the bathroom, and Jamie resumed his distractive talking.

Jane arranges her classroom in such a way as to offer her nontraditional students a more controlled and structured environment for purposes of learning. The activities and assignments she selects are related to her belief that all her students are learners, but especially so in a more controlled environment. Within a 90-minute block period, she conducts three or four learning activities around a single focus, for example, to improve revising skills. These activities might include the following:

- Journal writing in class about an event in the student's life or a reflection on a theme from a class reading
- A trip to the computer lab to convert their journal entry to a typed copy, with encouragement to make additions to the text
- Minilessons on some grammatical aspects of writing narratives, such as how to use dialogue with correct punctuation
- Instructions on what to do in the peer editing group with the typed copy
- Time for peer editing and individual help if needed by any student

Jane's lessons often include rubrics or check sheets that guide the activities and hold students accountable (see Figure 8.1 on page 129). Her method of instruction allows her to manage her classroom in the most positive and productive manner for her students. Jane believes that her method of instruction benefits all her students, including those like Ryan, Ray, and Jeremy who demand most of her attention.

Some Characteristics of Nontraditional Freshmen

Before we can begin to construct meaningful writing tasks for our students, it is useful to consider, among other important issues, the behaviors and attitudes of these students. In the following series of vignettes, we offer physical and behavioral details of our students in an effort to better describe to the reader some of the student traits and actions that could influence pedagogical choice and practice.

> Matt arrived each morning in Jane's classroom, hurried to Jane's desk to tell her about his latest ballgame, his new set of magic cards, or the ninth draft of his latest poem. He wanted her immediate attention. But when he saw that many other students wanted Jane's attention as well, he turned and sought out the first peer he noticed and started to repeat the same stories.
>
> Tasha, another student, was like most 14 or 15 year olds. She was naïve. Her physical appearance made her seem much younger. She was very small with a little girl's voice. In comparison, many of her young women peers were more physically mature. She was very quiet in class, and her literacy skills were lacking. Her lack of confidence with language forced her to consult Jane on every assignment. In fact, Tasha literally hung on Jane whenever there was class time for writing.
>
> —Deb's journal

Both adolescents in the previous vignette lacked self-confidence. They didn't want to be wrong. They wanted to be with their friends. They needed individual attention. Other students confided in us that they did not want to be moved ahead to a more advanced English class (even though they were capable) because they felt more comfortable with their friends and the pace they were allowed to learn at in their nontraditional classroom. Such was the case with Mark:

> Mark, physically more mature than his peers, had a vocabulary and verbal ability that a college student would envy. He started in Deb's honors section one year, but refused to complete any writing assignment—even though he demonstrated above average ability to perform at that level. After an emotional plea from Mark, Deb requested a conference with Mark's parents, both college professors. Shortly after, Mark was placed in Deb's nontraditional English class.
>
> —Deb's journal

Sitting next to the underachiever in the nontraditional classroom is often a student who does not possess grade-level literacy skills.

> Cliff was a sixteen year old in a freshman English class. He was there not because he had failed. He was smart. Yet, he had not attended school regularly for two years.

> When he returned to school, Deb's class was his only alternative to the juvenile system. A parole officer escorted Cliff to Deb's class every day. All Cliff really wanted to do was work with his older brother, who was a carpenter. For Cliff, whose reading and writing skills were at a fourth-grade level, school was a "waste of [my] time."
>
> —Deb's journal

Problems with self-esteem and identity are also common among adolescents and, we might add, natural among them. For teachers this means that "attitudes" may also be prevalent in a ninth-grade class.

> For Angela, high school was an opportunity to socialize—especially with more mature young males in her class. Her bouffant hairdo, her white, sheer cropped blouse made her stand out in class. But more noticeable was her resistance to learning. Deb moved Angela away from her male classmates after it became obvious that socializing was more important than writing or reading. Angela then decided to clean out her plastic purse, adjust her makeup, and talk whenever she decided she had something to say regardless of who was speaking or the classroom activities. She refused physically to participate in any dramatic improvisations or other activities like writing or editing her texts in the computer lab. Instead she stayed alone in the classroom with the door locked. Any attempts to reconcile the relationships she had with the class, with the teacher, or with her parents, who were divorced, proved unproductive toward changing Angela's classroom behavior. Angela remained uncooperative so eventually she had to be removed from the classroom.
>
> —Deb's journal

The preceding freshmen challenged us to think of literacy activities and programs that suited our particular students. Some of our students wanted careers in farming, hairstyling, truck driving, detailed painting, and the merchant marines. Many others had no definite career goals other than not going to college. Some thought they might go to college one day.

Helping Young Writers Make Connections

As writing coaches, we have discovered that all the literacy activities that we present in class must have a purpose relevant to our students' lives. Throughout the rest of this chapter, we offer the reader an extended exploration of an adolescent writer who often surprised us with his creativity in writing, yet at other times defied the most thoughtful and generally accepted pedagogical strategies for writing. Within the framework of this exploration, we will examine some successful writing strategies associated with three areas common to freshman writing classrooms: journaling, writing about literature, and writing in genres. In each examination, we offer examples of activities, suggestions, and questions so that our readers may generate ideas and think about how to create their own successful writing strategies.

As a starting point for each area of study that we examine, we will focus on one student whom we refer to as Michael Jay. His responses and approaches to writing assignments provide us with a lens through which we examine successful writing strategies.

A Portrait of Michael Jay

Jane led her English 9 class to the computer lab so that they could work on revising a journal entry. Ninth graders are like corks in a barrel of water; you push five down and the other twenty pop up darting in different directions. So taking 25 ninth graders to the writing lab, when every one of them feels that he or she is the only one in the class, is an impossible task for classroom management. On the way to the computer writing lab, Michael Jay happened to be walking behind a group of four ninth grade boys from his class. Three of the boys began to shove the smaller ninth grade boy between them—one would shove him into the other who in turn shoved him into the other boy. Words were exchanged.

"Hey wimp, wanna fight?"

"Naah!"

"He's too shrimpy for that. Aren't ya, boy?" Joe couldn't escape the height and weight of the other boys who shoved him between words and their bodies.

When Michael Jay heard this exchange, he stepped among the three boys and told them to leave Joe alone. From that moment on, Joe had a permanent case of sincere hero worship for Michael Jay. To Michael Jay this wasn't a problem; someone was picking on a classmate who couldn't defend himself. Before they reached the computer lab, Michael Jay told Joe, "Hey, man, don't let nobody talk to you like that. You stand up for yourself." Joe looked back at Michael Jay with a smile and a slight nod of his head.

Michael Jay is cool, but he doesn't feign being cool. He is quiet, but sparks of fire light up his eyes when he talks about basketball or his girlfriend Natalie or has the chance to do public speaking. The rest of the time, Michael Jay is somewhat quiet, sincere, and obsequiously cooperative in classes even when he is bored, which is most of the time. He is an underachiever. He takes the basic courses that really don't challenge him, but don't threaten him either.

In other activities, Michael Jay was the freshman representative to the Homecoming Court. Of course, freshmen candidates never "win" as king or queen, but Jane had the distinct impression that when Michael Jay becomes a senior he again would represent his class on the Homecoming Court and be crowned king.

On the basketball court, Michael Jay turns into a firebrand. He puts the energy he conserves during the school day into dramatic action on the court. Only the coach and the constant drills give Michael Jay's enthusiasm direction and purpose.

—Deb's journal

Journal Writing and Literary Analysis

At the beginning of each class, Jane would sometimes write single-word topics on the board such as *death, revenge,* or *worry* and let the students select a topic to write about. She believes that the students' readings and their writings should be connected to issues relevant to their lives. In addition to single-word topics, she considers broad themes from novels and short stories, such as *revenge, racist remarks that hurt,* and *justice for all.* As the semester progresses and Jane and students become more familiar with journal activities, she might begin a journal activity by saying:

> I want you to practice fluent writing and have a chance to write about any topic [you] want to write about. These are topics about your life. This is just for you. Two points for fluid writing, and I would like to see all of you write three quarters of a page today.
>
> —Observational Notes, Fall, 1996

After about 10 to 15 minutes of writing, Jane typically asked a student to share the contents of his or her journal entry. Then Jane moved on to the lesson of the day, which involved revising a journal entry based on sentence-level corrections on such topics as sentence combining, changing synonyms, and word selection and mechanical issues like commas and periods. After several days of writing journals, Jane asked students to select one entry and do more substantive revisions. This process involved peer review, peer editing, and the use of a rubric. Attached to the rubric is a check-off sheet, which is used by both the students and teacher to give feedback.

After all the students had finished in the computer lab, Jane then asked them to polish their drafts and grade their writing using a rubric called "Reaching for Excellence" (see Figure 8.1). Many students found this journaling process instructive because it offered them guidance through a structured series of rubrics during each phase of the writing assignments.

Alternative Models of Journaling

Journal writing for ninth graders needs to take on a multiplicity of purposes. Journaling has to have an immediate purpose for the students, as well as provide impetus for other related classroom activities. Teaching students to write a structured piece that is suitable for analysis or the competency exams would be futile if it did not have a purpose that engaged their expertise and their interests. Stephen O'Connor's research with inner-city adolescents shows a way to bridge interest and expertise into written compositions. From police reports and oral narratives, O'Connor focused the classroom writing tasks on the violence that his students often experienced in their own worlds.

A useful adaptation of O'Connor's activities is to use police reports or newspaper accounts of neighborhood violence or car accidents that involve teenagers as the focal point of student discussion and written assignment. The lesson plan in Figure 8.2 will guide teachers in planning and using this idea. The first part of the lesson may be completed during one class period, but the entire plan may take a full week or more to complete.

Reaching for Excellence

After rereading the revised journal entry from 9-25-96, a fair grade for my writing

would be _____ **because** _____

_____

A writing goal for this paper is _____

One specific suggestion from a peer is _____

_____

_____

_____

(Peer's name _____)

3 Specific Changes from 9-25-96 to this paper

_____

_____

_____

I accomplished my goal because _____

_____

My grade on this paper should be _____ because _____

_____

_____

_____
(signature)   (date)

FIGURE 8.1

Journaling with Police Reports
90-Minute Class Period

Learning Goal

- To think, analyze, and articulate a particular perspective
- To make the journal a sketch that can be rendered later into a more complex and finished piece of writing

Materials

Obtain police reports from the officer assigned to the school or local police departments. Students may also bring in stories from the local newspaper.

Activities

- Select a recent newspaper story or police report about some act of violence in the neighborhood. Have the students read the facts and underline the facts.
- Solicit information from the students who may have actual knowledge of the story not presented in the report. Allow them to tell their version of the facts, distinguishing between fact, supposition, and opinion.
- On the board or overhead projector, list the facts from the newspapers or report in one column and students' points of view in another column.
- Collect additional information by having the class take the role of an observer, judge, medical person, friend, parent, or sibling who might be affected by this situation. Analyze the scene as it occurred and affected each person touched by the incident. Compare the different facts and points of view.
- In a journal entry, have the students take a position regarding the case, based on the facts, about whom they thought was responsible and why.
- Ask students to reveal their positions in an oral discussion.
- Select a student entry to model. The teacher will show the students how to use the journal information and facts to create a piece of writing such as a short story, poem, play, or extended narrative.
- If time permits, take the students to the computer lab to write up their outlines.
- Students will work on individual pieces in the genre they have selected.

Assessment

The teacher will prepare a rubric that reflects the goals and stages of the writing.

FIGURE 8.2

Questions for Our Readers to Consider about Journaling in the Classroom

- Consider your purpose, assumptions, and reasons for using journals in your classroom?
- Consider carefully what kinds of writing and learning journal activities promote.
- How do you continue to find writing strategies that speak to issues that are of concern to your students?

Literature and the Teaching of Writing: Connecting to Students' Lives

Language arts teachers often use literature as a point of departure for writing. Jane uses themes and characterizations from novels and other pieces of literature to prompt writing and discussions of interpretation and to engage in literary analysis. For example, she invites her students to compare some aspect of their lives to the lives of the characters in a novel like *The Pigman*. We find that students gain a broader understanding of literature through writing if they can connect to the adolescent characters and themes in a personal way. In introducing *The Pigman* to her students, Jane asks them to compare their lives to those of John and Lorraine, two of the adolescent characters in the novel. Most of the students jumped into the assignment as they saw themselves in the characters and the situations these characters were involved in. Through the process of analysis, teachers assume that students will not only understand the literary aspects of the literature, but also find the personal connection to it that makes the literature relevant to their lives. Hence, they tend to engage in more analytical and thoughtful response and written expression. We caution our readers, however, to be aware that some students may not connect in the way that we might anticipate. Such was the case of Michael Jay during one related activity.

> I don't like comparing myself to somebody. I figure I am one person and nobody like me. It should be like that. Ain't nobody else like me. I'm unique. Nobody else like me. I'm my own man and I like it. All that stuff like that acting . . . Like my friends. They act cool and act the same. Just dumb, and I don't like that.
>
> —An interview

Despite his reluctance to compare himself to a character from the novel, Michael Jay complied with the nature of the assignment.

> I wrote me and John are somewhat alike and different in many ways. John and I are like this. In one paragraph I listed how we are alike, and second paragraph how we were different.
>
> —An interview

Later, Michael Jay admitted that he made up the being "alike" part. He could not, in staying true to his identity, say that he had anything in common with John. In *The Pigman*, John is a troublemaker who rides around at night in cars, and, after gaining Mr. Pignotti's trust, John and Lorraine literally destroy his house during a party bash they have in Mr. Pignotti's absence. Michael Jay comments are as follows:

> My parents are like strict. They don't like me going to parties. If it has something to do with school, I can go. But it's like somebody's house. They don't let me ride around while at somebody else's house. I don't play around in school and stuff . . . John and Lorraine they be. . . . Lorraine hops in everybody's car and rides around and stuff. John acts in school and playing all kinds of pranks and takes advantage of some old man. I couldn't do that.
>
> —An interview

Reflecting on Michael Jay's previous comments, we see how he has viewed the assignment as restrictive and contrived. Eventually, he completed a comparison–contrast paper for this activity, but he could not see a connection to his life in a way we imagined. Perhaps it was his strict literal interpretation of the assignment. We believe that for an activity to be most effective teachers must introduce a series of scaffolding activities throughout the year to build a framework that shows students how their lives may mirror the lives of the fictional characters they read about.

Sometimes our assignments appear to be broad, inviting students to participate in discussion from various points of view; but, in fact, such assignments are limiting from a student's perspective. For heterogeneous groups of students, we need to broaden the elements of choice within an assignment so that students can retain their identities. For Michael Jay, this means that if he had been able to choose any of the characters in the novel, he might have chosen Mr. Pignotti, whose moral behaviors were more like his own. In addition, the written task itself, like the choice of characters, limited Michael Jay's manner of expression. It appears that the comparison–contrast focus was too narrow for Michael Jay, and it prevented him from finding a style and form that he could comfortably connect with and use. Michael Jay's situation has helped us understand more clearly that form follows function. For example, if Michael Jay had been allowed to choose a character that he related to in any way, he may have been more inclined to work on the organizational structure for his ideas, which would have lead him to develop a form more suited to his interpretation.

Strategies and Activities for Interpreting Readings through Creative Drama

An effective strategy for teaching writing through the use of literature is to offer students prewriting opportunities in the form of creative dramatics workshops. These workshops take on a variety of shapes and are based on the notion that creative dramatic activities allow students to think more critically and to write more thought-fully about a story. Creative dramatic activities broaden how students begin to think about ideas and issues and provide them with a framework from which to write.

Certainly, academic writing may be one of the most difficult forms of expression for our ninth grade students to grasp. Our students are active and seem to be more comfortable with oral and visual forms of expression. A useful technique for soliciting from students multiple literary interpretations is to ask students to choose a character from a book or short story and then introduce creative dramatic activities that allow students to come to a greater understanding of the characters within the context of important issues and ideas. Figure 8.3 briefly describes a few creative drama activities that have worked well for us for this type of learning goal.

Creative Drama as a Bridge to Better Writing

By itself, creative dramatics makes sense only if students become more interested in ways to interpret texts. It's a welcome change for students who are more inclined to be active participants rather than passive participants in learning, for those with a kinesthetic learning style. We also find that creative dramatic activities encourage more detailed and descriptive writing from students. For example, as students use informal discussion and other informal methods to interpret the freeze frames, they become more aware of and more comfortable with a variety of perspectives about particular ideas and issues found in a story. Consequently, students are more apt to take a more varied and stronger stance when writing about these issues and ideas. These same students are also more likely to have looked closely at the detail and description that will help support their views.

Suggestions for Writing Assignments Using Creative Dramatics

- Rather than have the audience blurt out the meaning of the freeze frame, individuals can write a list of the details they observe from the freeze frame. They can also write freely a descriptive paragraph about what they observe. This kind of close reading provides readers with activities that help them improve their reading skills, including comprehension, and writing skills, including organization and detail.
- Students from the audience might select a character from the talk show who seems interesting and then interview that character to get supporting detail for a written essay, feature news article, or the like, that describes a character's role in a story.
- A student might try to describe his or her moral stance and point of view about how a young person might act in a certain situation, at the same time juxtaposing a character from the story with an opposite point of view. This written dialogue or conversation could be written in collaboration with another student or by a single student. The dialogue might appear written in opposite columns (Michael Jay's and John's from *The Pigman*) on a piece of paper.

Freeze Frame: Single Character

■ Ask students to choose a character and then find details in the story that describe the character's emotions, strengths, weaknesses, and positions on an issue. Now ask students to choose some outstanding characteristic(s) of this character and try to capture this in a freeze frame (a frozen pose) that will be interpreted by the rest of the class. Students enjoy trying to interpret the pose. They inspect the pose from their seats, then from close range, and from different angles. The teacher points out some of the detail that might have been missed. Students get involved and support their interpretations by alluding to the meaning being created by character's positions and gestures in the freeze frame.

Freeze Frame: Multiple Characters

■ A spin on the individual freeze frame is to have a group of students choose an interesting scene from a story that has several characters in it. Ask the groups to present a group freeze frame that represents the meaning of the scene. Again, the audience does close inspection of the freeze frame, argues about meaning, and gets a broader understanding of important issues. In the first stage of the preceding activity and other freeze frame activities, it is useful to ask the student character(s) in the freeze frame to hold their pose for a few minutes, then relax as the audience works to interpret what they saw. At this time, the student(s) in the freeze frame do not discuss with the audience the meaning they were making with their poses in the first stage. In the second stage, the students in the freeze frame hold their poses again as the audience goes back for another look. After taking notes once more, the audience then presents their interpretations to the freeze-frame group, who respond in a manner that clarifies what meaning they were trying to create.

The Talk Show

■ Create a talk show scenario in which the host interviews four or five guests (characters from the book) about a particular idea or issue found in the story. Each student does some thorough research about the character to make the characterization credible. This activity works best if students who are being interviewed also write questions for the talk show host. The audience, as guests of the show, can also write and ask questions of the host. Sometimes this activity works best if three or four students combine to find detail about a character and how they might respond to an issue or idea found in the book. Then this group chooses one of the students to represent the character.

The Interview

■ Everyone in the class chooses a character from a story and researches him or her. Ask students to pair up and interview a character they are interested in concerning an important issue or idea.

FIGURE 8.3   **Interpretive Activities for Reading/Writing Activities**

Indirect/Direct

This activity involves changing indirect dialogue from a scene in a story to direct dialogue. For example, here is how the narrative might be presented in its original form:

> As she entered the room she was introduced to other students one at a time. She asked them about the school, the town, and the strange rumors about the haunted house on the edge of town.

Changing the indirect to direct dialogue might result in something like "Are the rumors true about . . . ?" When students change the original dialogue, you are asking them to stay in character and within the limits of the idea. But you are also asking students to play with words and description in ways that reflect a particular perspective. We have found this exercise useful at breaking down a difficult scene or idea, and students find it fun trying to say explicitly what was implicit in the indirect dialogue. Students pay attention to words in the story, and they are encouraged to support their actions and choices.

Resources

You can locate many variations and renditions of these activities and more in the following resources, most generally geared toward children's activities, but very useful for creative drama activities with students of all ages.

Heinig, R. B. *Creative Drama for the Classroom Teacher,* 4th ed. New York: Simon and Schuster, 1993.
American Alliance for Theatre and Education found at the web site www.aate.com/welcome.htm

Creative Drama Tips Based on a Freeze-Frame Activity

Guiding Questions (for each activity, provide some guiding questions for the person(s) involved)

- What kind of body language will best convey the feelings you are trying to convey?
- What evidence are you basing your interpretation on?
- How does your interpretation of the scene help us understand the overall theme of the novel?
- How will the space and props you use to set up your freeze frame contribute to the meaning you are trying to convey?

Side Coaching

- Teachers should carefully listen to the audience responses to a freeze frame, and the teacher should encourage students during the freeze frame to expand not only on responses that get at some of the obvious meanings conveyed in the pose, but at subtle meanings as well.

(continued)

FIGURE 8.3   Continued

- Teachers should ensure that all questions from the student audience are positive yet probing as concerns meaning.
- Encourage students to get up and check out the pose from a closer view or different angles.

Considering Audience

- Ask students to always be sensitive to the performance and performers in the freeze frame.
- Ask students to take notes and work together in mining the meaning from the scene and the book as a whole.
- Ask students to focus on detail and how that detail contributes to a broader meaning of the theme, issue, or other feature.

Student–Teacher Feedback

Direct feedback to the performer might include written responses, but whatever the feedback from the teacher and students, it should be positive and directed at questions of interpretation and creativity. Examples follow.

- Ask the performer why she chose such an interpretation.
- Ask her why she chose such a pose to represent the interpretation.
- Ask audience members why they chose such an interpretation.
- Ask the audience how these new interpretations of a scene contribute to their overall understanding of the scene or book.

FIGURE 8.3   Continued

The previous double-voice activity allows students to achieve a greater depth of meaning in interpreting stories and writing about these stories, as Bruner suggests in *Actual Minds, Possible Worlds.* In fact, we believe that creative dramatics and the follow-up writing activities offer students a rich choice of options for thinking and writing about literature from their own perspectives. Students do not have to be dramatically inclined to participate in these creative dramatic activities. We have found that almost all our ninth grade students, the reticent ones, the boisterous ones, and the complacent ones, can find a role in creative dramatics that is satisfying and that serves the purposes of learning to communicate through some kind of physical and written performance.

Questions for Our Readers to Consider

- What strategies will encourage students to become more actively engaged in activities that use literature as a basis for writing?
- How can we ensure that the learning outcomes of these activities are directly relevant to the educational purposes of our classes?

Writing beyond Exposition:
Learning through Different Genres

> I like to find out for myself. I don't like to rag on people. Ask me stuff. I like to do stuff myself.
>
> —Michael Jay

When Michael Jay is asked to do a task, whether it is playing basketball or playing school, he makes it clear that he wants to have control over his actions and thoughts. In fact, he wants to be active. Teachers of ninth grade adolescents know that their students possess unbounded amounts of energy. Unbridled enthusiasm. Constant chatter. Playful, physical sparring. In the classroom, the teacher who has learned to corral that energy and give it direction and purpose, as in the structured activities of playing sports, is advantaged when working with nontraditional students. In the following example, we describe how to incorporate the physical energy that adolescents like Michael Jay possess into genre writing activities.

In the beginning of a unit on poetry and form, Jane asked her students to write their names vertically down the side of a sheet of paper. As Jane wrote her name vertically on the marker board, she said to her students, "I want you to write the letters of your name so that there is one letter per line on the paper." Her strategy for this poetry assignment, like many strategies she uses for teaching genre writing, was to assist the students in coming up with a word to begin each line of a stanza.

Michael Jay followed Jane's instructions to write the first letter of his name vertically on the paper. Then he sat at his desk for a long time without doing anything, nor doing any writing. He had trouble coming up with words. The letters of his name did not help him find words to start a line of poetry. Then he turned and looked up at the basketball poster that hung on the wall nearest his desk. Finally, he wrote "Believe in yourself." Then he looked up at the poster again and wrote "Strength on the outside comes only after." Here is his completed poem.

> Believe in yourself
> Strength on the outside
> comes only after
> Strength on the inside.
> Know your limits,
> then break through them.
> What you can achieve is only
> limited by what you can dream.
>   —Michael Jay

The first letters of each line do not even reveal Michael Jay's real name, much less his pseudonym. So what happened? He took liberties with the assignment when he saw the poster of the basketball player. Michael Jay completed the writing task when he co-opted the poster's words to express his own feelings about something he loved. An opportunity arose for him to combine the writing task with a subject of interest, and he engaged.

On the court, Michael Jay found connections, challenge, choice, and commitment of a kind that turned a disinterested student learner into a focused and committed student athlete. For Michael Jay, writing should be like playing a game: play, practice, and performance. In fact, in observing Michael Jay we think that students could benefit from *playing* with writing, enjoying the experience, practicing with certain genres, and performing the writing that they produce in some interactive way, as James Britton describes in *Language and Learning*. Thus, writing becomes threefold. Given opportunities, students like Michael Jay tend to create moments in the classroom environment that allow them to express themselves.

One such occasion presented itself to Michael Jay when Jane asked the students what they thought about the issue of respect from *To Kill a Mockingbird*. Michael Jay, usually a quiet and reserved class member, raised his hand. Jane called on him to answer, but when she recognized him, Michael Jay stood up and began to move toward the front of the classroom as if he wanted to lead the discussion. She allowed this. He talked about his views on respect until it became an extemporaneous sermon. Michael Jay's oral ability with language far exceeded anything he had written up to that time. It gave him an opportunity to demonstrate his knowledge through his verbal skills on a subject of interest to him.

Using Play, Practice, and Performance in Writing Drama

The previous scenario adds another dimension to creating successful writing. What is common to freshman students is that they do not have much practice or skill with the conventions of many genre forms, such as poetry, short story, novel, and drama, or even the four modes of discourse: narrative, description, exposition, and argumentation. So periods of concentrated seatwork in writing activities have to be directed and varied with periods of physical involvement that allow the students to learn concepts through tactile or physical engagement or application. We are suggesting that combining the need for purposeful and guided physical involvement can work with teaching adolescents about writing different genres. Michael Jay became engaged when he stood up and talked to the class. His speech would not have had the same passion and exuberance if he had delivered it seated in a desk.

Three elements at work in creating a successful writing assignment based on genre study: students need to play with the form, practice the form, and then have a performance of the form. What Michael Jay told about being successful in sports can be applied to teaching genre writing. Using a piece of literature as the model, we can introduce students to the actual construction of this genre as another tool for expressing their ideas about their world. The goal of writing strategies for genre writing is to use a genre model (drama in this case) and have the students learn the concepts about drama from physical involvement in the construction of it: playing with language, practicing the language skills in reading and writing and speaking, and then performing the written product (see Figure 8.4).

Lesson Plan for Writing in Specific Literary Genres (Drama)
90-Minute Class Period

Learning Goals

1. Use physical involvement and oral language to promote and encourage writing.
2. Represent lived experiences in a variety of forms.
3. Evolve a form (genre) through a variety of invention strategies.

Rationale

For high school adolescents, tapping into various forms of learning styles and manners of expression allows for language to be meaningful beyond common exposition and standard formal usage. Also, language learning by Vygotskian model encourages the processing of language skills from the external to the internal. These lessons parallel that pattern.

Activities

- Read a play and have students discuss the elements of plot, character development related to the plot, setting, and the play's message (theme).
- Discuss with students how a play is different in appearance from other genres, such as poetry, a short story, or an essay.
- List the conventions that make a play a play, for example, dialogue, stage directions, and the division of the play into acts and scenes.

Playing with Form

- Divide the class into groups of three heterogeneous groups.
- Divide the actual thinking and writing of the play into goals to be accomplished each day.
- Set the schedule on the board for the goals of the day and teach a minilesson on how to go about achieving that day's goal; for example, Day 1 was to decide on a subject. Once the group has decided, discuss the choice with the teacher. Day 2 might advance the process to writing a tentative message for the play and creating the characters who would carry the message. This state of the process is a consensus-building session through trial and suggestion until the group can reach agreement on the goals for that day. This division of goals proceeds until a first draft is completed.

Practicing the Form

- Students type up the transcript from the written text so that it resembles a play format. In typing, they revise and edit as they go through the play. Minilessons on how to revise a play also need to be part of practicing the form.

(*continued*)

FIGURE 8.4

- After the play is typed and copies have been run off, the group members solicit members of the class to be the characters in their plays. Group members become directors, editors, and managers of the drama.
- Together, group members create the scenery, find costumes, and schedule a time for videotaping the play.

Performing the Form: Performance Day

- Move classroom furniture, make sure the videotape machine is ready with a new tape, set up minimal sets, and have costumes ready.
- The class members not performing serve as the audience, usually sitting on the floor around the student actors. When one play finishes, the scene changes and another group gets ready to perform. Usually, one class period in a 90-minute block class is enough to film all the plays.
- Expect that the videotaping might be chaotic and often loud as students attempt to present their drama. Many of them lack self-discipline, and a chance to get up and act is an irresistible narcissistic moment.
- Show the whole class the videotaped plays, and provide opportunities for students to review the plays. Teachers can be very creative about doing the review activity.
- Each play runs about 5 to 10 minutes, depending on how much the student actors improvise their lines or how much they need to control their laughter and exuberance.

FIGURE 8.4   Continued

Figure 8.4 does not appear to present a description of a well-ordered classroom. However, the goal of such an activity is to engage the students so that they will be physically involved in a project with structured goals to be completed by the group. Writing a play not only teaches the conventions of drama (Moffett demonstrates this in his K–12 language arts curriculum: 1968, 1983), but involves peer cooperation, problem solving, understanding how to write dialogue, and the use of words to construct a message sustained through a series of conversations, acts, and scenes. Writing a play also utilizes the youthful energy of ninth graders. Laughter often accompanies the viewing of the video. Whether from embarrassment or frustration or real amusement, the students enjoy their efforts, now visible to them in written and spoken form.

Questions for Our Readers to Consider
- What features of literary genres, for example, dialogue, images, rhyme, word play, and story grammars, are your students most familiar with in real life? How can you use these features to create writing activities that teach students about literary genres?

- What kinds of activities might you design for your students that take advantage of their need to physically express themselves, and yet are useful and connected to writing tasks?

And Finally

We have presented a variety of classroom situations and writing strategies that we have used successfully with nontraditional students. We offer these examples as possibilities and patterns for thinking about meaningful writing assignments. We understand, however, that teaching writing to adolescents needs to be contextualized for each individual teacher and each unique group of students. Sometimes our need to be in control of the classroom and our need to know the answers and to direct the students in learning activities interferes with the wisdom that students convey to us about what makes learning exciting. Although we might agree that strategies for writing come and go and that some are more effective than others, one thing that we have found most effective is to listen to our students' voices about what makes learning exciting to them. When we listened to what Michael Jay and the other nontraditional students had to say about their own learning, our classrooms changed. We recognize that this pedagogy takes courage for both teacher and student but, as Michael Jay so eloquently reminds us in his own written words:

> Some day I plan to be one of the greatest men alive. Both at home and in the work place. As for school, the way you teach a student now will effect them later. So my advise to you is try to see eye to eye with the children. Stay on there level, don't try to go over there heads cause all that's gonna do make them hate you. And by doing that you loose their respect, and if they don't respect you they won't learn. Then you both loose.
>
> —Michael Jay

REFERENCES AND RESOURCES

Alvarez, Deborah M. "I Can't Teach Drama, But I Can Teach You How to Perform." Unpublished Manuscript. University of Wisconsin–Madison, 1992.

Atwell, Nancie. *In the Middle.* Portsmouth, NH: Boynton/Cook, 1989.

Bissex, Glenda. *Gyns At Wrk: A Child Learns to Read.* Cambridge, MA: Harvard University Press, 1980.

Brandt, D. "Sponsors of Literacy." *College Composition and Communication* 49.2 (1998): 165–185.

Britton, James. *Language and Learning.* Coral Gables, FL: University of Miami Press, 1970.

Bruner, Jerome. *Actual Minds, Possible Worlds.* Cambridge, MA: Harvard University Press, 1986.

Dewey, John. *Democracy and Education.* New York: Macmillan and Co., 1938.

Fine, M., L. Weis, and L. C. Powell. "Communities of Difference: A Critical Look at Desegregated Spaces Created for and by Youth." *Harvard Educational Review,* 67.2 (1997): 247–283.

Healy, J. *Endangered Minds.* New York: Simon and Schuster, 1990.

Heath, S. B. *Ways with Words.* New York: Cambridge University Press, 1983.

Heinig, R. B. *Creative Drama for the Classroom Teacher,* 4th ed. New York: Simon and Schuster, 1993.

Madigan, D., and V. Rybicki. *The Writing Lives of Children.* York, ME: Stenhouse, 1997.

Moffett, James. *Student Centered Language Arts Curriculum: K–12.* Boston: Houghton Mifflin, 1968, 1983.

Moll, L. "Literacy Research in Community and Classrooms: A Sociocultural Approach." In *Multidisciplinary Perspectives On Literacy Research.* R. Beach et al., eds. Urbana, IL: National Conference on Research in English, 1992.

O'Connor, Stephen. *When Will My Name Be Shouted Out?* New York: Simon and Schuster, 1996.

Romano, Thomas. *Writing with Passion.* Portsmouth, NH: Boynton/Cook, 1995.

Taylor, D., and C. Dorsey-Gaines. *Growing Up Literate. Learning from Inner-city Families.* Portsmouth, NH: Heinemann, 1988.

Vygotsky, Lev. *Thought and Language.* Cambridge, MA: Harvard University Press, 1971.

Zemelman, Steven, and Harvey Daniels. "Authorship and Authority: Helping Writing Teachers Grow." *English Education,* 18(4): 219–230 Dec. 1986.

9 The Reading and Writing Transaction

CARLA VERDERAME

In this chapter, Carla Verderame examines another of the challenging writing tasks: the response to literature. The students Verderame describes and offers strategies for are a population of college-bound students and thus more easily engaged. She offers readers an occasion to consider classrooms as places where students and teachers negotiate authority and, on occasion, exchange roles, where teachers become learners and students engage and teach one another. She investigates how such classroom experiences can help teachers move beyond their familiar practices and integrate the innovations that students can bring to learning.

Specifically, Verderame demonstrates the interaction that happened when she and her students interrogated texts together and celebrated their responses, particularly the written ones. She explores what happens, positively and negatively, when teachers and students attempt to write about literature. Verderame models her process, and that of her students, as she explicates three different texts: "The Lottery," *The Prime of Miss Jean Brodie*, and *Dead Poets' Society*.

An appendix to the chapter offers guidelines for using reading logs and offers assistance with writing descriptive, interpretive, and evaluative literary essays.

When I consider my first years as a high school teacher and the assignments that I developed for students to write about literature, I look back with some embarrassment. That is, I was an exceptionally conscientious teacher (my principal assured me) and an exceptionally popular teacher (my students assured me), but the activities that I assigned that I thought would engage students as readers and empower them as writers bored them and disappointed me. My students' responses to literature and their formal writing assignments reflected few original ideas or little evidence of the growth as readers or writers that I had been prepared to expect. While I felt that my teacher education program had prepared me well to teach literature and writing in the secondary classroom, I felt, at the same time, enormous pressure as a beginning teacher to cover the curriculum and to maintain control of my classes.

On occasion, there were creative activities that generated strong prose. We wrote letters from one character to another to help interpret characterization, address audience, and hone the written skills of persuasion. We enacted favorite characters' roles from favorite stories: we cried with Holden and traveled with Pip; we shared Scout's confusion and Frankie's isolation. But, overall, my students and I felt distanced from the entire process of reading literature and, subsequently, writing about it. The reading of a variety of age-appropriate texts (intended for both the middle and high school student) and the writing activities that followed such reading became a routine, formulaic procedure to satisfy both departmental and district curriculum requirements.

Happily, my teacher education program emphasized, among several models, the reflective practitioner model. I carefully considered what I had learned about the theoretical transaction between the reading and writing processes and examined my classroom in this light. Class discussions about specific texts flagged. Often, language did not serve my students or me as we attempted to analyze and synthesize our responses to literature. Written work lacked inspiration. As the teacher, I knew I had some work to do. I turned to my students for help.

To what extent do students shape curriculum? Do students have authoritative voices in our classrooms that contribute to the flow of conversation, and are they invited to shape curriculum by including their expressed needs and interests? In short, how do we invite students' responses? In my current teaching practice, I rely on students as useful prompts for reflection in ways that are less deliberate and more intuitive than I did in my early years as a teacher. That is, my students helped me learn how to establish a productive classroom atmosphere that welcomes the multiplicity of voices and contesting opinions that exist in the real world. I came to understand that not only the teacher presents the opportunity for meaningful interaction to occur, but also that students contribute significantly to a rich classroom environment and a successful time together. I learned to relinquish some of the responsibilities that I thought defined a strong teacher and encouraged my students to participate actively in all facets of our English classroom.

The classroom community directly affects student reading and writing. When students recognize that their classroom is a safe place that provides them with opportunities to succeed, they can learn to read attentively and to write cogent prose about their reading. One way to highlight that the classroom supports a community of learners and to ensure students' success when writing about literature is to invite students to generate their own topics that reflect the interests in which they are truly invested. Therefore, my students and I spend much time talking about possible paper topics. (See also Chapter 2 for the Write-Around Activity that can be used for fostering topics.) Our classroom conversation provides direction about how to refine a topic so that it is not too broad, and we study together where arguments need to be amplified and/or pared down. Students craft their essays based on topics and reading selections of their choice.

For example, in a secondary American literature elective course for juniors and seniors, students' interests dictated the stories we read and the writing activities that corresponded to our readings. The course demonstrated the success that students and teachers can achieve together when students contribute to curriculum design in concrete ways. In addition to selecting particular texts, my students responded to our reading selections in a variety of ways. Since responses to literature can be oral, written, aesthetic, or dramatic in nature, assessment did not take the form of traditional examinations or quizzes. Rather, it took the form of projects generated from students' responses to the titles and topics under consideration. For example, after having read and discussed William Faulkner's "A Rose for Emily," two students constructed a model of the "big, squarish frame house that had [become] . . . an eyesore among eyesores" (53). The students complemented their aesthetic response to the story by drafting a floor plan of the interior of Miss Emily's dwelling and writing an account of the parallel between the deterioration of the house and of Miss Emily's characterization as a "fallen monument."

Another student offered her aesthetic response to Toni Cade Bambara's "The Lesson" in the form of a watercolor painting. The student artist chose to contrast the opulence of F. A. O. Schwarz in the background with Sylvia, her friends, and Miss Moore in the foreground. The student's accompanying essay focused on Miss Moore as an unconventional though successful pedagogue who proves that sites of learning outside the classroom can be enormously instructive. Overall, the course showed students' high achievement when they are responsible for their own learning and participate actively in the life of our English classroom.

"The Lottery"

For an elective course to high school juniors and seniors, I decided to include a unit on violent fiction. I began the semester with Shirley Jackson's shocking short story "The Lottery," which includes a modern day stoning. I knew that some students would have read this short story earlier in high school and that I could rely on them to lead or at least generate discussion. Rather than choosing a more obscure story, one about which I would lead the discussion, I wanted to model immediately that I, as a teacher, was not the focal point of the classroom who would approve or disapprove of students' interpretations of the literature under consideration. Of course, I consider part of my responsibility as a teacher of literature to point out obvious misreadings, but I welcomed my students' different responses to our class texts in a lively exchange of ideas. The strategy worked.

Those students familiar with "The Lottery" compared their first readings to this present one; their contributions were particularly astute. Since they had already discovered the bad tidings that winning this lottery brings, they were able to focus on the more complicated aspects of personal relationships among the characters in the story. For example, at the opening of the story, the townspeople demonstrate tremendous camaraderie, only to betray each other later through the ritual of the lottery. "Mrs. Delacroix selected a stone so large she had to pick it up with both hands" (301). The villagers also violate their children's innocence by forcing them to participate in the ceremonial stoning. "The children had stones already, and someone gave little Davy Hutchinson a few pebbles" (301).

To work out the complicated levels of violence at work in Jackson's gruesome tale, my students and I shared responses to reading "The Lottery" through journal writing. By using journals, my students and I were not only able to communicate our thoughts with each other about violent fiction, but we were also able to work out our ideas about how complicated and ambiguous violence can be, especially in light of the various images of violence in the texts that we were reading. I support Toby Fulwiler's explanation of the important role that journal writing plays in the English classroom: "[O]ne of the most powerful reasons for writing is not to convey a message *to* someone else, but to find out for ourselves that we have a message and that we understand its shape and content. This is where journals come in: they are notebooks kept by writers and thinkers primarily for themselves as a means of methodically locating, collecting, and making sense of their own thoughts" (15, original italics). In our journals, my students and I worked out in writing our personal theories of violence and established individual working definitions of violence that were amended throughout the semester. Journals provided a forum for us to consider and to share our responses to the often disturbing stories that we read in class.

Other writing assignments that corresponded to "The Lottery" generated interesting ideas about the relationship between power and violence. As a pre-reading prompt to our study of "The Lottery," I asked students to write a brief response explaining the associations they make with lotteries. I wanted to know my students' opinions of participating in a lottery.

1. Were they positive or negative?
2. Was skill or luck involved in winning?
3. Are there strategies that ensure winning?

Responses varied, but the prompt began a lively conversation about the possibility to win unattainable riches, only for such fantasies to be dashed by Jackson's terrifying tale. Although some of the students had read "The Lottery" before, those who had not registered genuine surprise at its outcome. For those students who had not read the story, the prereading writing assignment helped them enter the text. Peter Elbow explains that writing before reading helps dispel the myth that "the role of writing is to serve reading" (194) and helps students exhibit the knowledge that they bring to bear on a text. "I . . . can make subtle but profound changes in the spirit of the teaching situation—if I put writing *before* reading and give ourselves permission to write imaginatively" (194). Asking my students to write before reading "The Lottery" urged them to refine their thoughts on a social practice that promises a bountiful return. Perhaps more importantly, however, the writing prompt visibly reinforced for students the logical connections between the reading and writing processes.

Our conversations about "The Lottery" indicated that the students found the story to be a quick but deceptively simple read. The juxtaposition of the frivolity of a neighborhood gathering and the horror of a stoning offers students an opportunity to learn about incongruity in fiction, particularly violent fiction. "[T]he whole lottery took less than two hours, so it could begin at ten o'clock in the morning and still be through in time to allow the villagers to get home for noon dinner" (291). Although the stoning functions as the central violent action in the story, violence also exists within the relationships of the people who gather in the village square on a clear, sunny June morning to stone to death one of their own.

Students who were unfamiliar with the story were astonished that the character Tess Hutchinson was stoned to death by her friends and neighbors, who resist change and adhere blindly to an antiquated tradition, the purpose of which none of the townspeople can identify. This story afforded us a beginning conversation, questions to ask about violence in a literary text, before we delved into longer works with more complicated representations of violence. "The Lottery" offered a substantive early lesson in predicting outcomes, a basic and necessary skill to read literary texts in general and violent fiction in particular.

> In order to make predictions, readers review what they have already inferred about a text and match that up with their knowledge of prototypical story development. For example, knowing a story is a comedy, they can predict that it will probably be resolved with a "happy ending." In working with students, it is important not to imply that there are "correct predictions." Rather, students should feel free to create any predictions. What is more useful is to help students define the basis for their predictions in terms of reviewing the text or their emerging text models. And, teachers could model ways of revising predictions according to perceived disparities between the predictions and the text model (Beach 85).

Beach touches on an important point about revising predictions that my students and I learned when we read "The Lottery" together. The horrific stoning at the end of the story forced my students and me to return to the text to look for clues that would suggest such an ending. We found, when looking back, details in the story that suggest the inhumane final scene. The verdant landscape, the presence of children, and other regenerative symbols were so in contrast with the final outcome of the story that my class and I learned to predict the strategies authors employ—counterpoints and foils—to diffuse explosive violence in their stories. We considered the tactics writers of violent fiction use to make the violence in their work bearable and the way that violence triggers a celebration of the commonplace and everyday. That is, because the violence in "The Lottery" is so overpowering, routine activities of the townspeople take on added depth and become more celebrated acts.

In addition to a discussion about the predictability of violent action, our early study of "The Lottery" generated a conversation about the reliability of characters' voices, the cues an author provides to advance her message, and, most importantly, the relationship of power to violence. The social body that comprises "The Lottery" wields its power negatively; it stifles language, severs community, incites violence, and, in the end, extinguishes life. "The Lottery" urged us to consider the following:

1. Who has power?
2. Who abuses power?
3. Who submits to power?
4. What is the relationship between power and violence?

Such questions prepared us to read and write about other titles, such as Flannery O'Connor's disturbing short stories, as well as the novels *To Kill a Mockingbird*, *Of Mice and Men*, and *The House on Mango Street*, each of which urges readers to consider the assertion of power that gets worked out through violent means.

Finally, our study of "The Lottery" helped students understand the way that reading shapes writing and writing shapes reading. After a close reading of the text and a discussion about the devices Jackson uses to shock her audience, students recognize that the act of writing about the story involves techniques similar to that of reading the story. They acknowledge that writers draw on reading skills as they write. Writers concern themselves with, among other writing concerns, organizational structure and logical coherence to ensure clarity for their readers. In turn, readers receive these cues in order to make sense of (meaning making) words on the page. To illuminate this connection between writing and reading, I ask students to draft their essays for a peer editor and for me. After receiving feedback, students revise their work. I emphasize strongly that the revising stage of the writing process is essentially an exercise in reading and that reading plays a large role in becoming an accomplished writer.

The Reading and Writing Transaction

Although it has been my professional experience that departments of English designate English courses as *either* composition *or* literature courses (thereby separating the reading and writing processes), my personal pedagogy resists such strict barriers between writing and literature. I applaud integrating reading and writing in the English classroom so that students come to see the connection between the two processes and that the two processes draw on a similar facility with language. The current research on composition and literature pedagogy bears this out. For example, Patricia Bizzell illustrates the link between the practice of reading and the practice of writing and the benefits of merging both disciplines in the English classroom.

> I don't think there should be any difference between the way we teach our literature classes and the way we teach our writing classes. What I want students to do is to study rhetorical strategies of persuasion in readings from a variety of genres, fiction and nonfiction ("literature"), and also to practice rhetorical strategies in a variety of writings of their own ("composition"). To maintain this position, I have to make two arguments: that literature should be taught in the composition class, and that writing should be taught in the literature class (167).

Clearly, uniting disciplines that naturally complement each other, reading literature and writing compositions, assists students in generating a topic, writing a cogent argument, and revising for clarity. While, as Bizzell, explains, it is our responsibility as teachers to provide models of rhetorical strategies through literary texts, we also need to help students acknowledge that they have access into literary texts, especially through writing. In the middle and high school English classroom, it is especially important to stress the correlation between reading and writing so that students become proficient in both arenas and acknowledge that skill in reading enhances writing and skill in writing enhances reading.

"Strategies like reading journals, collaborative learning techniques, freewriting, and argument analysis that are common in composition pedagogy are just as crucial in literature classes to give our students their own ways into the literature. Once in, we find that students are quite good at making connections and at navigating the troubled waters of interpretation" (George 165). I have discovered that the integrated language arts classroom targets students' needs and learning styles more readily and effectively than keeping the disciplines of reading and writing distinct. One effective method to integrate reading and writing and to provide students with a "way into the literature" is the consistent use of journals.

Using Journals to Clarify Thinking

The unit I taught on violent fiction included frequent reading and writing assignments. Journal writing, in particular, ensured that students reflected on the literature and attended class prepared to participate. But, more importantly, such writing assignments functioned as arenas in which students expanded their thinking and deepened their definition of violence.

> Journal writing is another kind of writing that is useful in gathering raw materials for papers and strengthening connections between writing and thinking. . . . Students can be asked to keep journals over the course of a specified period of time, making entries about whatever they are doing or thinking; but journals can also be used in a more focused way to record reactions while reading a book or working on a specific writing project (Gere et al. 155).

Not only did journal writing assignments help my students to clarify their thinking about our course content, but they also provided a starting point for discussions about the applications of our classroom to the world outside. The course became a forum to consider social action and social justice.

For example, as I reviewed my teacher's journal for the class, I discovered that my students never spoke about violence without mentioning power; both concepts worked in unison for them. One student offered this definition of violence: "Violence is a means to establish one's power over another and the result is always some kind of hierarchy of power" (2.17.97). Another student writes, "Violence is something that happens to a person. It is usually motivated by anger, frustration, or envy" (2.17.97). My students' journals indicate that, for them, power and violence are always linked. Their definitions suggest that power often functions as a catalyst or trigger for violence and that they view the perpetrator of violence as powerful and the victim as powerless.

Reading and Writing for Social Action

Another reason that rigid distinctions between literature and writing courses reflect poor pedagogy is that the literature classroom gets maligned as an arena in which social reform can be considered. "[W]hile students become social activists in the writing classroom, they often adopt a more passive role in the literature classroom, operating according to the familiar ritual of answering teacher questions. In the process, they lose their sense of purpose and motivation with membership in a writing community" (Beach 118). But this clearly does not have to be the case. Indeed, it was not the case when my students and I discussed violent fiction. The integrated English classroom that emphasizes both reading and writing as active processes not only helps students become strong readers and writers, but also helps them become agents of social change.

"Readers encounter the text, and in the encounter make meaning. To the act of reading readers bring conceptions, feelings and attitudes, hold them up against the work, and confirm, modify, or refute them in the process. Readers reshape their visions of the world—perhaps slightly, or perhaps dramatically—by assimilating the other visions the work offers readers" (Probst 62). Therefore, an integrated English and language arts curriculum offers students the opportunity to influence situations and events beyond the classroom based on their responses to readings and the way they work out such responses in their written work. The essays that students write address a problem or concern beyond their lives in school, and the basis for such essays is the literature they read.

To highlight the connection between the literature my students read and their lives beyond the classroom, I not only integrate language arts instruction, but also promote the language-as-a-social-construct framework in order for students to work out their responses to literature in light of their lives outside school. "In a language-as-social-construct classroom, the opportunity to explore topics of historical or cultural interest is seen as an important way to develop the students' sense of their place in the larger community. . . . The role of the teacher becomes that of a more experienced peer who questions and clarifies in an effort to assist the student . . . " (Gere et al. 188). The topic of violence and the subtopics that grew out of that topic (power, authority) dovetailed my global objectives for the unit particularly well. My students wrote compelling essays about power relations that affect their daily lives in the work force, in domestic settings, and in their neighborhoods.

The Prime of Miss Jean Brodie

In addition to the genre of the short story previously discussed, the novel occupies a prominent place in the secondary classroom. In a high school junior–senior elective course entitled "The Search for Self," I decided to include *The Prime of Miss Jean Brodie* by Muriel Spark on the reading list. The text not only offers an opportunity to consider universal adolescent struggles about self-esteem and interpersonal relationships, but also to investigate the relationships of power between teachers and students in classrooms. Since the majority of students in my class were second semester seniors looking forward to college, I thought we would approach the novel as a commentary on schooling, to help students think critically about the next step in their educational careers.

The backdrop of the Spanish Civil War, coupled with Miss Brodie's Fascist sympathies, generates interesting questions about totalitarianism in the classroom and Miss Jean Brodie's subversive pedagogy. Every year Miss Brodie decides on an exclusive group of six girls whom she will take under her wing, known throughout the Marcia Blaine School as "the Brodie set." Rather than implementing traditional methods of education more appropriate to the school's mission, Brodie schools the elect group by way of romantic stories and gossip. Miss Brodie's indulgent pedagogy and her possessiveness of the group yield ill effects on the young, impressionable girls. Miss Brodie informs her class:

> "It has been suggested again that I should apply for a post at one of the progressive schools, where my methods would be more suited to the system than they are at Blaine. But I shall not apply for a post at a crank school, I shall remain at this education factory. There needs must be a leaven in the lump. Give me a girl at an impressionable age, and she is mine for life." The Brodie set smiled in understanding of various kinds (15–16).

Brodie's announcement reveals her domineering approach to teaching in three different ways that my class and I address. First, Miss Brodie not only admits to, but also revels in, unorthodox instructional methods to no apparent end. Her teaching satisfies her own needs, rather than the needs of her students; students are invisible in Miss Brodie's classroom. Second, while Miss Brodie specifically identifies the Marcia Blaine School as an "education factory," the context of her statement implies that all schools are such. Her sweeping statement positions schools as mechanical warehouses that churn out a product, rather than sites of learning that nurture a person. Third, Miss Brodie openly displays her possessiveness of her students by admitting they are hers "for life." As we unravel Miss Brodie's story, we witness the lasting effects that she has on the girls.

Keeping in mind Miss Brodie's admiration for both Mussolini and Hitler and the subplot of totalitarianism that threatens Spain, we witness in Miss Jean Brodie a similar dictator. She is authoritarian and dogmatic in her teaching methods, instructing by informing her students how and what they should think. She queries the girls: "'Who is the greatest Italian painter?'" When the class responds "'Leonardo da Vinci,'" Miss Brodie replies: "'That is incorrect. The answer is Giotto, he is my favorite'" (18). I caution my students not to dismiss this dialogue as an innocuous exchange. Miss Brodie's "correct" answers are largely whimsical. She discourages independent thought and restricts conversation among the girls—or between the girls and herself unless she initiates the dialogue. In fact, she instructs her class of ten and eleven year olds that "speech is silver but silence is golden" (22). Miss Brodie's classroom represents the epitome of teacher-centered instruction that quells her students' collaboration and construction of knowledge. Essentially, Miss Brodie violates her girls by employing a personal pedagogy that silences them.

The second aspect of violation from Miss Brodie's statement is that she associates schools with factories. Miss Brodie suggests that schools merely reproduce the status quo. But Miss Brodie's teaching methods merely reproduce her personal agenda. For example, Miss Brodie encourages Joyce Emily to join her brother in Spain to support Franco's forces. The girl dies en route. Miss Brodie sharply criticizes Eunice for her decision to enroll in the modern rather than the classical curriculum in the Upper School. "'You will end up as a Girl Guide leader in a suburb like Corstorphine,' she said warningly to Eunice, who was in fact secretly attracted to this idea and who lived in Corstorphine" (92). Eunice chooses not to share her interests with Miss Brodie because she knows the fierce opposition that her teacher will assert. Eunice's silence literally depicts Miss Brodie's silencing of her.

While all the girls in the set endured criticism from Miss Brodie on some level, Miss Brodie's treatment of pathethic Mary MacGregor illustrates most clearly the emphasis that Miss Brodie places on social class and status, neither of which Mary MacGregor ever achieves. "Along came Mary MacGregor, the last member of the set, whose fame rested on her being a silent lump, a nobody whom everybody could blame" (13). Miss Brodie shows no concern for Mary's predicament or her place in the "set." For Mary, just being accepted in the group was a privilege; Miss Brodie fosters elitism within the school by choosing a set and within the set by marginalizing Mary. Mary's peripheral position in the group illuminates the manner in which teachers' oppressive practices can reproduce social class distinctions.

The third aspect of Miss Brodie's announcement speaks to her possessive, egotistical character; she claims that the girls are hers for life. The effects of Miss Brodie's influence play out most dramatically for Sandy Stranger, who decides to separate herself from the world by entering a convent. My class decides that Miss Brodie's oppression debilitates Sandy emotionally, causing her to flee the world she knows in favor of one that seemingly offers calm and isolation. My students not only admonish Miss Brodie for the violation of her set, but they also rightly accuse Miss Brodie of usurping her students' collective power by silencing them. Through our study of *The Prime of Miss Jean Brodie*, my students and I learn about psychological domination and its effects. Miss Brodie's influence influences the decisions the girls make in later life, giving credibility to her pronouncement "Give me a girl at an impressionable age and she is mine for life."

The students are particularly interested in *The Prime of Miss Jean Brodie* because of the controlled influence Miss Brodie inflicts on her girls. They identify Miss Brodie as a selfish teacher who oppresses her students, rather than a devoted teacher who fosters learning. "The Brodie set" functions as an audience set in rapt attention, who feed Miss Brodie's tremendous ego. Miss Jean Brodie's problematic pedagogy generates a productive classroom conversation about the danger of imposing on students in unfair ways and the dramatic results of stripping students of their power. (There is a more dire situation of disempowered students in *Dead*

Poets Society, which is why I pair these selections.) Since there is a highly regarded movie version of *The Prime of Miss Jean Brodie,* some students choose to compare and contrast particular elements from the movie with the book. Other writing responses include character analyses of the girls in the set, of the title character, and of the impact of minor characters in the text. Still other essay assignments include what I call "parts-to-the-whole" questions to help students understand the way that a particular episode or event functions in the novel. To get started, I urge students to form a question that they want to answer about the book. The class and I discuss possible questions that would lead to a productive essay:

1. What is the significance of Sandy Stranger's decision at the end of the novel to enter a convent?
2. What is the significance of Mary McGregor's death?
3. How does the backdrop of World War II function in the novel?
4. How does the text provide a commentary on social class distinction?
5. How do social class distinctions get played out in classrooms?

While my students and I make it a practice to consider paper topics based on students' responses during class discussions of the novel, such guidelines also assist students in reading closely and honing in on a topic to analyze.

Dead Poets Society

Although *Dead Poets Society* is not a literary selection, I occasionally include this movie among the titles I teach—often paired with *The Prime of Miss Jean Brodie* so that students can compare and contrast the portrait of teachers and teaching that they encounter in both selections. I include movies in this chapter because many district and state requirements expect nonprint media to be taught in the English classroom. Although the movie was a commercial success, and I know educators who applaud it as a successful model of innovative instruction, I find the characterization of the principal figure not only obvious and manipulative, but, frankly, dangerous—and the story similar to the pedagogical problems that we encounter in the study of *The Prime of Miss Jean Brodie.* However, the film serves as a worthy point of reference to help students write about a topic with which they are familiar—the process of schooling.

John Keating is a single, male teacher of English at an all-male, private, college preparatory institution, the Welton School. His avant-garde methods and alternative teaching style dazzle his students at first. However, Keating is blinded by what he considers to be creative classroom activities and, at the same time, is blind to his students' needs. He believes that tearing out sheets of a traditional textbook is innovative and that forcing silent students to write and act out a poem in front of the class will help them overcome their adolescent inhibitions. Keating makes no connection between a friendly classroom atmosphere and the objectives he pursues for his students to find their own voices and to solve and pose problems. In short, he wants his class "to resist the lives of quiet desperation Thoreau warned us about" (Bauer 305), but he offers merely frolic without a framework to which his students can refer. His classroom is fun but lacks substance.

Not surprisingly, the end of the semester brings unforeseen problems. Neil, whose domineering father wants him to focus solely on admission to a prestigious college and, eventually, to medical school, decides to accept the role of Puck in the school's presentation of *A Midsummer Night's Dream*. Neil's father is outraged at his son's defiance, disenrolls him from Welton, and makes arrangements to send Neil to a military academy the next term. Neil commits suicide. John Keating does not provide his students with productive means of understanding or changing their lives. Instead, he usurps his students' power, leaving them with no choice but to enact violence on themselves, demonstrated most dramatically in the film by Neil's suicide. "Keating [attempts] to counter the deadening of the intellect in the traditional disciplinary classroom. *Yet Keating's individualism is just another brand of authoritarianism*" (Bauer 305, italics mine). The fallout from the series of events demonstrates that Keating's classroom problems were obscure to him because of his limited vision about successful classroom strategies. Keating focuses on what he considers to be revolutionary activities in English classrooms, but fails to know his students or to teach English as an object of study. Essentially, he fails to teach his students anything. He merely transforms the English classroom; "he turns teaching English into game-show excitement" (Bauer 304). While the complicated act of suicide cannot be reduced to Keating's fault, he, as teacher, does nothing to prevent the tragedy. Like Miss Brodie, Keating is too self-focused to notice his students' needs; they are invisible to him.

Interestingly, Keating's students sell him out in the end. One student denounces Keating's alternative teaching methods to the administration, and other students follow suit. Keating is fired. I focus, with my class, on the students' betrayal of Keating because, although many students may embrace alternative methods and a "game-show" classroom, they want, in the end, to get down to business, to learn something. While learning and a fun classroom are not mutually exclusive, neither Jean Brodie nor John Keating knows how to accomplish both. Instead, they leave their students vulnerable by creating a superficial teaching situation that appears inviting to students when, in fact, it ignores the individual student. Keating believes that empowerment derives from merriment without developing a strong academic framework of reference. Additionally, John Keating displays poor pedagogy on two other counts. First, he fails to acknowledge that his approach is as authoritarian as the traditional methods he condemns. Keating merely takes one oppressive pedagogy and replaces it with another. "Students obedience to him is absolutely necessary for their self-exploration" (Bauer 304). Second, Keating underestimates his students' ability to recognize the falsity of his pedagogy. For all his pretense about educating to empower students and celebrating students' voices, he fails to give students credit for their wisdom or ability to see the pitfalls in their teacher's methodology.

Interestingly, my students embrace John Keating. While they take in my criticism of the lead character, they insist that Keating's methods and activities demonstrate his genuine interest in students' needs that they have not experienced in their own education. The movie generates comparative responses not only to *The Prime of Miss Jean Brodie* but also to my students' lives in school—with John Keating on the winning side. Although my intention is not to gain agreement, I want students to acknowledge the complicated enterprise that teaching is and how that point may become obscured through the merriment of John Keating's classroom. However, my students condemn Miss Brodie more than they do Mr. Keating. When asked why, they explain that they find Miss Brodie's traditional teaching methods oppressive and Mr. Keating's methods liberating. I continue to struggle with not wanting to impose my views on my students but to help them think critically about Mr. Keating's limitations, as well as the possibilities of his pedagogy. We consider whether gender influences my students' responses to Miss Brodie and Mr. Keating and generate topic questions that guide students to compose thoughtful essays about the novel *The Prime of Miss Jean Brodie* and the film *Dead Poets Society.*

Although beyond the scope of this chapter, using film in the English classroom gives students an opportunity to observe nuances of characterization and to consider interpretation and point of view more deeply. Directors' and actors' choices about how to present a character may differ widely from the texts students study. Such differences can deepen students' responses, thereby generating productive conversations and compositions about the literature they read. I have used the movies *To Kill a Mockingbird, Of Mice and Men, The Necklace,* and *Romeo and Juliet,* as well as other titles, with much success in the English classroom. (Of course, including film in the integrated English and language arts classroom offers possibilities in addition to a refined study of characterization. Incorporating movies into the writing and literature curriculum can offer points of contrast and comparison that assist students in thinking critically and in more complex ways.)

Suggested Activities That Prepare Students to Write about Literature

- Writing letters from one character to another helps students address audience, interpret characterization, analyze plot in relation to characterization, and consider setting, and it reinforces that setting reveals character.
- Maintaining writing portfolios enables students to keep drafts and revisions of all their written work together. The portfolio supports the process approach to writing; it suggests that good writing emerges from revision. Since the revision stage of the writing process is essentially an exercise in reading, students come to see not only the strong transaction that takes place between reading and writing but also the stages of their own writing processes. Papers that have been edited by peers and the teacher can be included in the portfolio.

- As described in the chapter (and in the appendix), reading logs and writing journals assist students in working out their responses to the literature they read. These can take a variety of forms. Students may write an excerpt from the text in their log or journal and comment on it. Students may respond to a prompt provided by the teacher. Students may save thoughts and reflections about the texts they read, the essays they write, and their reading and writing processes—and how those processes may change—over the course of a school year.

- Oral presentations, reports, and formal debates help students clarify the written arguments they want to defend about the literature they read. Articulating their positions in a public forum (that is, to the other members of the class) gives students practice in establishing and defending a position, while reinforcing the important connection among reading, writing, speaking, listening, and viewing.

- Projects that are artistic in nature, like the model of Miss Emily's house or the watercolor painting of characters from "The Lesson," referred earlier, provide students the opportunity to display their aesthetic responses to literature. An essay can accompany the projects to reinforce writing skills and to highlight the relevance of literature to students' lives outside the classroom.

- When studying how writers establish a credible and reliable voice (so that students are able to establish their own such voices in their compositions), we look carefully at the literary models we are reading. An activity I use with *The House on Mango Street* (the activity can be adapted for other texts) is to ask students to rewrite one of the vignettes in the novel in Esperanza's voice as an adult. Since much of the novel takes us through Esperanza's young life, this activity gives students an opportunity to work out the complexities of voice in a creative, fun way before they do so in their expository essays.

A Final Thought

In *Mystery and Manner,* Flannery O'Connor writes that "English teachers come in Good, Bad, and Indifferent, but too frequently in high schools anyone who can speak English is allowed to teach it. Since several novels can't easily be gathered into one textbook, the fiction students are assigned depends upon their teacher's knowledge, ability, and taste: variable factors at best" (137). While I chuckle at O'Connor's dire portrait of the teacher of English, I admit a healthy respect for O'Connor's criticism of the teacher who mediates instruction and demonstrates only self-serving interests, such as Jean Brodie and John Keating. What's more, I celebrate O'Connor's implication that students possess the capacity to critique their teachers, and I invite my students to do so. While making new discoveries about teaching as I work along with my students, I continue to rely on the discovery I made shortly after my first years as a teacher. I trust that my students will help me to help them as long as a space exists for them to bring who they are and what they know to our conversation.

APPENDIX

Reading Logs and Guides to Writing Essays

Some Ideas to Improve Your Reading Logs

Feelings: Give words that sum up your feelings about a piece of literature (e.g. sad, boring, exciting, intriguing).

Questions: Ask about the things that puzzle you—be in dialogue with the author, ask questions that you might want my response to—though I can't promise I will always have "the" answer; I will try to give some response. (For example, "I wonder why the author . . . ?" Or if you wish, use direct address, "Why did you?" Or question a character.)

Images: Take time to record what images you like or don't like—focus on the description writers use. (for example, what pictures do you get in your mind as you read? Describe these with full sensory responses.)

Favorite (or detested) words and phrases: Here you want to focus on the language writers use. Remember, repeated words or phrases are often conventions used to help convey the theme or other aspect the writer wants us to grasp.

Echoes: Of other books, stories, poetry, movies, television programs, headlines, songs.

Reactions: To characters or events (for example, why was Aeneas so cruel to Dido that he'd leave without telling her?).

Memories: How does the reading cause you to remember people, events, or places you've known?

Connections: How do you relate what you've read to other ideas, people, feelings, books, and so on?

Clustering: Put a key word—maybe the title of the reading—in the center of your page; circle the word and then branch off, giving related words or ideas as these come to you.

Note Taking and Note Making: With *note taking,* you are generally recording facts, such as the details of who a character is or the direct quote that gives the exact words of the text. With *note making,* you are providing feelings and responses that engage you with the text.

Write a Letter: To a character, to someone else who has read the text, to your professor—all these are possibilities for response.

Time Lines: Do a time line of events, putting the events you view as positive above the line and those you view as negative below the line.

Venn Diagrams: When setting up comparisons or contrasts, use Venn diagrams to see what overlaps from each.

How to Write about Literature

It might be helpful to have some reminders to assist you as you go about doing the papers for this literature course.

Most often you will be doing one of three things (and these three tasks frequently overlap): describe, evaluate, or interpret a text. Here's a brief description of each approach.

The Descriptive Critical Essay: The main question you are trying to answer with this kind of essay is how this literary text works. How does it get its meaning across? You are working here with *poetics,* the study of the codes and conventions, the recurring patterns and familiar structures, that make it possible for the text to have meaning. The advantage of the descriptive essay is that it gives you an entry into the workings of the text. The conventions and anticonventions you describe are not difficult to uncover and are relatively easy to defend or prove—they are there, in black and white, between the covers of the book. The disadvantage of writing a descriptive essay is that it can be tricky to develop your topic into an argument or thesis, an answer to the question "So what?" When you are accounting for the obvious, as many critics do, some creative thinking is necessary for placing your observations in an interesting, provocative context.

The Evaluative Critical Essay: This kind of essay asks about a literary text, "Is it any good?" It's a question that has no trouble addressing the "So what?" of criticism. If the poem, play, or novel is good, it is worth reading; if it's bad, it's a waste of time. But what keeps this criticism alive is that readers' standards differ.

The common form of the evaluative essay is the book review. You will actually not be doing the kind of book review that professionals do. Your first requirement for the evaluative essay is a clear standard or set of standards by which you are making a judgment. You need to make these standards explicit. You need to find textual reasons for whatever claim you are making, and it would be good to have a comparison of what is good or strong or whatever is the opposite of the critique you are making. The challenge of the evaluative essay is to write it persuasively, alluding to the possibilities for opposition to your argument and answering potential objections with specific commentary on passages from the text.

The Interpretive Critical Essay: This is the most common type of essay students do; the main question you ask is "What does this text mean?" A critical essay always raise questions about meaning. To write a descriptive essay is to address the question "How does this work transmit meaning?" To write an evaluative essay is to ask "Why is it worthwhile to think about this text's meaning?" And to write an interpretive essay is to ask "What does this work mean?" How you find and present a meaning will depend on the strategy of interpretation you choose to apply.

The best interpretive essays do three things: (1) they establish the strategy by which you choose to find meaning; (2) they "read" or "interpret" the work in question according to that strategy, giving lots of examples from the text; and (3) they make a point or an argument. Simply paraphrasing the work in your own words is not the same as interpreting it, because a paraphrase will not answer the question "So what?" You need to place the work's ideas in some context, in order to write persuasively about it.

Steps to Help You Develop Your Essay

1. Take notes: underline, highlight, star, or in some way mark all the passages that interest you.
2. Use your journal; this is an ideal source of inspiration.
3. Ask questions: "watch yourself reading," mark the parts of the text that you find moving, persuasive, confusing, or difficult. Write out your questions as they occur; these can lead to a thesis.
4. Look at the text's form; try to analyze the structure and see if it offers some significance.
5. Look for familiar moves. Identify the literary conventions of the text. Ask yourself where you've seen these conventions before. If the work you are studying is either remarkably conventional or noticeably unconventional, this could lead to a thesis.
6. Interpret figures of speech; think about the imagery or figurative language used in the text. What symbolic patterns emerge? What is the vehicle or the tenor of the metaphors you find? Is there any way to read the text as an allegory for ideas it doesn't mention directly?
7. Look up unfamiliar words. Especially with poetry and especially if the work was written before the twentieth century, it's key for you to understand the meanings of the words or the sense in which the words are used.

Formulating the Essay

1. Make connections. Look for patterns.
2. Create a thesis. Identify a "So what?"
3. Generate some ideas.
4. Formulate a thesis.
5. Organize the essay: shape your argument, build in transitions, don't suppress conflict.

REFERENCES AND RESOURCES

Arendt, Hannah. "Communicative Power." In *Power: Readings in Social and Political Theory*. Ed. Steven Lukes. New York: New York University Press, 1986.

Bambara, Toni Cade. "The Lesson." *The Compact Bedford Introduction to Literature*. Boston: Bedford Books of St. Martin's Press, 1997, pp. 136–140.

Bauer, Dale M. "Indecent Proposals: Teachers in the Movies." *College English* 60.3 (1998): 301–317.

Beach, Richard. *A Teacher's Introduction to Reader Response Theories*. Urbana, IL: National Council of Teachers of English, 1993.

Biddle, Arthur, and Toby Fulwiler. *Reading, Writing, and the Study of Literature*. New York: Random House, 1989.

Bizzell, Patricia. "Negotiating Difference: Teaching Multicultural Literature." In *Rethinking American Literature*. Eds. Lil Brannon and Brenda M. Greene. Urbana, IL: National Council of Teachers of English, 1997.

Cisneros, Sandra. *The House on Mango Street*. New York: Random House, 1984.

DeMaupassant, Guy. "The Necklace." Trans. Marjorie Laurie. *The Compact Bedford Introduction to Literature*. Boston: Bedford Books of St. Martin's Press, 1997, pp. 46–51.

Ebert, Teresa L. "The Romance of Patriarchy: Ideology, Subjectivity, and Postmodern Feminist Critical Theory." *Cultural Critique* 10 (1988): 19–58.

Elbow, Peter. "Breathing Life into the Text." In *When Writing Teachers Teach Literature: Bringing Writing into Reading*. Eds. Art Young and Toby Fulwiler. Portsmouth, NH: Boynton/Cook, 1995.

Epstein, Debbie. *Changing Classroom Cultures: Anti-Racism, Politics and Schools*. Stoke-on-Trent, UK: Trenthem, 1993.

Faulkner, William. "A Rose for Emily." *The Compact Bedford Introduction to Literature*. Boston: Bedford Books of St. Martin's Press, 1997, pp. 52–58.

George, Diana, and Saralinda Blanning. "Reading and Writing Back to the Future." *When Writing Teachers Teach Literature: Bringing Writing into Reading*. Urbana, IL: National Council of Teachers of English, 1997.

Gere, Anne Ruggles, Colleen Fairbanks, Alan Howes, Laura Roop, and David Schaafsma. *Language and Reflection: An Integrated Approach to Teaching English*. New York: Macmillan, 1992.

Jackson, Shirley. *The Lottery, or the Adventures of James Harris*. New York: Farrar, Straus, 1949.

Lee, Harper. *To Kill a Mockingbird*. New York: Warner Books, 1960.

O'Connor, Flannery. *Mystery and Manner*. Eds. Robert and Sally Fitzgerald. New York: The Noonday Press, 1957.

———. *The Violent Bear It Away*. New York: Farrar, Straus, and Giroux, 1955.

Probst, Robert. "Three Relationships in the Teaching of Literature." *English Journal* (1986): 60–68.

Shakespeare, William. *Romeo and Juliet*. Folger Library Series. New York: Washington Square Press, 1992.

Spark, Muriel. *The Prime of Miss Jean Brodie*. New York: New American Library, 1961.

Steinbeck, John. *Of Mice and Men*. New York: Viking Press, 1937.

10 The State-Mandated Writing Test

MARY WARNER

This chapter and the three that follow focus on topics for which teacher-to-teacher (or, in the metaphor of this book, coach-to-coach) wisdom is among the best means for achieving success. Although much of this chapter is based on North Carolina tests and what educators there are doing to address the state-mandated writing tests, there are many similarities from state to state; thus, the strategies offered are applicable for testing contexts throughout the United States. Mary Warner urges writing teachers to focus primarily on teaching students to think and to connect with texts; she also provides several simple premises, not the least of which is "know the rules in order to break the rules."

The preservice and in-service teachers speaking in this chapter, who suggest ways of guiding students to best manage the multiple pressures of these high-stakes testing situations, are themselves facing comparable testing pressures to those of the English and language arts colleagues nation-wide. Therefore, each speaker brings forward valid methodology. Jan Williamson, North Carolina State Department of Public Instruction Language Arts Consultant for Grades 7–12, demonstrates that not all state department personnel are "out of touch"; she discusses the rationale, which truly does identify common expectations for student writers.

Once again, Warner shows how the use of a children's book can be a viable catalyst to get a perspective on these tests. They are, after all, only one context among the many writing situations lifelong learners will experience. So, like Dr. Seuss's teacher Miss Bonkers, writing coaches need to confidently teach students "to think" and then we need not dread any testing context.

The third graders in my classroom are spending a great deal of time working on writing tests. Although I understand the importance in relation to evaluation and assessment, it seems that the children get so frustrated with the restrictions and limitations the test places on them. My teacher even seems to dread the test, although she works hard to prepare the students for it. Sometimes I wonder if this negative attitude leads to the distaste of the students. I am already nervous about the impending test. Many of them try so hard at writing that I do not want to see their self-esteem negatively altered by this test. (Britt 1999)

These words of Katrina Britt, an elementary education major in my Fundamentals of Teaching Writing course, about her observations and field experiences, raise major issues regarding state-mandated writing tests. In the following excerpt from Katrina's reading, writing, and activity journal for my course, written two weeks after the entry above, she expands on her concerns.

My teacher informed me that the children were disheartened about their writing test scores. When I inquired about the reasons why, the teacher told me that the test prompt isolated a particular place and time. She could not give me specific details, but she alluded to the idea that the children felt restricted because of the prompt specifics. Since the children are in the 3rd grade, their test scores are not "official," but the tests do indicate some measurement of skill. I was surprised how some of the most creative children froze on the test. (Britt 1999)

Listen carefully to the concerns Katrina raises: the time spent working on the test, the children's frustrations about restrictions and limitations, teachers dreading the test, negative attitudes and self-esteem, and, maybe most chilling, "some of the most creative children froze on this test." Add to this concern about stifling creativity the concern that the children about whom Katrina writes are only in third grade and are not even faced with the "real" test yet. For the children in North Carolina schools, the first "real test" comes in grade 4. They will also face state-mandated writing tests in grades 7 and 10. In addition, these third graders may well be "turned off on writing" simply by the massive pressures and restrictions placed on them; consider how they might feel about writing in the next years of education when they are already equating writing and testing. There are also school districts with policies about whether a student can pass tenth grade English (or seventh grade language arts) if that student fails the end-of-course tests. What does this pressure do to any interest or pleasure in writing? Those students who are at all aware of their teacher's feelings could also come to dread writing just because of the pressures they see their teachers experiencing.

I open this chapter on state-mandated writing tests with these excerpts precisely because they are indicators of the multiproblematic issue of the teaching of writing chained (and I use this verb with deliberate intent) to state-mandated and state-created testing. As difficult as it is to find ourselves as English and language arts educators continually barraged by external evaluations and evaluators, I do not see these publics simply going away; definitely, in this era of accountability in education, they are not going away anytime soon. One major theme of this chapter, then, is that English and language arts educators need *to know the rules, in order to break the rules.* We do have to meet the tasteless demands of the high-stakes testing flourishing nation-wide. Many times the test scores get tied to merit pay for teachers, school-wide or even district-wide. Even more problematic is that schools where students don't score high enough on the range of end-of-course tests (hereafter referred to as EOCs) can sometimes be deprived of funding—probably the very funds needed for more individualized learning programs to help students struggling with literacy.

The ostrich approach of finding refuge in the sand—avoiding such forces as the state agencies requiring the testing—is not a viable option. As is commonplace for teachers of English and language arts, we need to read and analyze; in this case the texts to probe are the expectations and regulations flooding our school mailboxes. We need to know the content of documents describing standards; we need to know how to juggle the ideals of our English and language arts pedagogy with the real demands of state-mandated accountability.

In many ways the writing tests could be a catalyst for a renewed look at Writing-across-the-Curriculum, and this would be a great renewal. When the scores on the English writing tests affect *all* faculty members of schools, maybe more of our colleagues will be willing to incorporate writing activities into their disciplines. Mike Lodico, one of the teachers cited in this chapter, speaks of ways the English faculty at Tuscola High School in Waynesville, North Carolina, works with all the teachers in their school to encourage writing in many disciplines, strengthening the writing that is demanded by the writing EOC.

A horror story from a student supervision visit this semester represents the other extreme, highlighting how often the English teachers of the school system carry the burden of teaching writing all by themselves. A cooperating teacher and I were discussing the writing tests. She related that in the previous school year the English 10 teachers in that high school were required to post their students' scores from the writing tests on the bulletin board in the faculty lounge. Scores were posted with each English teacher's name. We all know that students have a range of reasons for not being successful in standardized testing contexts. English and language arts teachers are even more aware of the challenges students face in writing exams, particularly those students with any kind of learning disability. The cooperating teacher reported that, fortunately, this year the scores would not be posted. Consider, however, how the English teachers must have felt, knowing realistically that no one will have entire classes of students scoring above the average 4, but not necessarily having that same understanding from their colleagues in other fields. We must therefore, learn a second key to dealing with these mandated writing tests: *to be supportive of our colleagues, K–12, since we indeed are "all in this together."*

Regie Routman addresses a number of the hot topics in language arts, and, among them, she speaks to the role of teachers to be articulate and visible on issues.

> As a society, we are skeptical of fads, trends, and innovations—especially when they involve educating our children. As teachers, we must begin to share with parents and community members the reasons we seek reform and changes in our teaching practices. We cannot let the media and outside voices be the only ones heard. Otherwise, we are doomed to backlash and failure. (55)

Particularly in the area of testing, many "outside voices" are being heard. Inevitably, reading scores and writing errors become the fighting words and arms of legislators, members of state boards of education, and generally anyone not involved firsthand in teaching English and language arts. My greatest frustration as an English educator of over 25 years is the constant attack on the writing skills of students, particularly when these attacks are raised by so many who have never considered the writing process, the cognitive demands of writing, and the amazing energy demanded to be responsive to student writing and to serve as a coach of writing. English and language arts teachers must become political enough to articulate what they see as the skill areas and in what ways the skills, particularly those of reading, writing, and thinking, can be most validly assessed. How many English educators are members of state boards of education? How often have English teachers taken the time (admittedly time is a precious commodity) to respond to editorials or other media exposés on literacy issues? Maybe we need to write editorials, just as we have our students use this writing genre; we surely have a real need to address the misconceptions.

Because one central premise of the response to these outside voices requires teachers being vocal about the concerns arising from mandated testing—and the concerns of Katrina's are merely a beginning of the list—we do need ways of "hanging together," as Ben Franklin expressed it, so that we "don't hang separately." The English educators in postsecondary institutions must also collaborate with, support, and defend their K–12 colleagues. One small but practical means for this support would be a moratorium on comments about student preparedness or lack thereof made by English educators; we would all do well to remember to meet the students we have "where they are" and "take them where they might go." There is sufficient disparagement about literacy scores from forces outside the field of English to discourage the most resilient public school language arts teachers; thus, university English educators and those preparing preservice teachers need to be equally informed and empathetic about the state-mandated writing requirements.

I have been working for the last several years in North Carolina. North Carolina is one of the high-stakes testers; in fact, the ABC's in this state refer to "accountability, basics, and control." I have stated, though, that reality calls for teachers to know the rules or, in this case, the state expectations in order to be able to respond to these. In this light, I urge teachers to be attuned to the expectations voiced by groups like the State Department of Public Instruction. This chapter offers the experiences of several English and language arts educators and, although each of the educators is from North Carolina, their experiences apply to any state-mandated English and language arts test. One of the voices is that of Jan Williamson, language arts consultant for K–12 at the North Carolina Department of Public Instruction. I asked Jan to write from her perspective about the state writing tests, fully expecting that these ideas would not be amazingly different from those expressed by others in other state agencies. Readers might be prompted to examine Jan's description in light of their own state standards and in light of the Standard for the English Language Arts as prepared by the National Council of Teachers of English (NCTE) and the International Reading Association (IRA). Readers can also develop strategies for integrating the demands of testing into their curricula based on knowledge of the overall state standards.

The North Carolina *Standard Course of Study* defines an effective literacy program which incorporates speaking, listening, viewing, reading and writing. All these strands work together for effective communication, with constant connections among the five strands in curriculum, instruction and assessment. For example, there should be a strong connection between reading and writing, not only because students who read become better writers and those who write become better readers, but because the reading and writing connection increase[s] engagement and motivation. Students who are engaged in both writing and reading activities understand that meaning is what the writer is trying to communicate, and thus they read for meaning and write for clarity and understanding. Writing helps students to understand purpose and audience, which underlie good writing; that understanding translates into good strategies for reading. Insightful writers make more receptive readers, and strategic readers make more informed writers. In similar fashion, listening, speaking, and viewing enhance and support reading and writing. (Williamson 1998)

The next segment of Jan's discussion of state-mandated tests gives a listing of the characteristics of a balanced literacy program. These characteristics are included in Appendix I of this chapter and should be used by readers as a guide for creating instruction that is grounded in multiple writing and reading opportunities, not simply instruction that "teaches to a test."

Williamson now addresses specifically the issues of the writing test requiring a response to literature.

In the sequence of high school courses, English I provides background for English II and the study of world literature. The reading and writing competencies of English I provide the foundation for the competencies of English II. For example, a competency in English I is to "recognize the presence of archetypal characters, themes and setting" and in English II a related competency is to "analyze the recurrence of motifs and archetypal characters, settings, and themes in world literature." Thus, the English II student is expected to apply, at a more sophisticated level and in the context of world literature, what he or she has learned about literary interpretation in English I.

The English II Test assesses how well students have mastered these spiraling reading and writing competencies. According to the "Scoring Guide, English II Essay, March, j98," the purpose of the English II Test is "to assess students' mastery of expository writing, the application of grammatical skills, and achievements in literary analysis." The End of Course Test provides an accurate and reliable score for each student's paper.

The test also fulfills another very specific purpose, one that is of major importance to teachers—"to provide information about school and school system achievement" by recording aggregate scores of schools and districts. Thus, schools and school systems can gauge the strength of their literacy programs, which should provide rich and consistent instruction, allowing students to master English II competencies by the end of the 10th grade.

Much of the earlier section of Jan's description resonates well with what many English and language arts educators believe they are doing and believe they *should* be doing. The elements of the balanced literacy program (see Appendix I) also highlight the ideal goals of reading and writing pedagogy. The challenge comes in that the wonderful lists of characteristics of balanced literacy programs seem to be negated by the "single-shot" writing exam or by the pressure placed on schools and districts and, of course, on the students and teachers in English and language arts to produce and score high. This clash of ideal and real expectations affirms another premise of this chapter, *that teaching for thinking and connection are key.* This premise will be explored extensively in the ending segment of the chapter.

Dealing with the clash of ideal and real expectations, with the forceful figures of state departments of public instruction and state boards of education and the legislators (the funding sources for public schools) looming over, teachers might create learning contexts in which the goal of lifelong learning through reading and writing is lost. The following narratives come from Dee Grantham, veteran English teacher at Smoky Mountain High School in Sylva, North Carolina, and from Mike Lodico, former head of the English department at Tuscola High School in Waynesville, North Carolina. Both teachers' stories represent the reality expressed by English and language arts teachers nation-wide and both offer advice validated by their daily experience in public high school. Dee Grantham identifies both the positives and negatives of state-mandated testing.

Dee Grantham's Narrative

Several years ago I embarked, somewhat willingly but certainly not voluntarily, on a journey which had as its destination and goal, the effective teaching of composition to high school sophomores. My home state of North Carolina had declared from the sacred halls of the Department of Public Instruction that this group of students would focus on reading world literature, writing in four modes (narrative, expository, descriptive, and argumentative) and using correct conventions in writing. The "world" in World Literature, according to the SDPI (State Department of Public Instruction), did not include America or Great Britain!

It did not take long to realize two important facts. First of all the textbook I had did not correlate with the state curriculum; I knew I would have to liberate myself from the text and would have to begin to develop supplementary reading materials. Secondly, since all sophomores would be given a two-day writing exam devised and evaluated at the state level, all of my sophomores, regardless of ability, interest or motivation, deserved equal access to the best materials and instruction I could provide. Therefore, I began to devise a curriculum of study that was the same for all, regardless of course level designation. Where once I was using a different textbook and supplementary for "lower level" classes, I now set out the same reading requirements for all. Please understand that the methods of instruction are different for various groups; I hope that is in response to my trying to meet the needs of my students. However, as I look back over the past decade of my teaching, unifying the curriculum for all ability levels has been one of the best changes I've made in my quest for quality. I've also raised expectations for all classes. The students heading for the work force or the community college were walking around with the same novels as those students headed for Chapel Hill! I would think this would be an enhancer for self-esteem, and with that in mind, I send a grateful acknowledgement to our State Department for demanding that I demand more.

Has the journey been difficult and stressful at times? Oh my, yes! Every fall at the state English convention, sophomore teachers gather to complain and commiserate over the test. What was the State expecting? How did the evaluators arrive at a score of 1 to 6? Was Pearl Buck's *Good Earth* considered World Literature? (No, we discovered.) Would the writing prompt require a response to literature? I truly believe a great part of the frustration and anxiety among teachers resulted from a lack of communication. Many of us felt Raleigh was just letting us flounder around and guess what was going to be expected of students. Finally after several years, we were able to determine that the first day's prompt would be expository in nature and would be literature-based. Why couldn't we have had that information early on? Why do we want to keep teachers in the dark? Is there a power struggle going on? We are the language caretakers—why are we not communicating better?

In our state we have now moved to one day of writing (maybe there is a lack of funding and time to try to evaluate two essays for each student). I know that the prompt will address expository writing and will require analytical skills applied to a student-selected work of World Literature. Because I have this information at hand, I can give my students instruction and practice in responding to theme or analyzing the effect that any element (such as setting, point of view, dramatic irony) has on the work itself—a rather sophisticated concept for a fifteen year old. This past summer the SDPI Language Arts consultants prepared a video for all schools in the state which does a fine job of explaining the nature of the test and the expectations of evaluators. I was thrilled to view it; I just wish I had had it about six or seven years ago.

Do I teach to the test? You betcha! But the test seems to address the skills my students need: analytical thinking, ability to gather and organize relevant information, proficiency in written expression, and use of correct conventions in writing. I've just completed a semester in which my students generally scored very well; next semester's end may find me in a pit of despair. "I gave the same instruction," I'll wail, "what happened?" I've come to the conclusion that much of all this is left to chance; if the prompt is a good one that lends itself to a work we've studied, students feel good about what they do. I've quit punishing myself and taking blame when the scores aren't what I wanted for my students; neither can I demand the credit when they're good. Good conscientious students in a writing mood, given a prompt with which they feel comfortable, remembering some of the tips I've given on writing right, an evaluator who likes the students' writing for whatever reasons (Does the evaluator give higher scores at the first of the grading day or toward the end?)—all of this works together and generally will bring good results.

And now I reveal my last secret. On the morning of the test this past fall, I was able to gather my sophomores in my room for—a last minute of instruction? Nope! We had a celebration of our efforts and ate a good breakfast! (Grantham 1999)

Dee's narrative reveals a number of pertinent responses, acknowledging both teacher and student frustration. She also recognizes the same essential visible in Jan Williamson's description of the ideals in a writing program. *The test does actually address common strengths required for good writing.* Teachers need to hold onto this premise in their anxiety about "teaching to the test." We want students who can analyze and respond to literature—to anything they read, in fact; we want students to gather, organize, and unify their ideas; we want them to be proficient in the basic conventions of expression and use of language. And we want them to have these skills for a lifetime, not only for a single test.

Note also that Dee demonstrates the premise of "knowing the rules in order to break the rules." She clearly explores what is expected by state tests; she confers with colleagues at local and state English teachers' conferences; she examines a variety of texts and evaluates her own teaching. Maybe most important, Dee has come to accept the human limitations of her students and of the scorers of the exam. She does not assume blame for the noncontrollable elements.

The *Scoring Guide English II Essay, March 1998,* a pamphlet accompanying the videotape Dee alludes to in her narrative, includes a good description of the qualities expected in essays, according to a 6–0 rubric. A copy of that scoring description is given in Appendix II.

The added challenge for North Carolina's tenth graders is the requirement to use World Literature texts. The opportunity to enrich our students' world view and global awareness is certainly welcome. Many writers of diverse cultures are worth exploring and should be introduced to high school students. But the additional aspect of cultural diversity adds a level of meaning to penetrate; for many noncollege-bound students, this barrier blocks their success in writing. Questions still remain: Aren't there other ways to encourage and develop writing skills? Aren't there other texts on which to base the writing? And aren't there other ways to assess that would more consistently acknowledge the writing process?

Earlier I spoke of the necessary collaboration among postsecondary institutions and the public schools. Dee has been among the public school teachers who participate in Western Carolina University's Model Clinical Teaching Program. This program arranges for team teaching that pairs a university methods faculty member and a public school teacher. I have had the good fortune of having Dee teach with me in Methods of Teaching English and in Fundamentals of Teaching Composition. In the latter course, Dee has frequently brought student essays from her sophomore classes for my students to read, respond to, and score. This allows the preservice teachers to get a realistic sense of the tenth grade (or middle grade or elementary) students' writing potential. From the preservice teachers' standpoint, there is also the advantage of becoming familiar with the scoring procedures for state-mandated tests. The better the preservice teachers are acquainted with the state's curriculum, the more these students can serve as additional audiences for the public school students preparing for testing. The valuable one-on-one conferencing, which is nearly an impossibility for the single teacher in a classroom, can become more feasible if a student teacher or intern, well-schooled in the writing requirements, can aid in the process. One-on-one conferencing with Dee's students has worked because she has scheduled conferencing of practice drafts when preservice teachers can work in her classroom; each person then can work with about four or five student papers and offer more individual response than a single teacher can provide.

We hear now a second narrative, another perspective on the writing exam. Mike Lodico outlines a series of strategies applicable for meeting any state's requirements. Lodico and a colleague who teaches tenth grade English also participated in the Fundamentals of Teaching Composition class this semester. They provided handouts and explanations of the state writing assignment for all the English secondary education majors. A middle grades teacher presented information about the seventh grade writing test; an elementary teacher addressed the elementary majors, covering the fourth grade writing exam.

Mike Lodico's Narrative

Just about any English teacher can recite a litany of complaints about writing tests that are delivered from on high: ETS developed tests, state tests, or system-level tests. Among the likely gripes are questions of validity, e.g., "Does this test measure the skills which I have tried to develop in my students?" as well as those of reliability, e.g., "How do I know that my students' writing will be graded fairly?" Frequently concerns about such issues cannot be and should not be laid to rest. Teachers need to be actively involved through their school systems and professional organizations to ensure any such "institutionalized" writing assessments are fair and appropriate.

Many writing teachers are concerned as well about the anxiety and pressure that students feel about writing. Many of us want to use writing as means of empowering students; institutionalized writing assessments tend not to be rooted in a student's need to convey a cogent message to a real audience—the goal of most written expression.

The wheels of change move slowly, however, and the next test is likely to be on the horizon before any protests from the last test have been heeded or even heard. What can a teacher or school do to make impersonal writing tests a vehicle for meaningful writing instruction? The experience of the English Department of Tuscola High School in Waynesville, NC, may prove instructive.

Integration: The state curriculum's emphasis on literature-based writing has fostered better integration of the English curriculum. No longer do teachers do a "writing unit"; instead, writing instruction is embedded in the year's work (or semester in the block scheduling) from the beginning and, as a result, becomes a thread that ties the year's activities together.

Teamwork: The state of North Carolina gives a writing test involving literary analysis to all tenth graders. Tuscola's tenth grade writing teachers meet at least twice a month as a team during a common planning period to discuss issues in their literature and writing curricula. Individual teachers have done mini-presentations on works of literature and on specific instructional strategies. This group has become the driving force for a writing across the curriculum effort in the high school as a whole. Each English teacher has worked with another department as its "writing buddy" to aid non-English teachers in developing, implementing, and evaluating writing activities.

Parent Communication: In order to let parents know of the importance of writing in the curriculum, Tuscola sends home a letter during the first semester to parents of all tenth graders explaining the nature of the state writing test and some specific strategies for parents to monitor their child's progress in English. A second letter is sent to parents of students who performed poorly on the school's practice writing test.

Practice: Individual teachers make sure that students have ample opportunity to practice their writing skills. About six weeks prior to the actual state writing test, Tuscola gives all tenth graders a practice test which simulates actual testing conditions as closely as possible. Teachers from various departments are trained to score the practice tests. Because student numbers are used, there is little danger of halo effect. The papers are returned to the individual teachers for follow-up.

Follow-Up: The Tuscola teachers develop a roster of low-performing students from the practice test. The parents of these students receive a letter explaining times when special writing test prep sessions will be held. Some students need individual attention; teachers meet with them in review sessions that involve a variety of activities designed to increase students' familiarity with the demands of the state writing test. These sessions are set up for any student who wants to hone his skills in dealing with the writing test.

Through the above methods, Tuscola's tenth grade English teachers have created a greater understanding of the demands of writing instruction in their school and community. As a result, Tuscola teachers have fewer students who "just won't write." Too, they are seeing teachers in other departments incorporating writing into their areas. The teachers still have many concerns about a writing assessment which involves neither a full writing process nor a real audience. Nonetheless, they have worked hard to turn the stressful state writing test into a vehicle for student growth. (Lodico 1999)

Again we see a number of positives expressed by Mike; surely any increase in communication among teachers, parents, and students, especially adolescents, is a plus. Also, the reality of increased awareness among teachers in all disciplines about the necessity of writing is a distinct advantage. Mike also reinforced my earlier premise of knowledgeability; I underscore his recommendation to participate in state and national English organizations. The NCTE and the state councils of English teachers are two strong support systems. A similar concern to Dee's appears in Mike's narrative: the state writing test does not work with writing as a process nor does it allow writing for a real audience.

To the many good and practical strategies and approaches that Jan, Dee, and Mike offer, I add my ultimate premise of advice regarding the state-mandated writing tests. I encourage writing that calls for a union of thinking and feeling, of head and heart, of analysis and relation. I do see the value in writing that is embedded in literature, and the literature should be a site for the connection of students' experience and response. Regarding the North Carolina requirement of World Literature as the basis for the writing test content, I maintain that if students can connect with or relate to at least one literary character or one text they will be able to write about that work. Maybe they relate to the young man at war from *All Quiet on the Western Front*, or maybe they can see in Elie Wiesel's *Night* something about the need to hold to deep meaning in life in order to survive some of its inexplicable horror, or maybe *Oedipus Rex* comes alive for them as a tragic experience of one who thinks he sees but is blinded. Maybe it will take paralleling a young adult text with characters more real to a more classic work, but somehow, somewhere we as teachers of English and language arts need to help students find that connection; we need to ignite the passion we hold for reading and writing in the lives of those we teach. We need to validate students' experiences so that they will want to write narratives, descriptions, and arguments about their values and valued memories.

At a state conference of the North Carolina English teachers in the fall of 1998, I again became aware of how we need to empower our students' abilities to think: to think through, to think about, to think around the issues, the ideas, the problems, the texts they confront. I had the privilege of hearing North Carolina's English teacher of the year, Pamela Freeze Beal, present her best ideas for teaching World Literature, the reading content background for the English II writing test. She introduced me to a wonderful children's book, *Hooray for Diffendoofer Day!* by Dr. Seuss, Jack Prelutsky, and Lane Smith. In the typically enjoyable Seuss fashion we are introduced to Diffendoofer School, where, the narrator proclaims the students are learning lots of things not taught at other schools, particularly because the teachers at Diffendoofer School are remarkable and "make up their own rules." Among the list of creative things the students at Diffendoofer are taught are listening, smelling, laughing, yelling, and "tying knots in neckerchiefs and noodles," and in Miss Bonkers classroom they are taught "everything."

The day comes when the principal, Mr. Lowe, a particularly sad man, announces that all students from all around must take a special test to see what they've been learning and "to see which school's the best." Mr. Lowe is terribly depressed since he knows if Diffendoofer School does not do well, it will be torn down. Worst of all, the Diffendoofer students would have to go to school in Flobbertown. Flobbertown is "miserable" and Flobbertown is monotonous and lacks innovation. But spectacular Miss Bonkers, the most "different-er" of the teachers at Diffendoofer assures the dismayed students that they've learned the things they need to know to pass this test and many others because, among the many creative things these students have been taught, they have been taught the most important skill of all: they have been taught to think.

The students of Diffendoofer discover when the test is handed out that it is filled with all the things they know they know. And, of course, when the results of the exam come back, Mr. Lowe can proudly report that Diffendoofer School got the very highest score.

Beal uses this book in her tenth grade English class early each semester; I used the book in Fundamentals of Teaching Composition with the K–12 preservice teachers of writing. After reading the book aloud, I asked my students to create a writing prompt that they would use in their particular teaching context. This allowed them to practice creating writing prompts; more pertinent to their preparation though, is Miss Bonkers' pungent statement, "We've taught you to think." When students have been encouraged through probing questions, through engagement with texts, through frequent writing that allows them to explore what they see, view, read, and hear, they are grounded in the ability to think. When they are focused "thinkers and feelers," "analyzers and emoters," when they are connected and able to relate to at least one text or one issue or one experience, the state-mandated tests will not daunt them. They will bring to this isolated writing experience the vast resources of the reading and writing and thinking they've done in our classes. Then teachers of English and language arts will not dread the exams and our student writers will not necessarily "freeze" in writing under pressure. Our largest task is to help them see the connections and spark the flame.

APPENDIX I

The Balanced Literacy Program

Jan Williamson,

NC State Department of Public Instruction

In a balanced literacy program, students learn to write with control and clarity when they

- write daily and have opportunities to share their writing.
- write regularly for real, personally significant purposes and for a wide range of audiences.
- have rich and continuous reading experiences, including published literature of merit and the work of peers and teachers.
- have access to models of writing and writers at work.
- are given instruction in the processes of writing.
- can collaborate with peers for ideas and guidance in writing.
- have one-to-one writing conferences with the teacher.
- have direct instruction in specific strategies and techniques of writing.
- are taught grammatical usage and mechanics in context of their own writing and speaking.
- are given ample opportunity to revise works to develop stronger drafts.
- write as an extension of literature study as well as write in diverse genres such as autobiographical/biographical sketches, narratives, journal entries, personal responses, business letters, feature articles, research reports, scientific/technical writing, process essays, editorials, formal speeches, letters to the editor, fables, folklore, myths, short stories and poems.
- practice and use writing as a tool for learning in all disciplines, not just in English.

Students who are given this type of writing instruction, beginning in kindergarten and continuing in every grade, will be ready and able to write in diverse ways. They will be able to choose their own topics and they will be able to write to a constructed prompt. They will be able to generate and organize their ideas without using a formulaic approach.

In a balanced literacy program students also

- read extensively, in class and out of class, in all disciplines, not just in English.
- read in different ways—shared reading, silent reading, guided reading.
- have a print-rich environment with multiple types of text available to them.

- have multiple opportunities to talk about and write about what they have just read.
- are explicitly taught reading strategies when they demonstrate a need for them.
- are read aloud to regularly so they can hear proficient, fluent reading and experience complex language and ideas they may not be able to read for themselves.
- understand their own strengths in reading and build upon them in a reflective way.

With this strong literacy background, students will have the foundation they need for English I, which also combines reading and writing in an introduction to literature that is a study of genre, literary terms, and literary analysis. Literacy development is continued in English I as instruction provides rich opportunities such as the following:

- Students are allowed to write in genres of their own choice as well as in assigned genres.
- Dialogue, where every student has a voice, is encouraged.
- Students learn to pose problems to discover why authors from certain time periods wrote things as they did; they learn how to make connections by using familiar themes to connect texts to each other and to their own lives.
- Grammatical usage and spelling are dealt with in mini-lessons and individual conferences.
- Students learn about elements of literature such as theme or characterization in discussion and writings about the text.

APPENDIX II

Expository Composition: Focused Holistic Score Scale

Score Point 6: The response exhibits a strong command of expository writing. It is focused and has a fluent, clear progression of ideas and evenness of development. There are strengths in all four criteria. The writer provides specific, relevant details to support ideas. These papers exhibit a strong command of an expository writing strategy. The writer clearly develops all parts of the prompt and uses an appropriate and highly effective approach (i.e., tone, point of view, originality). An appropriate sense of audience exists. Sentence structure is varied and effective, and word choice demonstrates the ability to use a large vocabulary skillfully. If a literary work is referred to, the work must be from world literature (other than American or British literature). There is a sense of overall completeness.

Score Point 5: The response is focused, progresses logically, and exhibits a command of expository writing. There are strengths in all four criteria. There is no break in progression. The writer uses specific details and clearly links events and relationships. A few minor flaws in coherence may be present. The writer addresses all aspects of the prompt and uses effective vocabulary and sentence structure. If a literary work is referred to, the work must be from world literature (other than American or British literature). An appropriate sense of audience exists. There is a sense of overall completeness.

Score Point 4:   The response is focused and establishes progression of ideas and events although minor lapses in focus and progression may be present. The papers have elaboration and support in the form of specific details. Papers scored "4" have an organizational pattern, but minor flaws may exist. They may have minor weaknesses in coherence. The writer clearly addresses the topic and supports it, but some aspect of the prompt may be missing. If a literary work is referred to, the work must be from world literature (other than American or British literature). In some responses, a sense of audience may exist.

Score Point 3:   These responses exhibit some progression of ideas and events and provide some elaboration and support. The elaboration may be flawed, but it has relevance to the requirements of the prompt. Papers scored "3" have a generally organized pattern but contain minor flaws. The papers are generally coherent although minor weaknesses in coherence may be present. These papers are focused on the prompt; some may not address all aspects of the prompt. Some papers may tend to summarize at times or have a list-like quality, but they should have concrete, supporting details.

Score Point 2:   There is evidence that the writer has seen the prompt and responded to it, although the response may be unclear. Some responses may have little or no sense of connection between a controlling idea and supporting details relevant to development. Other responses may have a sense of focus but lose it. Some "2" responses may be extended lists or lists with some extension. The writer has some sense of organization, but the composition may be too sparse for a higher score point. Some of the compositions do not directly address all aspects of the prompt, and some lapse into summary.

Score Point 1:   There is evidence that the writer has seen and attempted to respond to the prompt. However, the response may not sustain focus on the topic. The writer may attempt to support ideas, but there may be no sense of strategy or control. Many responses exhibit skeletal control but are too sparse to be scored higher than a "1." Some responses lack coherence and/or have an inappropriate strategy (i.e., pure summary, pure list).

Score Point 0:   The response addresses a literary work but is incorrect in its perception of the literary concept.

Non-Scorable: The response is off-topic, unreadable, or blank.

REFERENCES AND RESOURCES

Britt, Katrina. Writings from her journal in English 414: Fundamentals of Teaching Composition. Western Carolina University, Cullowhee, NC, Spring 1999.

Dr. Seuss, Jack Prelutsky, and Lane Smith. *Hooray for Diffendoofer Day!* New York: Knopf, 1998.

Grantham, Dee. "Narrative" on the English II Writing Test. English teacher, Smoky Mountain High School, Sylva, NC, January 1999.

Lodico, Mike. "The Dreaded State Writing Assessment." English teacher, Tuscola High School, Waynesville, NC, January 1999.

Mayher, John S. *Uncommon Sense.* Portsmouth, NH: Heinemann, 1990.

Motivating Writing in Middle School. Standards Consensus Series. Urbana, IL: National Council of Teachers of English, 1996.

Routman, Regie. *Literacy at the Crossroads.* Portsmouth, NH: Heinemann, 1996.

Scoring Guide: English II Essay, March 1998. North Carolina Department of Public Instruction, 1998.

Standards for the English Language Arts. A Project of the National Council of Teachers of English and International Reading Association. Urbana, IL: National Council of Teachers of English, 1995.

Teaching Narrative: Write on Grade 3–5. North Carolina Department of Public Instruction, 1994.

Teaching the Writing Process in High School. Standards Consensus Series. Urbana, IL: National Council of Teachers of English, 1995.

Williamson, Jan. Language Arts Consultant, K–12, North Carolina State Department of Public Instruction. Description of the NC Standard Course of Study in English/Language Arts, November 1998.

A series of handouts from the 1998 National Council of Teachers of English Conference, November 20, 1998, Nashville, Tennessee, is available.

"A History of the Nevada Writing Assessment."

"English Language Arts Curriculum Framework, K–12," State of Tennessee Department of Education.

"Virginia's New Writing Assessment," Virginia Department of Education.

Any state's Department of Public Instruction or Department of Education is an important source.

11 The Grading Game and the Teaching of Writing

STEPHEN TCHUDI

Something English and language arts teachers dread even more than state-mandated writing tests is grading. In this chapter, Stephen Tchudi first helps readers see the distinction between *grading* and *assessment,* assuring us that students are indeed able to do assessment. Tchudi moves on to offer six principles of assessment-based writing, and from his vast experience as an English and language arts practitioner, he provides a variety of assessments connected to each of the six principles; the assessments are primarily writing based.

In the second part of this chapter, Tchudi presents grading systems for the teaching of writing; he suggests four systematic approaches to grading: rubrics and grading guides, credit and no credit "grades," contract and achievement grading and point systems, and portfolio assessment and grading. In discussing the advantages and disadvantages of each system, Tchudi establishes an excellent grading foundation for teachers and students of writing.

In some respects, I'm the wrong person to be writing a chapter on the grading of compositions. My position is this: *Grading of writing should be abolished.* Not only should it be abolished for writing, but for the English and language arts in general and, if I had my way, for the entire educational establishment. I'd like to institute universal pass–fail or credit–no credit classes, courses, and programs. Simply put: If people do the work and do it well, they get credit. Instead of single alphabetic grades, we'd substitute comprehensive assessment systems, what's been called "twenty-six letter grading": written assessments by instructors matched with self-assessments by students.

Twice during my career I've been able to teach briefly in nongraded systems, and in both cases I felt that my ability to talk with my students was enhanced and that we were both working for a common aim—learning—rather than feeling conflicts about the inevitable question, "What will I get on this paper?"

But for the vast majority of teachers, and in my own day-to-day teaching, grades are required. So the second element of my diatribe on grading is this: *I hate grading and do it only under duress, but I do grade.* Much of what you will read in the remainder of this chapter, then, will be based on the conviction that grading is something that teachers need to work around. That is, while meeting the requirements of the system to grade, teachers need to be responsible to their own pedagogy and strive to make grading as fair as possible. I call this being *aggressively cooperative.*

Why this almost fanatical resistance to grading? I believe the grading "game" has traditionally been a lose–lose enterprise for both teachers and students of writing and, as implied, in all education. In a volume I edited, *Alternatives to Grading in the Teaching of Writing,* author Lisel O'Hagan did a thorough study of the research into grading practices and found that generations of study clearly showed that grades seldom enhance or catalyze student performance, although they occasionally induce artificially high or paralyzingly low effort through threats and artificial rewards. Grades often interfere with student–teacher communication about what really matters in writing. If you have doubts about the negative effects of grading, I encourage you to read Lisel's essay.

Or take some time and do a little free writing about your own experiences with grades as both student and teacher: Write about the feelings you experienced when you received a grade that was poor or unfair. Recall times when you were mystified by what the teacher wanted in an assignment, with the threat of a grade hanging over you. Write about when you were conflicted over what grade to assign a student or about the feelings your students had when you—of necessity, of course—had to give them a bad grade.

The fact that you are reading this book and are a member of the teaching profession suggests that you probably are a *survivor* of the grading game, maybe even a good player at it, and that your negative responses may be fewer than those of other people. Many of us are teachers because we did well at school and were among the high achievers who received good grades and the praise that goes with them. Even so, you can carefully assess your experience in writing: What did you ever learn from a grade? What did an A or a C+ teach you about actual learning? What have you learned in life without grades? How did that learning differ?

To add just one more bit to this assignment, I strongly encourage you to interview some students about grades, students with both high and low averages. I predict that you'll collect stories from both the high and low achievers about the negative effects of grading. Even students who do well under a grading system are pretty guarded and qualified in their response.

I don't expect that you will necessarily share my grading phobia, so this chapter will be based on the more modest proposition that, like any teacher, you're concerned about the possible negative effects of grading and, in any case, want to make grading as fair as possible. My aim will be to outline ways in which teachers, within the constraints imposed by the educational system, can work their way to equitable and productive grades, not only in writing classes and courses, but with implications for other areas of teaching as well.

Before proceeding, however, I want to make an important distinction between two terms that are often conflated: *grading* and *assessment.* I personally have no objection at all to *assessment* as part of the educational process. Nor does assessment necessarily have the kinds of negative effects that I associate with the narrower phenomenon of grading. Assessment at its best collects a wide range of data or information that students and teachers can use to reflect on performance.

In colloquial language, assessment asks "What's happenin'?" "How's it goin'?" "What next?" People assess naturally in their lives, literally every minute of every day. We read body language to see what people are thinking; we carefully scrutinize what we're doing at the moment we're doing it; we monitor the effects of our actions to see whether we're producing what we intended to. Moreover, I argue that most students come into our classroom with very well developed assessment skills, even though they may not be conscious of these skills or apply them systematically for school learning. They size you up the moment you walk in the door; they assess their relationships with peers and strangers; they weigh the value of what you've asked them to do and what they'd prefer to do and then make decisions about how to spend their time.

Grading essentially debases the assessment process. It takes a wide range of assessments and reduces all that data to a single letter or number. The complexities of assessment—and, again, students are intrinsically good assessors—are diminished, and the reductioneer is always the teacher, dispensing the final grade.

My claim is that if grading is placed in a broader context of high-quality, informative assessment, and if assessment is placed in the still broader context of good, motivated writing activities, teachers can reduce the negative effects of grading, provide careful evaluation, support their students' writing growth, and help the students themselves become skilled assessors of their own writing, thus preparing themselves for writing activities beyond the classroom.

In the next section of this chapter, I'll make six broad claims about an assessment-based writing program and suggest ways in which we can productively assess student writing, not just at the end of the project, but throughout the entire writing process.

Toward Assessment-based Writing

Here are six principles for assessment-based writing:

1. Base writing (and other composing) activities on genuinely productive assignments.
2. Discuss criteria for success early in the assignment.
3. Provide frequent opportunities for in-process feedback.
4. Guarantee that teacher and audience will respond.
5. Demythologize correctness in rhetoric, grammar, and usage.
6. Grade growth, not papers.

Provide Productive Assignments

In my high school days, writing assignments often consisted of a quotation on the board and a mandate to write 500 to 1,000 words about it. Composition theory has considerably improved on such assignments. There is widespread agreement that good assignments generally include provision for student selection of topics, real as opposed to teacher-only audiences, and a choice of discourse modes and forms. Poor grades often begin with unmotivated assignments, unreal assignments, or write-for-the-teacher or write-for-the-grade assignments. There are, of course, times in life when one has no choice about the assignment: The boss says "do this"; a teacher in another class says "write this." But it stands to reason that the grading–assessment process will go more smoothly if the writing is motivated. Other writers in this volume have gone into detail about the early stages of the writing process from an assignment-making perspective. Here, I simply want to outline some of the forms of *assessment* that can come into play from the very beginning. Note that most of the assessments are *writing based*, so even as students are preparing to write, they are using writing, gaining fluency, and seeing that writing is a tool for learning.

Students can assess the following:

■ *Their areas of interest and concern.* I regularly begin writing classes with a variety of interest inventories and free writings. What concerns you? What do you like to do with your time, your life? What are the top five worries in your life? What are your achievements? What do you want to do next? Frequently, such generic assessments provide a long list of writing ideas.

■ *Their background knowledge and understanding.* Whether we're studying the Victorians or space travel or the English language, students can do free writing that discusses what they already know about the topic, what they assume is interesting about it, and the questions they might want to explore.

■ *Possible audiences for their writing.* Other than the teacher, who might be interested in reading about the Victorians, space travel, or the English language? What is this audience like? What do you suppose they would want to know? Where can you send work to get a readership? What are the possible audiences among fellow students? community members? friends and parents? public officials? celebrities? other interested people? "Who," to adapt from the Little Red Hen, "will help me read this writing?"

■ *Ways of reaching these audiences.* What kinds of writing or composing would be the most appealing to an audience? In terms of the classical rhetorical partition of appeals, to what extent might I be able to reach these readers through *ethos* (establishing my own credibility), *pathos* (appealing to their emotions), or *logos* (logical argument)?

■ *Possible modes of composing.* Some days the good old essay may be the best way to reach an audience. But what about composing my ideas as a poem? a story? a video? a hypertext computer document? Writing about writing, which is the essential function of this and the previous suggestion, helps raise students' consciousness of writing processes.

■ *Their skills.* What skills and abilities do I bring to this task? What are my biggest successes as a writer? How can I build on them? How can I use my own human relations skills to build a bridge to my particular audience?

Assessing Criteria for Success

The chalk-it-on-the-board assignments of my youth gave no hint of what was required for success. "Write a paper. Hand it in. Grades will follow." Clearly, if students are required to learn in maximum ways from writing, they need to think about criteria for success even before they put pen to paper. Help students decide, in advance, what will constitute effectiveness in a given subject. If you are placing letter grades on individual papers, it's especially important to outline the criteria for success. Many teachers, alas, confuse assessment with a distribution of points, such as 40 percent for ideas, 40 percent for organization, and 20 percent for surface conventions. But *points* and *percentages* are not *criteria;* they don't tell how the teacher will read the paper and pass out the percentages. What do we mean by ideas? by organization? How do we know whether a paper has good ideas or not? (Later in this chapter I will provide a sample grading rubric that presents criteria as well as percentages.)

To engage the assessment engine at this stage, you can have students do the following:

■ Collect examples of the kind of writing they propose to create, and then do free writing describing some of the characteristics they observe. What makes a good or successful essay? What makes a drama or a short story work for you?

■ Predict outcomes. If my paper is successful, what will the audience say or do when I'm finished? What steps can I take as I write to ensure that I'll get the response that I want? Students can often write fascinating imaginary responses to their own work in advance of doing the writing!

■ Discuss and write about evaluation and grading criteria. If 40 percent of a paper grade is to be given for ideas, what does this mean? How do we recognize a good idea? What are the traits of a well-organized paper? In particular, you can encourage students to contextualize their own writing: If they're writing, say, letters to the editor about the need for more youth entertainment activities, what kinds of organization would be appropriate? Whatever system of grading you use, engaging students in *discussing* and even *generating* criteria helps to demystify the process and increase student engagement in learning.

Providing Feedback in Process

Such feedback can include teacher–student, student–student, and student–audience. One of the nagging problems with criteria for assessment is that they are necessarily decontextualized. I cannot tell a student precisely in advance what a good idea is or how a well-organized paper will look. While we can offer general criteria, the specifics will emerge during the process of composition, as a student shapes a paper about birds or bees or global issues or personal concerns. As theme graders, we can often recognize the absence of the necessary traits: "Bad organization: C–." "Terrific ideas: A." But such after-the-fact information is seldom very helpful to novice writers. A highly productive middle ground is to provide in-process feedback for students. Instead of waiting for a paper or even a draft to come in, the teacher can proactively engage the students in process feedback. In written or oral form students can do the following:

■ Generate critical questions for their peers or the teacher: How am I doing so far? What do you think of my opening? Are you still with me?

■ Provide focused feedback. Various books by Peter Elbow are filled with ways of providing such feedback, often in very creative ways. One of Elbow's strategies I've frequently adapted is "the movie of your mind." The reader describes images in his or her head and describes responses, page by page, scene by scene, as he or she works through the text. Students can also provide one another focused feedback on beginnings, middles, endings, organization, voice, style, creativity, and so on.

■ Discuss the criteria for success (the second guideline) within the context of the writing at hand. So what does good organization mean *now* for a paper on "Ethics and Cheating" or "My Summer Vacation"? How can we make generic criteria specific to this paper, written for this audience, at this time?

■ Propose alternatives. Without taking over the paper, readers can suggest possible ways of proceeding: where to go next, what to say, how to end, and how to get out of a writing bind.

■ Compare drafts. How did my second draft improve over my first? Have I lost anything? Am I getting closer to success with the paper?

■ Write imaginary responses. Write from the perspective of the proposed audience members. Write a letter from a famous personality to the writer of the paper. Write an imaginary letter from the writer to him or herself. Imagine a short story as a film, a poem as a story, or an essay as a piece of platform oratory.

Provide Teacher and Audience Response

As noted previously, we've presumably already made provisions for students to write for audiences other than the teacher. But even audiences need some *education;* that is, although we want students to write for genuine purposes, real-world audiences can at times be very harsh, perhaps as a result of previous conditioning by English and language arts teachers. The teacher can often help control this process by encouraging audiences to respond in particular ways. Thus students can do the following:

- Send their writing to volunteer community readers, who are instructed to write a letter of response (not a critique).

- Solicit response to their writing and compare it to their earlier projections of how an audience should respond.

- Engage in pen pal correspondence with audiences.

As much as we'd like students to write for real, it's not always possible for us to get a response to writing from outside the classroom. Students can write only so many letters to editors and politicians before that fountain runs dry. In many cases, students in the class can also serve as an audience or mock audience by:

- Writing as if they were the audience itself: Martians responding to an appeal, politicians responding to an appeal, the general public appreciating a poem.

- Writing carefully constructed critiques, reacting to papers, and offering suggestions, not "trashing" the piece and its writer.

- Serving as editors and editorial boards for publications of class writing: books, anthologies, and broadsheets.

And at this stage, we must also recognize that, in the end, students are the best audience for their own work. They can write the following:

- Self-assessments, including narratives of their own writing process.

- Brief discussions of problems and pleasures, what they think went well or badly in the paper.

- Comparisons of their projection for the paper and how it turned out, emphatically *not* always or even necessarily for the worst. Indeed, writing often pleasantly surprises the writer with its directions!

Demythologizing Correctness

Note that this concerns *demystifying*, not *dismissing*, correctness. It is important for us to show students that correctness matters, that not adhering to the conventions can draw negative fire. But we must emphasize that correctness involves polishing papers *after* the substance of content and style has been worked out. Students can do the following:

- Compile usage directories of their most common problems.

- Develop rubrics for conventions, for example, ways of checking for mechanics, usage, and spelling.

- Study the standard English of publications, including the use of slang and colloquialism.

- Write on the issue of people's rights to their own language or on related issues, such as bilingualism and English only.

- Create their own minilessons on mechanics, usage, and spelling, with those who know teaching and with those who do not.

- Turn textbook advice on correctness into posters for display, elements in a class web site, or a set of leaflets on proofreading strategies.

Grading for Growth

I am personally opposed to putting individual grades on individual papers. The focus of the individually graded paper is, too often, the rights and wrongs of the present paper. Moreover, if a teacher gives any grades less than an A, she or he must devote most of the explanation for the grade to what was allegedly done wrong. By contrast, there are ways in which grading can be done to emphasize growth over time, and several of these are discussed in the next section. Meanwhile, if it is mandated that you grade each individual paper, I hope that the suggestions in this segment have helped make it clear that grading need not be a negative process, provided that students have been engaged in assessment throughout the writing process. Although a letter grade isn't a particularly good descriptor because of its one-dimensional nature, when based on careful discussion of the aims of a writing assignment, the predicted outcomes and criteria for success, plenty of in-process feedback, and lots of good audience response, grades seldom traumatize.

Grading Systems for the Teaching of Writing

The key word in my heading here is *systems*, for if we are to think of grading for growth, we need to think not only of ways of assessing individual papers, but also of finding ways to ensure coherence from paper to paper, even semester to semester. There are numerous ways for grading papers. Probably, in one form or another, they all work more or less successfully. The only system I would outlaw, however, is one that was submitted to me some years ago when I was editor of *The English Journal*. Modestly entitled, "The Perfect Grading System," it was an outline of major and minor writing errors, each linked to a point value so that by docking students systematically for spelling errors (½ point) on up to sentence fragments (I think the penalty was 2½ points), the teacher could reliably and consistently grade compositions down to the half-point. Let's not go that way.

I offer four systematic approaches to grading for your consideration:

1. Rubrics and grading guides
2. Credit–no credit grades
3. Contract and achievement grading–point systems
4. Portfolio assessment–grading

Rubrics and Grading Guides

Students need to know in advance how they will be assessed. Whether you are grading individual papers or groups of papers, creating rubrics or heuristics provides a degree of direction and, most important, encourages, even forces, the teacher to articulate criteria in advance. I have developed the generic grading guide in Figure 11.1. It lays out precisely how a paper is to be graded and the weights or percentages that will be assigned to each aspect of a composition. With this rubric, I adjusted the numbers and percentages so that the possible points add up to 100. A middle school friend of mine is of the conviction that "middle school kids like points, big points"; thus she designs her rubrics so the points total 1,000! You could just as easily design a rubric with 1 million possible points, or to amuse the students and complicate your grade book, you could have the points add up to an odd or peculiar figure, say 1,066 or 5,280. For the scheme in Figure 11.1 (probably most appropriate for nonfiction), I divided the grade among two major and one minor part: content, style, and conventions. Both content and style categories could be further subdivided to give more direction to the students. In this generic guide, I have suggested criteria in the form of the questions a reader–grader might ask. You could also use *trait descriptions* in which you offer the criteria for a low, middle, or high score. One trick I've used in this particular model is to start the scoring of "good" or "competent" at about 7 on the scale of 10, ignoring 1 to 5 and rarely using 6; I give my students mostly 7s, 8s, 9s, and the occasional 10, which means that I am acknowledging that even the least successful papers in a class are not disasters.

In grading guides of this sort, I also leave ample room for teacher comments following each numerical rating. This has a twofold effect: First, it forces me to articulate the reasons for my score, so I can't get away with just circling a number without explanation. Second, and more important, is that it provides the student with an explanation to go along with the score in an effort to de-emphasize the numbers and to focus on editorial comments.

I leave it to the reader to see how the general format could be adopted to virtually any writing form, genre, or product, including the so-called creative genres.

When I've used similar grading guides, I've made it a practice to distribute the guide at the beginning of the assignment and to involve students in both discussion of the criteria and their appropriate weights; in fact, the guide shown in Figure 11.1 was developed around criteria developed by my students.

Grading guides are also interesting because they reveal a great deal of a teacher's philosophy; indeed, a teacher should be able to demonstrate the philosophy underlying the distribution of grades along a rubric.

Having given this description of grading guides, I now have to say that, after experimenting with them off and on for years, I have rejected them as a mode of grading. If you are required to put single letter grades on single papers, you may

1. Content (30%). Is the content of the piece clear? Rich in details? Showing evidence of careful observation or research? Is it original? Are there signs of creative use of materials and interpretation? Is the organization clear? Does the piece hang together?

Low   0   1   2   3   4   5   6   7   8   9   10   High × 3 = _____

Comments:

2. Language and style (30%). Does the paper have voice? Does it avoid clichés? Is it an easy or comfortable "read"? Do some expressions amuse or surprise or delight the reader? Is the choice of formal versus colloquial diction appropriate? Are words used appropriately and naturally?

Low   0   1   2   3   4   5   6   7   8   9   10   High × 3 = _____

Comments:

3. Audience (20%). Is this paper accessible to the reader? Is there evidence that the author cares about the audience and is working to reach it? Are there signs that the writer has thought about what the audience knows and needs to know?

Low   0   1   2   3   4   5   6   7   8   9   10   High × 2 = _____

Comments:

4. Conventions (10%). Has the paper been carefully proofread? Are there any obvious problems with [ ] spelling   [ ] punctuation   [ ] mechanics   [ ] usage?

Low   0   1   2   3   4   5   6   7   8   9   10   High × 1 = _____

Comments:

5. Extra considerations. Here are some things I think you did especially well in this paper.

6   7   8   9   10   High × 1 = _____

Comments:

Total score for this paper: _____

FIGURE 11.1   A Generic Composition Grading Rubric

find the grading guide helpful. But if you're like me, you'll encounter some of the following problems:

■ No matter how carefully you describe the criteria, they are still *general.* Whether you are awarding points for clarity or voice or originality, the criteria never fully describe your expectations.

■ Note my authoritarian language immediately above: Rubrics still are a matter of *awarding* points, placing the teacher in the usual position of being the award-meister, the dispenser of values, which, in turn, may undercut efforts to make students independent writers.

■ Rubrics seldom allow adequate room for individual differences. If I am consistent in my grading, a 7 is a 7 is a 7. Thus, I am trapped into being unable to reward Charles, a C student, more than 7 for his terrific effort, while Osgood, the traditional A student, pulls down his usual 9 without lifting a finger.

■ The whole of a paper seldom is reflected in the sum of the scores. Often, after doling out the points as fairly and equitably as possible on a grading guide, I find that the sum total just doesn't seem right. I want to tweak the final total to make it match my impressions. This means that I, like many teachers and most readers, am grading "whimsically," rather than by the fragmentary parts, no matter how carefully articulated the components.

A kind of scoring that recognizes this holistic phenomenon calls for a single grade or score to be put on the paper. This method rightly acknowledges that writing is too complex to be broken down into itemized criteria. However, holistic grading really brings us back to ground zero, for it often appears to the student to be arbitrary, and it conveys almost no specific information about what has been done well or badly. Once again, I observe that my language in the previous sentences, *well* and *badly,* is being driven by the grading game away from my pedagogical desire to avoid such crass generalizations.

Credit–No Credit Grades

There are a number of variations to this approach, which is actually holistic in the sense that it calls for a yes–no judgment: The paper is up to snuff or not. Successful—unsuccessful and pass–fail grading schemes are variations, and I'm convinced the educational world would be much better off if we went to a universal P–F, Cr–NCr, or S–U grading system.

Another variation within this approach is A–incomplete or B–incomplete; here the teacher says that a paper must be written up to an A or B level before it is accepted. Some A–I teachers literally give only A's in their courses, and the student, Charles or Osgood, works until he's reached that level for himself. B–I operates on the same principle, with the teacher sometimes reserving the right to award—there's that word again—an A for especially well done work (by either

Charles or Osgood, by the way). Sometimes an overall grade may be, say, five credited papers, that's good for a C, while doing more work can raise the grade higher. In this way, quantity plus quality combine to lead to grades. The teacher, meanwhile, is relieved from quibbling over scores—is Charles's writing a 7 or a 7.2 or possibly a 7.4½ + or –?

To avoid arbitrariness in Cr–NCr grading, the teacher must provide detailed discussion, again involving the students, over what makes a basically acceptable or creditable project. What are the characteristics of a good editorial or sonnet? What do we look for in an essay that we, as readers, will accept as basically satisfactory, or more? As with other grading systems, spelling out such criteria can be abstract and decontextualized, but the S–U, P–F systems offer a pedagogically interesting way out of that dilemma: Students don't "flunk" or get bad grades; they keep working until they have achieved a satisfactory level of performance. Granted, the teacher is still the final arbiter of what passes for up to snuff, but his or her comments and suggestions are no longer linked to traditional grades, no longer associated solely with failure. And the comments are contextualized: If a paper is not yet Creditable or of B or A quality, the teacher can articulate on the draft fairly accurately what needs to be done for it to receive credit.

Detractors from this system sometimes claim that Cr–NCr variations result in a lowering of standards, promoting *quantity* over *quality* or accepting the mediocre. I claim that, to the contrary, Cr–NCr raises standards, for, in essence, it eliminates the "gentleman C." One can structure such a system so that mediocre work is simply not accepted, not credited. Conventional grading, with its willingness to dish out D's and F's, can make no such claim to high standards.

Contract and Achievement Grading–Point Systems

I first learned about contract grading when I was a high school teacher in the early 1970s, when, incidentally, concerns about the negative effects of grading were gaining national attention in the profession. In contract grading, the student, with guidance from the teacher and within the requirements of the class or course, essentially proposes what he or she will do to earn a C, B, or A. The contract usually contains provisions for the amount of work to be completed, the criteria for acceptance or success, and a timetable for completion. A contract could be written for an individual assignment or for an entire course, class, or semester. The student submits a proposal for a contract, the teacher may ask for modifications, and eventually the teacher and student work out an agreement. A generic sample contract is shown in Figure 11.2.

For me, contract grading solves a great many traditional problems associated with the grading system. Students are involved in assessing their own aims and goals right from the start, and the student gains a sense of control over his or her work. Most important and salutary, in my opinion, is that contracts, sometimes almost magically, put student and teacher on the same side of the grading fence. Once a contract has been signed, the teacher steps out of the judge-and-jury role and becomes a coach–helper. The teacher's goal then becomes helping the student

To the student: As we discussed in class, you can control the grade you earn on this project. Completing the basic requirement, on time, with careful quality work pretty much guarantees you a C. If you choose to put in additional effort—to write more, to read more, to add elements beyond the basic requirements—you can earn a B or an A. If you decide to go for a higher grade, you'll need to describe your additional work. The blanks in the form below allow you to create a proposal for your grade. I will review this proposal, perhaps suggest alterations, and, once we've agreed, this becomes your contract. If you complete it, you will have well earned your grade. If you think you are going to fall short, let's talk.

1. **Aims of the project.** Briefly outline what you plan to do and why. Give me a working title for the project and explain what the project entails and why you are interested in it.

2. **Grade.** You can opt for a C, B, or A, the latter two being optional.

[   ] For a grade of C, I propose to do the following:

[   ] In addition, for a B, I propose:

[   ] And going all the way for an A, I would, in addition, do:

3. **Timetable.** List the stages of your project and when you will submit drafts, revisions, and final copy.

Student signature: _____

4. **Instructor reply:**

[   ] Accepted as is.

[   ] Accepted with the following modifications.

[   ] Not yet acceptable. Please see me for a conference.

Teacher signature: _____

FIGURE 11.2   A Generic Contract Grading Form

successfully negotiate the contract by providing whatever help is necessary to earn the selected grade.

No grading system is perfect, and that includes contracts. One drawback is the dilemma a teacher faces if the student chooses to work on a low grade. What if Charles says all he wants is a C out of the course? A student-centered teacher, it seems to me, will want to argue Charles out of that choice, to have him work for a B or an A. Students often earn high grades under contracts! Charles, who may never have earned an A in his life in language arts, is suddenly in a position to earn that grade, since everybody in the class is invited to write an A contract. Straight A averages, or very high averages, may be frowned on by some administrators, but I personally regard them as a sign of successful teaching. If the contracts are legitimate and the students meet them, the A's and B's are deserved.

Another, more serious problem is that sometimes contract grading requires an expertise on the part of the students that is beyond them. A student who is not yet an accomplished writer often has difficulties identifying needed areas of growth and may have considerable problems identifying criteria for success. When I use contracts, I often find students writing things like this: "I don't know how to judge the success of this project, but you and I will know when it's done, I guess." The student has a point, I think; and thus I moved in my own teaching to a variation of contracting that I call achievement grading: I take more responsibility for blocking out requirements and criteria, but encourage students to increasingly take individual initiative to earn higher grades. Indeed, the criteria for higher grades *become* the students' ability to move out on their own.

In achievement grading, I block out a set of minimum or basic requirements for a class or course; such requirements may be linked to state or district curriculum or standards, in fact. A generic achievement grading form is given in Figure 11.3. Typically, to earn a C, a student must attend regularly, participate actively, turn in most assignments on time (I usually give students a "wild-card" late paper), complete certain self-assessments, and possibly pass a final examination or final writing. The B often requires regular commitment to course-related activities over time; frequently for my classes, this will involve keeping a logbook, journal, or notebook throughout the term. The A calls for an independent study or research project, something that shows that the student can apply concepts from the course in new areas. I'm pretty comfortable with these criteria. Compare the typical meaning of grades with those in an achievement system:

Grade	Traditional	Achievement
C	Average	Completes minimum
B	Above average	Consistent work beyond minimum
A	Way above average	Independent and creative work

Achievement grading, for me, relieves some of the ambiguity of contracts while still pushing for the same goals: encouraging students to set their own goals, providing

Grading for this class is done on an achievement system in which the more high-quality work you do, the higher your grade. All work for the course is thus "graded" Credit–No Credit. If the work is well done it is Credited; if I do not feel it is up to quality standards, I will mark it No Credit. All NCr work may be redone until it is fully credited.

For an Achievement Grade of C:

1. Attend class regularly (no more than x unexcused absences).
2. Participate actively in class activities (if I think you're not participating, I'll notify you).
3. Complete all readings and note taking as outlined in the course syllabus.
4. Complete the assigned drafts and final copies of papers as shown in the syllabus.
5. Compile your work in a midterm and final portfolio.
6. Create an introduction to your portfolio explaining what it contains and what it demonstrates of your skills.

To earn the C, your work must be good enough to demonstrate that you have achieved the basic course goals as outlined in the syllabus.

For an Achievement Grade of B:

Complete a term-long project for which you collect materials related to our topic and write thoughtful commentaries at least twice a week. You can clip newspaper and magazine articles, write about television shows, interview people, visit museums, etc. In your writing, you'll need to explain how these materials relate to our course topic. Turn in your materials every week (except two; you can take two one-week holidays). Save all your materials in a loose-leaf binder. At the end of the term, your binder will be on display with those of others who have elected this option.

To earn the B, your work must be consistent and steady, and it must demonstrate that you've been willing to go beyond the minimum expectations for the course in some depth.

For an Achievement Grade of A:

Do an independent study project that shows you can take the ideas you've learned in this course and apply them in a new or fresh situation. There are lots of possibilities for this project. For example, you could

- Read additional books by the authors we're studying and write a series of reports.
- Read a couple of books by one of these authors, read his or her autobiography, and write a paper connecting the life with the writer.
- Write poems! How many poems? Enough. Let's discuss your plans.

FIGURE 11.3   A Generic Achievement Grading Description

- Write short stories or short plays.
- Go online on the web and research a topic of interest, or create your own web site.

The A-project is open to anybody in the course, and I expect that everybody here is capable of earning the A if he or she wants to put in the time. High-quality work is expected, not a project thrown together in haste to raise your grade. To propose a project, submit a proposal that includes the following parts:

- Working title.
- Brief description of the project.
- Your aims and goals, explaining what you want to learn.
- Discussion of why you think the project is appropriate to this class.
- Timetable for your work.
- Criteria for evaluation: How will you and I know you have completed the project successfully and well?

FIGURE 11.3   Continued

opportunity for individual initiative, and changing the role of the teacher from judge to mentor.

In a sense, these grading systems reward quantity, and I tell that to my students: The more you do, the higher the grade. Some critics have argued that the mere quantity of the system plays into the hands of students who are the most diligent, the drones who have been well trained in the teacher-centered ways of conventional schooling, who are good boys and girls and shoot for the top. I grant that concern, but counterargue that the system also opens up opportunities for A-earning by the students who have never been diligent.

It is also extremely important to emphasize that the work done under an achievement grading system must be high in quality; this is not a matter of simply cranking out assignments. Although the teacher in these systems is primarily a mentor, at times he or she must be a traditional judge and turn back work, saying "No, this simply isn't good enough. This is not creditable." However, in contrast to traditional systems in which such work would simply earn a D or an F, in contract–achievement grading the teacher can supply specific information about what must be done to bring the work up to snuff; it then is left to the student to determine whether he or she wants to make the effort.

Mere quantity may be the problem with one variation of these systems that I'll mention just briefly: point systems. In this scheme, students get fixed amounts of points for doing things: showing up for class, participating in a discussion, reading a book, writing a paper, and so on. Teachers identify the points associated with various projects and the students have at it. Some projects may still be required in a class, say a certain number of papers or journal entries or books read. Optional projects for various kinds of points are offered for additional work. The points add up and students earn grades according to a predetermined scale; for example, if the teacher likes the "lots of points" concept, 1 million points might be good for a C, 2 million for a B, and so on. With experience, teachers learn to adjust the ranges so that the distribution of grades is appropriate.

The drawback to this system is simply that students sometimes become obsessed with points. "How many points for a B?" "Can I get double points for a long book?" "What if I write 750 words instead of 500?" With time, teachers can figure out ways of solving these problems, and, in my experience, any contract–achievement point system needs to be accompanied by a set of ground rules that clarify the teacher's position on common questions and anticipate possible misuses of the system.

Portfolio Assessment–Grading

In a sense, the portfolio is *not* parallel to the previous three categories, which are concerned with ways of stating criteria and arriving at grades. The portfolio is a way of collecting data; it can be used with any of the systems described above: students can present a portfolio or collection of their work that has been graded by a rubric; they can collect all their creditable or passed work in the portfolio in support of their grade; they can use a portfolio to demonstrate that they've accumulated sufficient points to earn a particular grade.

As I use it, the portfolio starts out as a file folder: "Save *everything*," I tell my students. "Save every scrap of paper you generate for this course." At various points in a class or course, the students then winnow out extraneous material, and the portfolio becomes a demonstration of their work. It might contain drafts, revisions, and final copies, depending on the teachers' priorities. A portfolio can also go beyond *paper* records: Students might submit audio- or videotapes, photographs, even artifacts that they create as part of their work, for example, a photograph of a city park renewed by a community service initiative. A portfolio will also contain a good deal of self-evaluation by the students (recall the emphasis on self-evaluation in the first half of this chapter).

Many teachers (I am not among them) have developed the practice of *grading* the entire portfolio as an alternative to placing individual letter grades on individual papers. Students do not receive grades on work throughout the marking period, and teachers conduct, say, a midterm and final portfolio grading. For such an enterprise, we can develop a grading guideline that reflects both quantity and quality of the work required for the course. In general, grading across a portfolio is more productive than individual paper grading because, once again, the discussion can be on growth and development, rather than on the strengths and weaknesses of individual artifacts.

My own decision not to use portfolio *grading* is based on two principal reservations: First, I'm skeptical of having grades deferred over a long period of time. Too often, such a practice simply heightens grade anxiety and, instead of moving the teacher out of the judge-and-jury role, merely raises the judge's bench a few meters higher. My preference for contract and achievement grading, as noted, is that students know exactly what's required for a specific grade at the very beginning.

Second, student self-evaluation is considerably more productive and even sincere when it involves assessing the contents of a portfolio rather than putting materials together in support of a grade.

While acknowledging, then, the success of grading portfolios, I much prefer to make the portfolio a demonstration of achievement, rather than an appeal to a judge.

The Perfect Grading System

In a sense, this chapter has been a narrative rather than an essay. Although some of the story line has been masked under the appearance of exposition, my generalizations and classroom illustrations, by and large, grow out of personal struggles with the grading game. I don't suppose or propose that any teacher would want to adopt my strategies without careful consideration of their implications, especially their links to an overarching pedagogy. Assessment must, in fact, reflect what we articulate as a philosophy of teaching. I must also add that the stories of my own grading games have not ended; not a term or course goes by that I don't struggle with the elements of the grading system, making efforts to link payoff for students with the aims of my teaching, trying to minimize the negative effects of the grading, while acknowledging its reality in systems where I teach. I frankly don't expect to ever win the grading game. I don't expect I'll ever find the perfect grading system. But if you do, for heaven's sake, please drop me a line and tell me how it works.

REFERENCES AND RESOURCES

Atwell, Nancie. *In the Middle: Writing, Reading, and Learning with Adolescents.* Portsmouth, NH: Boynton/Cook, 1987.

Black, Laurel, Donald Dalker, Jeffrey Sommers, and Gail Stygall. *New Directions in Portfolio Assessment.* Portsmouth, NH: Boynton/Cook, 1994.

Cambourne, Brian, and Jan Turbill. *Responsive Evaluation.* Portsmouth, NH: Heinemann, 1994.

Elbow, Peter. *Writing without Teachers.* New York: Oxford University Press, 1973.

Graves, Donald, and Bonnie S. Suntein, Eds. *Portfolio Portraits.* Portsmouth, NH: Heinemann, 1994.

Hillocks, George. *Teaching Writing as Reflective Practice.* New York: Teachers College Press, 1995.

Jackson, David. *Continuity in Secondary Education.* London: Methuen, 1982.

Morris, Paul, and Stephen Tchudi. *The New Literacy.* San Francisco: Jossey/Bass, 1996; Calendar Islands Press, 1998.

Tchudi, Stephen, Ed. *Alternatives to Grading Student Writing.* Urbana, IL: National Council of Teachers of English, 1996.

———. *Planning and Assessing the English Language Arts.* Alexandria, VA: Association for Supervision and Curriculum Development, 1989.

White, Edward. *Teaching and Assessing Writing.* San Francisco: Jossey/Bass, 1994.

12 When Coaching Is Teacher to Teacher: The Collegial Journal

TERESA BERNDT AND DONNA FISHER

Teresa Berndt and Donna Fisher are middle and high school English teachers who are "right there, right now." They address the teacher of writing and the preservice teacher of writing, sharing their own powerful discovery of the collegial journal. The style of the chapter, then, varies a bit from the other chapters, which present teaching strategies aimed at students; Berndt and Fisher present strategies for the writing *teacher*. They capitalize on writing's powerful quality of reflection, and they convincingly and skillfully guide readers to use writing, particularly the naturally self-reflective nature of journal writing, to address all the issues facing teachers of writing.

Berndt and Fisher have a strong message: Without caring for the "I" who is teacher, we cannot educate the "Thou" who is learner. Their ongoing journal experiment began from the time when Berndt was a student teacher and Fisher was her mentor; thus, preservice teachers, as so many of mine have discovered, are an audience who will find this chapter a "must read."

The Journey

When Teresa Berndt responded with candor and enthusiasm to an invitation to journal with her cooperating teacher Donna Fisher, neither realized that a routine preservice experiment could become an enriching and permanent professional tool for both of them. Now six years into their journey together, Donna Fisher, a 20-year veteran of high school classrooms, and Teresa, now a middle school teacher in the same district, urge other teachers to adopt the colleague journal as a means of praxis reflection on their own work as teachers of writing.

They use their journals year round for many purposes:

- "Big picture" reflection about the teaching profession and their own growth as writers

- A vehicle through which to vent about and to celebrate their experiences
- A professional, practical, and personal means to energize their teaching lives

Professional journals Donna read underlined the need for openness between student teacher and mentor. Absorbed in her own students, Donna feared Teresa's need for reflective conversation might get lost in her harried schedule. Furthermore, she knew some questions and opinions might be easier for Teresa to ask on paper than to offer face to face. Donna suggested a journal as a way to manage the difficult questions, feedback, and observation. Journaling built intentional sharing into their relationship.

In a little "welcome to teaching" journal, Donna wrote this entry to Teresa:

> Will I be able to show you what you need to know, to offer just the right mix of counsel, challenge, and comfort? For you: question, search, push, try, and especially fail now and then so you'll know that's OK, too. For me: watch, listen, and let go—and especially, take the opportunity to reflect and study. For us: let's keep a record in this journal; you get to keep it when the journey's ended. Welcome to my precious turf, Teresa. I'm opening my hand and offering to share what I love—my kids and my vocation.

Teresa responded to the journaling invitation with eagerness. In the journal she struggled with scope and sequence, coped with students' failing grades, and battled publication deadlines and spring-break mania. Her questioning encompassed individual lessons and particular students; queries also involved observations about issues of personal privacy and administrative policy. Donna saw opportunities for teachable moments, framed as questions, but with space to allow for cool down and breath catching before she responded in her role as cooperating teacher. Already the dynamics of their partnership had begun to change. Donna wrote as follows:

> I want to let you know how much I appreciate the freshness, vulnerability and honesty with which you approach both this journal and your teaching experiences. Those qualities will be your best tools because they'll help you make the strong human connections so essential in teaching. I feel a little guilty that I've pushed you into such deep water, but when I see how strongly you swim through it, I'm really optimistic about your successes as a teacher. Now we move from student–teacher to apprentice–mentor!

Parker Palmer in *The Courage to Teach* affirms that "Mentoring is a mutuality that requires more than meeting the right teacher: the teacher must meet the right student" (21). Almost from the beginning, this match felt right. However, what neither Donna nor Teresa expected was the power of the journal to make connections about practice not only in the teaching process they shared, but also within themselves. Clearly, both veteran and mentee must feel comfortable with such an evolving relationship in print.

Wincing a bit about the toll her own consuming commitment to her work might be making on her young colleague, Donna made discoveries about her own teaching in Teresa's observations:

> When I first started student teaching I thought, Wow! This woman never gets tired, never gets upset, can deal with anything no matter what and it never phases her at all. I'll never be like this, is what I said to myself. I felt intimidated by your abilities to handle it all—I realize that you can deal with tons of things at once, but I've seen the way it does affect you. I'm still impressed with the way you handle situations and the great way you phrase your responses. I admire those qualities but have come to the conclusion that even the awesome Mrs. Fisher has limits too. That makes me feel better about my downfalls.

By this point, honesty and even vulnerability were essential components in the success of their experiment. Donna felt comfortable in acknowledging weak spots:

> I chuckled with the "do-it-all" observation and my legendary energy. Remember that you don't see me come home and collapse into zombiedom. I'm not sure energy relates to getting lots of work done either. I know quiet, deliberate people who accomplish loads of work. Even energy is a matter of style and each person must work and move at the pace which feels right. I do believe, however, that usually an energetic teacher is able to transfer that energy to the students she works with. For sure the lethargic teacher will be an energy sapper, not an energy giver.

As her college graduation approached, Teresa measured the value of the collegial journal:

> The journals are the most memorable for me. If we hadn't taken the time then, [the experiences] would be forgotten by now and the learning opportunity would have been missed.

When Teresa's student teaching ended, both agreed they wanted the journaling to continue. Teresa's being hired as a teacher in the district's middle school made the exchange of journals easier.

Convinced now that their journal was an essential professional development tool, they continued to write throughout the summer. Donna, particularly, experienced the push from an energetic young colleague who read professional journals regularly, "You can't possibly imagine what a boost this is . . . I really appreciate your snagging articles and sending them my way." A few months later, she wrote again about reflection:

> So few take time to reflect with each other. And so rarely do our supervisors genuinely remind us [of] the incredible difference we can make in a child's life. I've got you, Girl! Am I glad! How blessed I am at this stage in my teaching career to have an energetic colleague I respect and admire as a partner in this venture of praxis.

The journal had evolved into a working tool by which two professionals examined not only their own writing curriculum, but also explored ideas to influence colleagues inside and beyond their departments. Both, however, continued to share triumphs and frustrations.

Rationale: Why Journal?

> After three decades of trying to learn the craft, every class comes down to this: My students and I, face to face, engaged in an ancient and exacting exchange called education. The techniques I have mastered do not disappear . . . , but neither do they suffice. Face to face with my students, only one resource is at my immediate command: my identity, my selfhood, my sense of the "I" who teaches—without which I have no sense of the "Thou" who learns (Palmer 10).

When Palmer Parker's *The Courage to Teach* was published in 1998, his words gave professional and philosophical validity to what we had experienced through the journal for more than 4 years. Palmer's words suggest both a warning and an invitation. For eleven chapters this book, *Winning Ways of Coaching Writing*, has offered invaluable content, tools, and techniques. But we argue from our own experience that Palmer speaks the truth and that, for us at least, we cannot teach without the process of understanding the "I" who teaches. The collegial journal offers both the new teacher and the master teacher a place of continuing exploration of the "I" who teaches.

As praxis, as a safe place to vent and celebrate, as a buffer against the loneliness and isolation inherent in the teaching profession, this collegial journal is a lifeline. Teresa concluded

> In five years I've learned a ton through reading professional magazines and attending conferences, but I still feel so lost in so many areas. Without the journal, I truly wouldn't have made it. I'd be like the new teachers still struggling or out of the field by now.

The journal forces praxis (reflecting on practice) and provides both method and energy for continuing good practice. Our why, how, and what if discussions not only clarify instructional purpose, but also enrich methods for our students, who differ widely in intellectual and social maturity.

Although the early years of teaching writing can be both exciting and intimidating times, veteran teachers will continue to struggle with fears and questions. Because writing with our students and the intimacy of the writing process in general are so risky, perhaps such fears and questions are natural for both veteran and novice teachers. Being able to place these fears and questions on the page allows us the opportunity to know where we need to focus. The daily rush of teaching becomes a fierce reality for us. The journal forces us to slow the pace long enough to use this reflective tool.

Jim Burke, in *The English Teacher's Companion,* calls writing

> an activity that forces thought: You cannot write without thinking, for to arrange language into meaningful units . . . is to use the mind. True, we might not be conscious of our thinking . . . however one reason for using writing to think is precisely to bring the unconscious more to the surface, where we can "see what we have to say" (140).

In journaling, each teacher captures both the triumphs and disappointments so often lost in the daily rush of teaching writing. The trust between journal partners allows each teacher to examine the feeling of the moment by telling her journaling partner. Again Palmer's words in *The Courage to Teach* strike sparks of recognition: "We must talk to each other about our inner lives—risky stuff in a profession that fears the personal and seeks safety in the technical, the distant, the abstract" (12).

When a first-year teacher realizes that teaching is often accomplished in isolation, the mentor journal can be an antidote for feelings of aloneness. Like so many new teachers, Teresa realized how isolated she felt from colleagues, and she turned to the journal to reflect on those feelings:

> I guess the hardest part is that I feel so alone. I feel like I'm winging it. I'm the new kid and I'm walking on tiptoes for awhile till I know whom I can and can't trust.

On hectic days with no time to converse, the journal provides access to each other. The journal "create(s) interactions in which two minds can unite to bring about new understanding, new ideas, new possibilities. A dialogue means continuity of discussion, until the meaning of a topic has been worked out; dialogue means unpredictability and novelty . . . " (Staton 54).

For the preservice teacher, for his or her cooperating teacher, for the English methods instructor, and for education departments, the collegial journal offers these benefits:

- Practical and intensely personal ways to influence a new generation of teachers
- An energizing vehicle for teaching veterans who must encounter new tools and theories
- An interactive platform for professional partnering

If the preservice process does not require a collegial journal, the student teacher may want to invite the cooperating teacher to try it as an experiment.

Clearly, the professional commitment we made to each other changed both of us. Not all veteran teachers believe that working with student teachers or new teachers is a way to touch the future. Some view it as a burden requiring time without increased pay. Those veteran teachers that do believe in working with the "new kid on the block" not only assist the future of education, but find ways to rejuvenate their own teaching in the process (Weinheimer 66).

The *English Journal* dedicated the entire September 1996 issue to veteran teachers and their advice. "Ten Tips to Keeping Your Teaching Life Energized" recommends supervising a student teacher or mentoring a new teacher in the building. New teachers will let "you see yourself as you were when you began your teaching career—idealistic, happy, optimistic, and full of the belief that you can make a difference . . . and to realize that passing the baton to the new generation is part of life" (27).

Veteran cooperating teachers, take note! Rose Weinheimer's advice in her *English Journal* article is to "hang out with the new kids on the block [because] they have their thumbs on the pulse of new educational theories and practices and always have the most refreshing outlooks. . . . Sharing with them keeps me vital and prevents cobwebs from settling in" (66). Recognizing that others can change their points of view, challenge belief systems, and justify methods makes one a stronger educator.

The chance to "dance" with a partner to the music of shared reflective writing gives every teacher of writing a powerful advantage. Through our journals, we illustrate what Parker Palmer affirms in *The Courage to Teach:*

> Mentors and apprentices are partners in an ancient human dance, and one of teaching's great rewards is the daily chance it gives us to get back on the dance floor. It is the dance of the spiraling generations, in which the old empower the young with their experience and the young empower the old with new life, reweaving the fabric of the human community as they touch and turn" (25).

The journal "is designed to create interactions in which two minds can unite to bring about new understandings, new ideas, new possibilities . . . " (Stanton 54). Our journal transforms our lives. Not only does it provide us with a place to reflect, but it also provides us with a place to grow both personally and professionally.

We encourage other teachers to commit time to journaling with a colleague across the hall, with a student teacher, or with a former teacher that touched one's life. Journaling changed our lives: it has the potential to do the same thing for you.

Before we move to excerpts from our journals as models of the larger purposes of the collegial journal ("big picture" reflecting, venting and celebrating, and energizing), let us discuss what journaling is not. Hear us offer warnings about the pitfalls we experienced. Learn several options for finding colleagues with whom to journal, and discover practical suggestions for topics to write about.

What Journaling Is Not

While the journal may be therapeutic, using it as a counseling tool may not be wise. We consciously limit our journal to experiences and issues of our teaching lives—Palmer's "I" of teaching—not the counseling-type issues like family identity. We learned to keep it professional.

Our journal is not an organized idea file, although we often use the journal to trade ideas about resources, choice quotes from professional reading, or questions about methods. What gives the journal its true value, however, comes from its reflections—our "teaching" hearts and souls on paper—not from its listing of resources and methods.

Using it as a record of routine memos, as a notebook of lesson plans, as formal instruction or evaluation—all these will change the collegial nature of the journal. Obviously, these kinds of materials will be shared frequently between colleagues, between the preservice teacher and mentor, but the journal is not the place for such an exchange.

Pitfalls Exist; So Beware

Writing in the journal has one big obstacle and that is *time*. When we committed to the student teaching journal, we knew that it required dedication to write or to respond daily. Indeed, the entry dates showed that "daily" did not always happen. However, we learned that we must correspond at least a couple of times a week. And the benefits from these entries far outweigh the time invested.

Once our relationship moved to colleague–colleague, time devoured opportunity. Daily entries turned into weekly, then biweekly, and sometimes only monthly, but we, believing in the value of the entries, compiled lists of interesting items to be written about in the journal. Phone conversations become another culprit to our journal's continuity. Calls sometimes ended with "Stop right now! Go write this in the journal. It's good stuff we've gotta have!" We learned that writing forced a kind of reflective practice that telephone conversations did not accomplish.

After being invited to present our journal project at the South Dakota Council of Teachers of English state convention, we began to reread the early journals. We discovered we could not use the quotes we'd shared because we had failed to record page numbers or titles. Although our journals still had great personal value, our shoddy documentation limited their professional use. We learned to document.

Moving some of the written conversation into cyber space, Teresa joined Donna on e-mail. When Donna questioned the "seduction of e-mail" and its lack of reflection, Teresa agreed. Distance from the moments of planning, teaching, writing, and reading student work emerged as important to genuine praxis. What evolved was combining pen and paper journaling with printing out and saving significant e-mail dialogue.

Discussions included departmental or district policies involving what and how writing was really being taught among our English colleagues. We realized that using school e-mail to exchange journal entries might have been naïve. If our confidential exchange had been read by someone whose trust we did not share, these private reflections might have damaged relationships. We wrote because we needed to discover what we really believed. Our views, however professional they might have been, were not yet ready for public airing. We learned that we needed a secure method of journal exchange.

With Whom Might I Journal?

Many settings lend themselves to the collegial journal model. We suggest these, but your personal as well as professional situations may inspire other models. Get a journal and invite someone to join you. If you don't like the J-word, see Chapter 5 for alternative labels.

Student Teacher–Mentor

Student teachers might persuade cooperating teachers to participate in a journaling experience. Try these topics to prompt discussion and eavesdrop on our early dialogue.

■ *What do I grade on writing projects and why?* Grading is teaching, Donna reminded Teresa:

> Know why you're marking something, or look it up when you're not sure. One secret is to focus on certain kinds of errors, telling students that you won't claim to catch everything. Don't be afraid to admit an error, but keep pushing yourself on mechanics. You ask about the balance between mechanics, content, and style—for us there is no balance because I believe we should know it all. You'll notice that while I emphasize that content/organization/evidence are primary, I also suggest that solid mechanics are a given—basic to good writing anywhere, anytime. "A" papers must have great mechanics, but great mechanics alone do not ensure the "A."

■ *How do I manage the paper load?* Donna responded with ideas from business:

> Borrow Stephanie Winston's *Getting Organized* from a library and snoop for ideas. It's not the newest thing but her TRAF (Trash, Read, Action, File) is a model I use—sort of! I need to do more trash and less read and file though. Shut up! You're laughing already and I can hear it. Ok, so I'm under a grand delusion that I'm semi-organized, but isn't it rude to laugh out loud?

■ *What's the difference between doing writing and teaching writing?* After her first round of grading major compositions, Teresa turned to the journal in a panic. Having considered herself a fairly skilled writer, she discovered the gap between doing and teaching writing. She felt stupid, she said. Donna wrote

> Keep that feeling and use it to motivate yourself every time you prepare to teach. However, I remember feeling incredibly stupid, especially about the fine points of grammar and usage. Live with the stylebook and memorize William Safire's *Fumblerules* and Strunk and White's *Elements of Style....* The only caveat I have on grammar is to practice and prepare, ensuring that you know the concepts you're explaining before you face the class. For example, you'll want to thoroughly prepare for Daily Oral Language because each sentence covers many grammar and usage possibilities.

Cooperating teachers might request a journaling experience for their student teacher's benefit as well as their own. Consider sharing some of these more philosophical issues:

■ *Should I teach?* Teresa's early questions reflect student teacher angst:

> I'm trying to decide whether to apply for a teaching job or try for another English career. What do I really want to do? What can I handle? One day I love to teach, the next day—never! This personal struggle weighs heavily on me at times. Can I do the job I want to do as a teacher? There is so much I don't know.

With years of experience and a love of teaching, Donna's words reached out from the pages of the journal:

> I'm glad that you're wrestling with these feelings now. You'll make a good decision if you choose teaching. All those gifts and graces—determination, stamina, enthusiasm, courage—you have already. Both skills and knowledge will continue to grow from experience. But there is one key question to ask yourself: Is the act of teaching, the interaction with kids basically nourishing—"feeding" for your spirit or is it strength-sapping, draining? I don't mean whether you get tired or discouraged or even angry or just plain bummed. You've surely seen me in all those circumstances. But somehow being with the kids is energizing and exciting and worth it all. If this isn't true, don't teach.
>
> Most of us, who are "born" teachers, teach in our sleep, teach everything to somebody else the minute we learn it, and learn always so that we can teach something more. We didn't choose teaching; it chose us. We're addicts. If you can STOP teaching, then you can be just as happy and considerably less stressed doing something else. If secretly you absolutely love seeing someone else take your bit of knowledge and make it his or her own, then teach!

College programs should be encouraged to incorporate the collegial journal into the student teaching experience. Department members might consider questions like these:

■ *What written products will build effective bonds between the student teachers and mentors? How does the collegial journal differ from the personal journal?* With a new round of student observers visiting in both Donna's and Teresa's classes, their journal entries turned to preservice preparation for teachers of writing. Donna wrote

> The college still doesn't get it that real observation takes time. All secondary preservice teachers get is a hint of what might be happening. Then sadly, what they bring to their own teaching are only the ways they themselves were taught. Times are a-changing, the demands are huge and if [these pre-service students] want "in,"

then give US the time! The "hell" they call observing cannot compare to the "hell" of Year One if a new teacher has no foundation.

Colleague to Colleague across Buildings and within Departments

Writing provides ongoing discussion based on reflection responses from daily situations. Talking cannot provide the same reflective tool that a written response offers. Try an exchange of questions like some of these:

■ *May I steal resources from other teachers . . . or let's call it pirating.* After a busy first year in the classroom, Teresa wondered about using the ideas and materials of other teachers:

> I feel like I'm stealing from everyone. As a new teacher overwhelmed by everything, it's hard because I need time to research all the things I'd like to do. I've got some great ideas from you and many from the magazines I subscribe to, but I always feel that somehow I need to make them mine yet. I can't wait until summer so that I can spend time revamping things I've already done.

Donna agreed.

> Steal girl, it's the mark of an open and collaborative style. Just because *you're* teaching the idea, you'll be making it yours. Also if we didn't "steal," why would anyone publish?

■ *What do I do with so many teaching ideas to choose from?* An enthusiastic innovator, Teresa bewailed how to choose from among the possibilities. Sometimes a journaling partner will only respond with more questions. Donna wrote

> I suspect it's the curse of the information era, so many possibilities for doing, thinking, reading, resourcing, and even fewer minutes to process them. I'm not good at selectivity. With so much new stuff to learn, how do I make good choices for what really counts? It's certainly the dilemma of teaching—boy, it was easier and I felt less guilt-ridden when I let the textbook publishers make those decisions for me.

Journaling provides links within the department and from an elementary or middle high level to secondary level and beyond. Experiment with questions about scope and sequence:

■ *What writing-researching skill must be mastered and when?* Using the journal, both teachers described research unit plans and discussed outcomes. Teresa listened as Donna mourned the lack of information integration skills in her juniors. In response, Teresa began to expand her curriculum beyond paragraph writing and nominal research because of what she'd learned about performance expectations in high school. Teresa wrote

> Library research and writing will be done and I'd like to try a mini-manual for order and instruction concepts. I'm not talking three page essays, but if they don't learn it now, they'll be lost in 9th grade. . . . I want to do a very short tech type paper on career interests. Only facts and information, no opinion really, but how do you research without note cards? It frustrates me that we don't teach library or research skills until they're in high school; by 11th or 12th grade, they get so upset by the mechanics and steps that they don't get to enjoy the research.

Introducing a substantial eighth grade research unit was a triumph for Teresa:

> The kids have done better than I had anticipated with bibliography and note cards. Notes are still confusing, but we did an exercise that I hope helped them to think of categories that go together and the format style. I'm proud of their progress for the first time being exposed. Why do we underestimate the power of these children? Teach them all things while they're still excited about learning because down the road they may go into shutdown and then it's too late.

■ *How can we be "on the same page" within our department?* Our journals discussed the importance of using rubrics for both large and small projects, while developing more global expectations for the year as a whole. Teresa wrote

> [My principal] paid me a nice compliment. She said the strong point I have is that I know where I'm going with my lessons and am able to do a better assessment because I have my goals and expectations established early on. It comes in handy to know where you're going in teaching.

Donna affirmed this broad perspective:

> As for global vs. specific in lessons you need both. The standard, the benchmark, the specific target, teaming with other disciplines—Yes! Knowledge integrated becomes understanding and, maybe some day, wisdom.

Professional: District to District

Journaling can provide continued dialogue between teachers in the same district or from a secondary to university level. Discipline-wide issues fit perfectly into partnering through journals because perspective beyond one's department becomes essential. Pose questions like these:

■ *Do we have a consistent language arts curriculum within our district and across our state? How are state-mandated writing assessments going to affect my classroom and yours?* In South Dakota statewide writing assessment in grades 5 and 9 was mandated about the same time that state universities began implementing language proficiency testing. Students needed to be able to respond fluently and quickly to writing prompts. Teresa discovered that her students had been taught very structured paragraph writing in relation to their reading:

> This would explain the difficulty I encounter with eighth graders being able to think and write on their own. I allow some freedom in what they're writing on and then have structured projects too. I follow [Nancie] Atwell's philosophy of letting them write what's interesting to them. However, if the writing process isn't focused upon in all grades 4–7 below, it is no wonder then why they struggle in my class with multiple paragraphs and creative thoughts. I'm not trying to pass the buck, but feel we need a more consistent writing program.

■ *How can we help students do well in mandated assessments? Must we teach to the test?* As the teaching community buzzed over our governor's involvement in state and national content standards, our journal reflected frustration surrounding language arts implementation. Donna had been a member of the language arts standards writing in its first phase. She worried on paper about forced implementation, yet sounded cynical about teachers being willing to change curriculum to what the standards demanded:

> Time is the issue. "We DO that!" is the cry. To implement standards seriously, we need time and a facilitator who will make us tell HOW we do it! I know, for example, I am not teaching persuasion/argumentation as well as I once did. I am doing a better job on literary analysis which colleges scream for in Freshman English. Solution— persuasion/argumentation forms could be taught thoroughly in sophomore speech—yeah, right!

Teresa described her own fears about losing the vision:

> Our greatest [fear] is will teachers begin to teach to the test to keep their jobs and show high scores. Will everyone need to teach the same then to meet the test questions? Those who choose to bury their heads about standards are going to have a huge awakening. They think it will all pass and they can teach as always, but I don't see that being the case.

Journaling on Paper Won't Work? Try This . . .

- Join an online discussion group or listserv. The National Council of Teachers of English offers a variety of online discussions, as do your state's writing project, the National Writing Project, the U.S. Department of Education, and state and teacher organizations.
- Start an electronic journal with teachers you meet at conferences and in university courses.

Warning: If you are using a written journal and an e-mail journal, remember that e-mail can be a seductress. The immediate feedback is tempting, but it may detract from the actual thought-provoking written entries.

Why Does the Collegial Journal Enrich the "I" Who Teaches?

- It forces big picture reflection about the teaching profession and our own growth as writers.
- It provides a vehicle through which to vent and to celebrate.
- It offers a professional and personal means to energize our teaching lives.

"Keep your eyes on the prize" makes a great mantra for teachers of writing, but to focus successfully on the big picture in the hurly-burly of a real classroom requires experience, support, and miracles! Years of journaling nurture the habit of reflection about our writing curriculum. Our journals show movement from mundane details toward pedagogically significant discussions of content and sequence, assessment, and mandated standards. Through, and perhaps because of, our journaling discipline, we are forced into skills both for ourselves and for our students. Donna wrote the following:

> The best thing I do for myself at year's end is asking kids to write me letters answering these three questions: What did I do that made learning more difficult? What did I do that made learning more effective for you? What suggestions do you have for making this class better? Many sense the integration concept and the goals of preparation for school and work. Many have learned some things about themselves. More than a few say things that bring misty eyes and caught breath. And two or three scare me because I realize I might just have made a critical difference by the smallest comment or word of encouragement. We truly do touch the future, Girl, in ways we can't possibly know. I think it's important to give students some way of telling us how our teaching has affected them because we need to be energized for a new group of students.

Although no strangers to the writing public, both Donna and Teresa had become involved in a variety of writing experiences. Teresa found new confidence and incentive through the Dakota Writing Project. She wrote the following:

> This summer has been so good for me—at times very stressful, but outstanding for me on a personal and professional level. Realizing that I can sit down and produce stories, poems, quick writes, etc., was very exciting. I'm setting my goal to really sit down and write with my kids, share my stuff and let them rip it apart as well. I've kept copies of the revisions I've done and want to show kids that writing is hard work and never seems to be just the way you want it.

With another English teacher in another community, Donna wrote a State Humanities Council grant to research and produce a state literary map and accompanying web site. Contracts, proposals, and funding requests, plus the actual copy on the map and web site, meant that her writing was exceptionally public, clearly modeling for her students the vulnerability and risks of the publishing process. For the fifth season, she created an Elizabethan-style script, partly in blank verse, for a "town and gown" holiday madrigal, another highly public venture. Donna wrote the following:

> It occurs to me that all of these "authentic" writing experiences give me credibility with my students that teachers who aren't writing "in the real world" may not have. What do you think? I'm so pleased that DWP renewed your "for public view" writing confidence. Publishing—that final stage in that writing process list we put on posters all around the room—is frightening for English teacher types like me. We slap grades on things playing the comfortable role of judge and juror. Do we realize how our kids' stomachs churn when we pass back those papers. Will they get it? Will I sound stupid? I know I'll make some mechanical errors. The words aren't right—too many, too weak, too clumsy, too cliché. Every time I write for "publication"—web pages, the community madrigal, the newspaper, the map—and I hand over those pages to the printer, I want to run and hide! Only feedback tells us whether we communicate fully. I'm convinced that only suffering the stresses of being a "real" writer can give the teacher real empathy for students' writing.

The moments that frustrated them and inspired them and all those rare moments that made their hearts sing were written down and shared within the journal pages. A collegial journal offers partners a context in which to realize that all teachers have similar frustrations, dreams, victories, and defeats. It is what we can learn from all the little moments that enhance our classrooms. Teachers' lives are often misunderstood. The journal captured a sense of the roller coaster that teaching is.

No matter what their subject area, teachers hear about the heart-breaking situations with which students cope. Writing teachers, in particular, sometimes feel overwhelmed by what they hear in students' papers and journals. Sharing the pain helps, even for veterans like Donna:

> They're good kids with no dreams, no energy, no desire to excel and tremendous need to demand attention and assign blame. They're frustrating me—and some of them are breaking their parents' hearts, I think. I've made more calls to parents on grades this quarter than I have in two years. What I have to focus on—if I'm not going to say the hell with it—is not how I'm feeling. I'm feeling so tired, so pushed, so unprepared some days, so unsuccessful so many days. I have to think about how I want to feel and then act as if I feel that way! Ugh!! It's work!!!

Widely reported low writing assessment scores and confusion around the implementation of state standards, paired with local administrative changes, can drive even enthusiastic professionals to a point of frustration. The collegial journal offers a haven to vent without risk. Teresa wrote the following:

> I've been disillusioned by people placing demands on teachers with little assistance, shaking things up, then walking out the door—never looking back to the damage they left. That's probably how education works, but it makes me feel bad and makes me question why I keep taking it all.

Sometimes just seeing one's disillusionment and frustration in print helps manage it; at other times a trusted colleague's response helps restore perspective.

> Don't get discouraged by all this crap, Girl. Been there, been there, been there . . . and I've learned a couple of things. Kids matter—in fact, kids and learning are all that really matters. Garbage doesn't last and even if the bad guys win a round, better doors open for the good guys in the next round. Read what Sarah Breathnach says in *Simple Abundance:* "Every time we cope with whatever real life throws our way, it's another deposit of confidence, creativity, and courage in our self-esteem account. So congratulate yourself each night for handling the unexpected with finesse."

The inherent loneliness of teaching, particularly that faced by teachers of writing, who must deal with stacks of student papers in solitude, threatens genuine community. All too often failure to release these discouraged and energy-sapping feelings means a closed heart, a sad thing for a teacher of writing. Parker Palmer suggests another way: "the courage to teach is the courage to keep one's heart open in those very moments when the heart is asked to hold more than it is able, so that teacher and students and subject can be woven into the fabric of community that learning, and living, require" (11).

But Then There Are the Things That Make Your Heart Sing

Most importantly, the collegial journal becomes a place to tell somebody the good things about one's teaching and know that the result will be cheering and camaraderie and not turf terror and jealousy. What a totally great and necessary thing for a teacher of writing to have, as Teresa affirmed.

> I think the best thing about teaching and the only thing that keeps me sane is the fact that I love these kids! I've realized for the first time since graduation that I truly feel like I'm "home" so to speak. Every day has been a new challenge, and although I haven't mastered the grading part yet, I feel like this is definitely the right path for me. I doubt myself at times, but I feel alive when I'm in class with the kids. I thank God that I have them. . . .

Like no other vehicle that we have encountered as professionals, the collegial journal helps us to see what we have to say, to learn where we've been, to recognize what we feel, and to know where we must go. Donna reflects

> After 22 years, I still teach some days as if I'm a novice. But the other side of this feeling is a sense of "getting it," of knowing how to reach most kids, of how and when to prod and cajole and praise. Some days the sense of knowing propels me along even though I'm tired to the point of whimpering or swearing. Some days!
>
> This life we call teaching, when its done right, is NOT a profession. It is a calling, a vocation, maybe even a sacred one with vows of poverty and, to some extent, of obedience. Here's a quote from Hannah Hinchman's *A Trail through Leaves:* "A delight in the obvious, the daily still rescues me from dangerous ground . . . these are the acts that knit the world together." Isn't this true for us, too? The importance of noticing the face lighting up with understanding, the flicker of delight, the flash of anger that turns to resolve, the apprehension of words that really sing, little moments. The big picture—standards, sequence, rubrics, integration—all so important, but let's not lose the little joys of teaching either.

REFERENCES AND RESOURCES

Atwell, Nancie. *In the Middle: Writing, Reading, and Learning with Adolescents.* Portsmouth, NH: Heinemann, 1987.

Breathnach, Sarah Ban. *Simple Abundance.* New York: Warner Books, 1995.

Burke, Jim. *The English Teacher's Companion.* Portsmouth, NH: Boynton/Cook, 1999.

Hinchman, Hannah. *A Trail through Leaves: The Journal as a Path to Place.* New York: Norton, 1997.

Palmer, Parker. *The Courage to Teach.* San Francisco: Jossey-Bass, 1998.

Safire, William. *Fumblerules, a Light-hearted Guide to Grammar and Good Usage.* Garden City, NY: Doubleday, 1990.

Staton, Jana. "The Power of Responding in Dialogue Journals." In *The Journal Book.* Ed. Toby Fulwiler. Portsmouth, NH: Boynton/Cook, 1987.

Strunk, William, Jr., and E. B. White. *The Elements of Style.* New York: Macmillan, 1979.

"Ten Tips to Keeping Your Teaching Life Energized." *English Journal* (September 1996): 25–27.

Weinheimer, Rose. "Six Mileposts along the Highway to Successful Teaching." *English Journal* (September 1996): 65–66.

Winston, Stephanie. *Getting Organized.* New York: Warner Books, 1991.

———. *The Organized Executive: A Program for Productivity: New Ways to Manage Time, Paper, People, and the Electronic Office.* New York: Warner Books, 1994.

13 Learning to Diagnose and Prescribe for Success in Student Writing

STEWART BELLMAN

Stewart Bellman, retired professor of English, provides a wonderful chapter to conclude this book. Bellman's strategies, arising from over 30 years of teaching and learning with his students, are based on the following premises: use gentle trickery in teaching; fun is an essential!; everybody writes, the teacher, too!; own what you write; teach students to exercise judgment about writing; walk a mile in the students' shoes; and find constructive ways of teaching. One particular methodology he offers is the use of teacher-composed writings to be used for student revision and response.

Bellman includes actual student writing and models the activities he advocates. These two aspects of his chapter add reality and practicality to what he suggests for success in student writing.

I am retired now. After 32 years of reading and grading student compositions and seeking ways to help students discover their voices as writers, I have time to ponder the challenges of teaching writing. This chapter offers suggestions from my experiences as a composition teacher for those who are preparing to take up the task. One course from my college student days, not a composition course, provided memorable and long-lasting lessons that I carried along with me through the years.

A Teacher Who Puzzled Me and, in Puzzling, Taught Me for Life!

Way back in 1954, Dr. Recht, my astronomy professor at college, introduced his students to Writing across the Curriculum, although he didn't call it that and I doubt that the term had been coined yet. Dr. Recht, a credible scientist, was a memorable classroom teacher. Two things he did that first year of my college career have stuck with me for four decades. The first caused me to wonder at his sanity and to remember him always with affection and curious bewilderment.

On the day before Thanksgiving, Dr. Recht walked into class carrying a worn little book and a box of M&M candy packages. He passed the M&Ms around, instructing us to take one package each and to enjoy munching on the candies during the class. Then he opened the book and told us he had something important to share with us that day.

He read the title of a short story, "The Gift of the Magi," and told us the author's name, O. Henry. He proceeded to read aloud to us this story that he apparently loved. As he read, he wept, tears running subtly down his cheeks. I do not remember how he ended the class; I do know that of all the class sessions I have attended and taught since that one class session, in which a science professor did something so out of character and out of context, has endured as memorable. I learned something that day about being a teacher: A teacher can offer gifts to students; a teacher can reveal a loving vulnerability to callow youth; a teacher need not explain or justify all that he or she does. That idiosyncratic moment returned to me at key moments throughout my years of teaching. Although I cannot offer a sensible explication of its meaning, it touched much that I did with students. I credit it with making me a more caring and generous teacher.

Questions: *Spend some time listing teachers who have been important to you. Can you remember one or more who did something special and memorable, a Dr. Recht in your student life?*

Who was this teacher?

What did the teacher do that was puzzling and/or memorable?

Why do you value what this teacher did?

How do or will you use the experience with this teacher in your life?

Gentle Trickery in Teaching

Dr. Recht's second lesson more directly influenced my work as a teacher of writing. We freshman students in Dr. Recht's astronomy class struggled to remember the vocabulary of astronomy, and we struggled to comprehend the "science" he was teaching us. Many of us found the subject foreign and irrelevant to our interests. Then, one day, he made us teachers. He was, he explained, writing a book about astronomy for people who didn't know anything about it but were curious to learn.

His problem was that as a professor who had taught and practiced astronomy for decades he just didn't know how to present his subject in a way that laypeople would understand. Could we help him? We eagerly volunteered to help. He gave us an assignment. From now on in the course, we would study the subject with him, listening to his lectures, reading the textbook chapters, and discussing our questions in class. Then, we would each write a version of what we had studied in language that our parents and brothers and sisters back home would be able to understand. We would become the intermediaries who would teach him how to put the abstractions of astronomy into language for nonastronomers. Our status as students would make us expert interpreters and translators. He would read our papers and then use what he had learned from us to write the chapter of his book. Wow! What an exciting challenge that was. And our very ignorance became a tool that would help our teacher!

Dr. Recht probably never wrote the book for which he enlisted our aid. He was more interested in having us, his students, master the content of the course he was teaching. The lesson he taught me was that students could be enlisted in their own learning. One way to do this is to trick them, but trick them gently and in their own interest. Gentle trickery has been one of the more useful and fun tools I have used with students.

Questions: Review your list of memorable teachers. Has a teacher ever "tricked" you into learning? Who did this? When?

How did you react when you learned you had been tricked?

How did the trick help you learn?

Fun, an Essential!

A high school English teacher once shared a key insight with me. She had been a teacher for 28 years. One day in class she realized that the lesson bored and irritated her. When she thought about why this was happening to her, she realized that she wasn't having any fun. It occurred to her at that moment that if she wasn't enjoying what she was teaching the students probably weren't either. Thereafter, she would insist that if she couldn't make a lesson fun (which can also mean interesting) for herself, then she would not teach it. She had discovered a basic tenet of teaching: *the teacher and students should have some fun along the way.* Although writing is a serious endeavor and students will write serious and important pieces during their studies, their learning can be advanced and enhanced by some pretend and humorous tactics. Students of all ages possess a surprising amount of savvy and insight. The trick is utilizing this savvy and insight to help them learn and to help them perform at the level of which they are capable.

A Letter-Writing Activity

Here is an example: One day I walked into class and shared my befuddled state of mind with my students. My former students and colleagues, I explained, besiege me each spring with requests to write letters of recommendation for them in support of their applications for jobs. But writing letters of recommendation had become unrewarding for me because I had no way of knowing if my letters actually helped anyone. Therefore, I had done some research and learned that virtually no one for whom I had written had ever gotten the job. It occurred to me that something must be wrong with my letters. Perhaps my current students could help me revise one of my letters so that the candidate I was supporting would have a better chance of being hired. I told them that I would value their advice. Here is a letter I circulated among the students once when I used this ploy.

My Letter

Freddy Fraidco Auto Parts
111 Main Street
Little City, USA

Dear Freddy,

Hi, Im writing to tell you what a great guy Sam Sportnut is. Hes a guy who really like to play sports basketball and track being his special areas. Sams really gung ho about being on a winning team. He spends hours up at the high school practicing, and he runs just about every place he goes. Our principal is always shouting, "Hey, Sportnut, slow down, no running." But Sam never hears, he just charges on in his enthusiastic way.

Well, anyway, Sammy would sure like a job. He heard that you hire kids to shag parts and to help unload freight and maybe do counter work. Sammy really likes to drive you can't hardly get him away from his old Camaro Z-28 which he works on whenever he's not practicing for his sports. Don't get me wrong though, Sam cares about school too. I am his computer technology teacher, and he is great whiz at surfing the net. Actually, he developed a good stock control plan for a sporting goods store for a business class he took from me using a computer data base in an original and creative way.

Need I say that Sam is strong? He has really developed himself with his sports training, so he is great at stockroom work and at loading and unloading freight. During the summer he works on his grandpa's farm helping with the harvest, so Sam is not a stranger to hard work.

All of the kids I know at the high school seem to like Sammy a lot. He can always be found joking with the guys in the parking lot after school, and I often here girls calling him a dreamboat. He is good in class about helping other students with problems on the computer, and he always says "hi" to his teachers when he meets them around town.

He is pretty regular in attendance and gets his work in on time most of the time. The coaches praise him lots and say he may be chosen as captain of the basketball team this year. Even his English teacher said she was impressed when she saw him reading a book in the library on day this spring.

Sam Sportnut will be a good employee. He is respectful, and he learns real quick. You will be glad that you gave him a chance.

Sincerely,

Rod Megabite
Business and Computer Instructor
Little City HS

After the students finished their revisions of my letter, we talked about what they had done to the letter. In most cases, the students made the letter more formal. They often recognized that the person writing the letter should introduce himself early in the letter and offer his credentials for writing the recommendation. Sometimes, they added detail. When I asked why they added the detail, they explained that an employer would want illustrations rather than generalities about Sam's abilities. And they had also changed the way Sam's attributes were described. They recognized that the language I had used and the way I had phrased some of my comments about Sam made him seem immature and not ready for a serious job. They thought that I could look more deeply into the qualities I commented on. Very few students referred to Sam's English teacher in their revisions. In fact, the students' revisions allowed me to help them identify four principles for revising writing: *rearrangement, addition, deletion,* and *substitution.*

Four samples of student revisions follow (I have omitted the inside address and the closing signature).

Letter 1

Dear Mr. Fraidco,

I'm writing this letter in regards to Sam Sportnut. He is interested in gainful employment as a deliveryman. I have personally worked with Sam and his additude towards his schoolwork is very enthusiastic. I know he has good human relation skills as he communacates excellent with his classmates and peers. He can be trusted with tasks as he exzemplfed that through the Sports Department, creating structoured stock controled plan for the atheletic gear. He is excellent physical condition, as to handle part handling. I appreciate your consideration in this matter. Any questions please contact me.

Sincerely,

Letter 2

Dear Freddy,

Hello, I am writing to tell you about how good a person Sam Sportnut is. He came up to me and asked me to write a letter of recommendation. I thought it would be a great way to tell you how much of a hard worker Sam is.

He has always been on time for my class. And the only days he has missed was when he was sick with the flu or when his father died. He has also handed in his work on time. And he has an A average in my class.

He has works for his grandpa in the summers, helping with the harvest. So I would say his upper body strength is very good. He would be a great asset to a company like yours. He would be able to unload freight with ease; he is a good person so if you had him working at the counter, he wouldn't make you lose any customers.

Sam Sportnut will be a great employee. He is respectful, and he learns very quickly. You will be glad that you hired him.

Sincerely,

Letter 3

Dear Mr. Fraidco:

My name is Rod Megabite and I am Sam Sportnut's computer technology teacher. I would just like to share with you my experiences with Sam. I have found Sam to be very dedicated individual in and outside the classroom. Sam strives to be the best he can be mentally, physically, and spiritually.

In the classroom Sam has displayed great mental achievement. He is well educated when it comes to computers. In fact, Sam has developed a very accurate stock control plan for a sporting goods store using a computer database. I must say that I have never seen something so successful and creative. Sam has excelled tremendously in class. He is among the top three in his business and computer classes.

Physically Sam has reached the goal of being in ultimate shape. Sam is very dedicated not only in school but when it comes to working out also. Sam has enjoyed sports throughout high school with basketball and track being his special areas. In the off season he is constantly training. His muscle strength development would be an asset to your company. He would be a great help in loading and unloading freight. Sam is no stranger to hard-dedicated work.

Sam is spiritually matured. Family and friends are among his top priorities, and he is well liked by the faculty and his peers. His coaches chose him as captain of the basketball tem this year and have many wonderful praises and comments to share about him. Sam is often found joking with his fellow students and his presence is always enjoyed. Sam is helpful not only in school but with his family too. He has lent a helping hand on his grandfather's ranch for the last four summers and is spoken highly of by his parents and siblings.

Thank you for your time. Please consider Sam as an employee for your company. He is dependable, respectful, enthusiastic, and learns quickly. I feel that Sam would be an asset to your company and it would be a mistake not to have Sam as an employee. If you have any questions feel free to call me anytime.

Sincerely,

Letter 4

Dear Mr. Fraido,

I am writing to recommend Sam Sportnut for a job position in your business. I am his Computer Technology teacher and have known and observed Sam in school and out of school. He is a very involved student being on both the basketball and track team. He is also very dedicated, spending hours at the high school practicing, and constantly working to better himself. Sam is a leader, having a chance of being chosen as team captain of his basketball team. He is also well liked by his friends, classmates, and coaches, and teachers and he uses his great people skills to help others, often helping students in my class when they have problem on the computers.

Sam is a hard worker and is well qualified for the job. He has worked summers doing farm work and has developed sufficient strength through his sports training which would be of use in helping to unload freights and for stockroom work. He also knows his share about cars, owning an old Camaro Z-28 that he works on whenever he is not practicing for his sports. Sam also has a good head for business. In one of my business classes, Sam developed an excellent stock control plan for a sporting goods store using a computer database in an original and creative way.

Sam Sportnut is a fast learner and will be an effective and sufficient employee. I highly recommend him for hiring.

Sincerely,

The students who wrote these revisions used their classroom computers. I was interested that many of the students in this class did not use the spell-check or grammar-check features of their word-processing programs. Thus, while they corrected my errors such as "Im" to "I'm" and "like" to "likes," they committed similar errors of their own.

Clearly, most of the students in this class need to work on editing, something they can learn to do using the computer. They could also work together on editing the language, punctuation, and mechanics of their letters.

The revised letters that classes produce for this exercise demonstrate a variety of perceptions and values. Some students write much briefer letters, while others write letters nearly as lengthy as mine. The briefer of the four samples you have just read get right to the point and offer general support for the recommendation. The longest of the four letters adopts an organizational schematic: The essay begins with an introduction of the writer followed by a thesis that introduces the focus of each of the paragraphs of the body—Sam's mental, physical, and spiritual qualities. Having the class members explain reasons for the approaches they took to the rewrite proves to be most instructive. Class discussion of students' revisions can also provide an opportunity to examine and teach formal concepts, such as how to address the prospective employer. Some student revisions of my letter used the familiar "Dear Freddy," and others used the more formal "Dear Mr. Fraidco." Teachers frequently offer strict prescriptions for issues such as the greeting. A class conversation about the writers' reasons for the greetings they chose can lead to a more rational understanding of issues of form and formality.

This exercise started as fun because my students laughed when they read "my" letter. The introduction I gave to the request that they revise it tipped them off that I was talking "tongue in cheek," and when they read my letter, they laughed out loud. I had invited them into a charade that amused them but that became more academically serious as we progressed. Thus, fun led to learning. The rewriting of a letter of recommendation has usually led to a fairly serious discussion of composing and revising writing. A whole-class conversation about the rewritten letters allows an excellent opportunity to identify four principles of revision. Fun led to success.

Questions: *Reflect on teachers you have had through your school years from elementary school through college. Do a 5-minute free write in which you recall writing activities or assignments that were fun or playful. Or think of something a teacher had you write that could have been fun, but wasn't. What grade level did or could the activity occur at? What made it fun? Did it, and how did it, become a learning activity? Don't limit yourself to just English classes. Think of other subjects in which you have written. For example, a special education educator I know asks his students the following question: If you could choose an IQ for yourself, what would it be? Why would you choose this IQ? How would you benefit from your choice?*

Everybody Writes, the Teacher, Too!

Another tenet of teaching writing that has been important is that teachers should be participants in the writing that occurs in their classes. In the letter revision exercise, my students worked with a sample of my writing, although they quickly recognized that it wasn't a representative sample. They were able to recognize my playfulness because of the introduction I gave to the activity, but they had also read other samples of my writing and knew something about me as a writer.

Years ago I witnessed an illustration of the importance of a fourth grade teacher writing with her class. I, two of my college students, and a fifth grade teacher whom I admired spent a day at a local elementary school doing a writing activity with fourth grade classes. In each class, one of the two college students read a poem about a dancing clown to the students. As the student read the poem, our fifth grade teacher, who was dressed as a clown, danced and mimed the poem. We then asked the fourth graders to write something. Although I forget the specific assignment we made, I remember that the poem and the dancing clown (playful fun) elicited willing writing from the kids. All the fourth graders wrote willingly, but two of the classes stand out in my memory. In one of the classes, the students were noisy and undisciplined, and their teacher spent a lot of time giving orders and admonishing them—with scant results. When we asked the students to read their work aloud, they were reticent to do so. This was a new request for them. This class was unpleasant for us.

In another class, the students jumped right to the writing. When we asked the students to read their work aloud, they willingly and even eagerly did so. But they also asked in chorus that their teacher read what she had written. They knew that she would have written with them for she always wrote with them, and she shared her writing just as they did. I probably don't need to say that this class was a smoothly operating community of learners in which the teacher did not have to scold or admonish. They were *all* writers, and writing was fun for them.

I recently received another illustration of the value of this principle. At Christmas last year, I received a letter from a former student. He included in his letter a writing assignment he had made for his high school juniors. He was anxious to receive their responses. For several weeks, he had been reading a book aloud to his students, a chapter every few days. The book, *Tuesdays with Morrie,* by Mitch Albom, tells of fourteen Tuesdays that Mitch visited his professor, Morrie Schwartz, who was dying of Lou Gehrig's disease. The Tuesday visits became an ongoing dialogue about important questions that humans encounter: death, love, pain, joy, purpose, and the like. Though the book was sad and brought tears to the reader and his students, I assume that hearing it was in some way "fun." My friend had developed a three-question prompt for the students to write an essay for which the reading of the book had prepared them. He included in his prompt an essay he had written in response to the prompt.

I was also deeply touched by his essay. In it, he named me as his "Morrie." The label was especially touching because I had just returned from a stay in the hospital and was recovering. The kindness of friends was very important to me just then. I was pleased and a bit embarrassed by his words, but I accepted them as sincere and flattering. How could I respond to him in a way that would be appropriate? It occurred to me that since I had just finished reading *Tuesdays with Morrie* myself, I was qualified to write in response to the three questions Mike had asked his students. So I wrote the assignment and mailed it. Our old practice of writing together in classes continued to serve us. I don't know if my friend shared my essay with his students; I gave him permission to do so. I do know that I greatly enjoyed writing in response to his assignment and that I admired him for having read aloud to his students and for having written in response to his assignment. I hope his students were also pleased that he had done this.

Questions: *Have your teachers written with you in classes, and have any of them shared their writing?*

How did you and other students respond to the teacher's writing?

If you felt that the teacher was showing off, what caused you to feel this way?

What did you enjoy about what the teacher wrote?

How did the teacher's writing support your writing?

Think of teachers who didn't write with or for their classes. How might their having written with or for their classes benefited the students?

Own What You Write

When my friend read the book *Tuesdays with Morrie* to his students, he was investing time preparing his students for his writing assignment. The assignment he eventually made was a bit abstract, inasmuch as he asked his high school students to write about topics that they might not have thought about or that might embarrass them. The book about Morrie's last fourteen Tuesdays provided some concrete experience with the topics about which they would eventually write. The conversations the class had with their teacher about *Tuesdays with Morrie* served as a sort of prewriting session in which they examined ideas and shared experiences. They made connections that would allow them to approach the writing assignment as a familiar topic and not as something foreign and new. Their teacher accomplished *yet another important tenet of teaching writing: He prepared his students to write with authority based on experience with the problem.*

Perhaps the most important realization that I have experienced as a teacher and writer has been to *own* the task. A problem that student writers face is how strictly to follow the guidelines of the assignment and how much liberty to take with the assignment. Students try so hard to please their teacher that they do not take license to approach an assignment from their own knowledge and value base. A colleague of mine demonstrates the process of taking ownership of an assignment. After he gives an assignment to his class, he begins writing his response to the assignment on the chalkboard. As he writes, he begins to define the assignment within the framework of his own background and understanding. The assignment necessarily changes a bit as he discovers his unique access to it. He models the process of moving to ownership.

A very effective ownership strategy that I have observed occurred in the fifth grade. A teacher who attended my state's Writing Project reported this strategy. Each year, her class did its own version of a Broadway musical. The year this teacher attended the summer institute of the Writing Project, her class had performed *Cats*. They had looked at photos of the show's set and spent part of the year decorating their classroom as a junky alley where the cats might live. Some students served as set builders and technical crew; others tried out for and were given roles to portray. Finally, one day, parents came to class, and the students gave the show. It was a huge success. A "real" writing assignment occurred when each of the students wrote a letter to a character or crew member of the Broadway production currently showing. The students generated and asked questions and told about their classroom production. In return, each student received a written response from the person he or she had written to on Broadway. The actor who played Old Deuteronomy on stage recognized something special about the lad who was playing Old Deuteronomy in the fifth grade. (The boy had a learning problem that revealed itself in his letter.) The stage Old Deuteronomy wrote a nine-page response in which he talked about the character and his values. Think about what a special letter that must have been. Other students received letters in which the cast members talked about how thrilled they were to be on Broadway, about their careers, and about their lives. The fifth grade class made up a scrapbook, which stayed with the teacher for future classes to read as they began their fifth grade theatrical projects.

One of the more effective strategies I devised for this taking ownership quest involved the way I graded essays. In a composition course of gifted students, I distributed very specific criteria for the grade of B. These criteria spelled out formal, developmental, stylistic, and editing expectations. I gave no criteria for other grades, explaining that a C paper would fall short of the B criteria. A papers, on the other hand, had to violate the criteria in some purposeful way. Their authors had to risk failure. They had to venture into unexplored territory. The students that term were particularly attracted to science and problem solving. Several accepted the challenge of discovering how to approach the assignment in a manner that would result in the grade of A, while departing the criteria for the grade of B sufficiently to risk missing the point of the assignment. Their challenge became a scientific one of positing a thesis and controlling the variables while stepping outside the parameters of usual and accepted practice. One intelligent student, who succeeded in writing several A papers that term, started by writing a paper that embarrassed her because it challenged the norms of her previous education.

She wrote an essay about her introduction to profanity and to irony. The narrative at the heart of her essay took her readers back to her elementary school education in a Roman Catholic parochial school in a rural midwestern community. A boy from Chicago joined their class, and he introduced the class members to the exclamation "Holy shit!" "Holy" seemed an appropriate word, but the students had never heard the other word before and had no idea of its meaning. So the phrase became a playground expression until one day in class the teacher, a nun, addressed a question to a student who had no notion of the answer. The young man responded, "Holy shit, Sister, I don't know." Well, you can guess the outcome of his outburst. The students learned that something called profanity existed, and they learned that one can be punished for crimes of which one is essentially innocent. My student's essay was humorous and purposeful. It got its point across, but my student quaked about using the word in her essay, fearing retribution from me. She presented me with the opportunity to reward her writing and to help her learn that profanity can be used appropriately when it is pertinent to the writer's purpose. The chance she took helped her future compositional experimentation and her ability to judge the appropriateness of the risks she would take.

Questions: *Reflect about successful writing you have done in school. Describe a technique that a teacher used that helped you write an assignment with confidence and authority?*

Think of a writing assignment that you found difficult because you lacked experience and authority on the topic (I think here of an assignment in which I asked students to write about how to reform the American medical care system without recognizing that my students had little or no concrete experience with that system). What was the assignment, and what prevented you from success?

Students Learn to Exercise Judgment

The story I just related about my students learning for themselves what might violate the rigid norms of a B-level piece of writing to achieve the challenge of producing A writing leads me to *one more tenet of teaching writing: Students can become reliable critics of writing and, in so doing, they can learn to evaluate and control their own writing.* Critiquing and judging writing can take several forms. Students can read and critique each other's papers; they can judge the quality of writing by people not in their class—students in other classes or schools, writers seeking response to and criticism of their work. Students can develop the criteria of evaluation for valuing or grading writing. And students can assess the performance of published writers.

A successful and playful (to return to my first tenet of teaching writing) strategy that I used in my class was a ghost-writer named Trevor. Trevor didn't attend school, but he was very interested in writing and in developing his writing skills. He was a friend I saw almost daily, so he often wrote the assignments that I gave to my students. He had lots of free time, so he asked me to enlist the students' help in critiquing his work, and then he would revise the work so I could let the students read it and decide if he had improved the piece. Unfortunately, Trevor was a superficial fellow who had trouble engaging a topic. Invariably, his early responses to an assignment were recognizably trite and vague. He suffered from a range of errors that he committed in his writing. But he was willing, and he would revise earnestly and quickly so that he could hear more advice from the students. As we engaged in the assignment in class and worked with versions and revisions, Trevor's work provided us with a measure by which we could gauge our own writing. He listened to the advice my students offered and slowly improved his essay or story. Here is a sample of one of Trevor's early responses to an assignment and then a revision following the students' critique:

Assignment.   We have just read a story about a lonely widow whose friends have died and whose children and younger friends are so busy with their lives that they rarely remember to offer her the gift of quality time together. Write an essay about some of your own experiences with loneliness and the value or meaning that those experiences had for you.

Loneliness
Loneliness affects all people. It takes many forms and people react to it in different ways, but everyone experiences loneliness in their lives.

I have experienced loneliness in my life. The time I felt it most was when I went to a summer workshop while I was in high school. I had been looking forward to getting away from home. I wanted to be on my own and away from my parents. I thought it would be great not to have them always asking about everything in my life.

After they left me at the college where the workshop would be held, I got really lonely. My roommate didn't arrive until late that first night, so I spent the afternoon sitting in the room alone wondering what would happen the next day and who my roommate would be. The next day, I didn't know anyone, and no one really took time to talk or to make friends. Then I started talking to another kid who sat next to me in two of the classes we were taking.

My grandmother was lonely during the last years of her life. All of us lived too far away to go see her very often. I always felt sorry when we went to see her. She was sort of forgetful, so it was hard to talk to her, and us kids got pretty bored. When she died, I realized I would never see her again.

I have never liked being lonely. It's depressing. I try to keep busy so I don't have to feel that way. People who are lonely are left out of life, and it's easy to pick up bad habits like drinking or thinking negative when you are alone. It's much better to appreciate people in your life and stay close to them.

My students were able to ask Trevor questions that helped him revise the essay. They wondered if he could find a way to make the beginning of the essay less general and more focused. They commented that the first paragraph was vague and fairly obvious. The entire essay was too self-pitying. Transition was needed between the part about the workshop and the part about the writer's grandmother. All the essay needed more specific development. Some concrete examples would help. Eventually, Trevor's essay became this essay:

Alone But Not Lonely

The day was sunny and blue—an ideal spring day. For me, it might as well have been gray and rainy; I had just experienced my first funeral. I had loved my grandmother, and my brothers and sisters and I had always looked forward to going to her home for a visit, even though we hated being cooped up in the car for the five hours it took to drive to her house. When we got there though, the cookies and goodies she always had ready for us caused us to forget the boring drive, and we enjoyed playing in her barns and roaming the grove of trees beside her home.

On the day of her funeral, I was understanding for the first time that I would never see my grandmother again, and I was lonesome. Her death may have been the first time when I realized I was lonesome. I am sure I had been lonesome before, but the feeling had never had a name until then. Since that time, I have experienced many forms of loneliness, and though I haven't learned how to avoid it, I have begun to understand how to cope with it and even to realize that while being lonely hurts, the capacity to feel lonely is in many ways a valuable part of being human.

As children, we experience many lonely moments. I remember being lonely when my friends were away on vacation or busy with their families. At the time I didn't know it was loneliness that I was feeling. I remember being lonely when I chose not to go out for a school team. My decision separated me from my friends who did go out. Often when they were practicing or away for a game, I regretted my choice. But when my friends returned from their vacation, I was happy to see them and to learn what they had done. When I didn't join the team, I was taking piano lessons. Today, my ability to play the piano is important to me, so by choosing my own way, I gained something valuable to me.

It was also lonely when I attended a music workshop on a college campus one year. I had been eager to get away from home and to try out living independently. But the first evening after my parents left for home and my roommate didn't arrive, I was miserable and depressed. How pleased I was when my roommate arrived and I had someone to talk to and to know I was there. The campus was strange the next day because people were in a hurry and didn't say hello. I got through that first day and then I made some friends at the workshop, and by the end of the week I had a new group of friends. Some of us still write to one another or call each other once in awhile.

I know that I have only begun to learn about loneliness. I understand now how lonely my grandmother must have been those last years when the family didn't visit very often. I know she would have liked to have been with us kids more, but we were off playing. Loneliness is a strange and sometimes surprising emotion. Sometimes it hurts, and sometimes it angers, but often it teaches and enlightens. Though being lonely confuses us, I doubt that any of us would want to live without the capacity to be lonely.

Trevor's final essay probably exceeded the advice the students were able to give to him, but it did respond to that advice by becoming more concrete and less focused on self. It was structured more strategically, and it utilized language to lead the reader from one part of the piece to another—it included transitions. The point of having Trevor write and revise is that Trevor's work was instructive. In its early drafts, it needed criticism and advice, which the students were able to give. In its later drafts, it became a model of what the students were attempting to do in their own essays.

The fun of Trevor was that Trevor didn't exist. I was Trevor, and eventually students caught on to this. Then Trevor became a shared joke among us, an obvious teaching ploy. But the Trevor drafts continued to provide us with neutral territory for criticism and experimentation. In a sense, perhaps, we all became Trevor. Trevor helped my students become critics of writing and helpers of writers. But there's another benefit in the teacher doing writing that approximates the ability levels of the students in the class.

Walk a Mile in the Students' Shoes

It's worthwhile practice to write in the manner of our students. When the teacher actually writes an essay that approximates the average-ability student in his or her class and other essays that approximate the above-average and outstanding-ability students, then the teacher comes to a deeper understanding of how the students think and approach assignments. It is fairly easy for a teacher to tell students why they receive the scores the teacher assigns to their written work. It is more difficult to help students understand why they are achieving at the level that their score represents. When the teacher writes as a student, the teacher more consciously examines the student writer's challenges and becomes better prepared to diagnose problems in the student's writing and then to prescribe ways of responding to these problems. When the students have also participated in reviewing writing and in recommending ways to improve a piece of writing, they too are better enabled to diagnose and improve their own writing.

Questions: *Have you ever written as though you were another person? Write a brief essay in which you assume the persona of a tenth or eleventh grade student. Your essay should represent what you imagine an average tenth or eleventh grade student might generate.*

Assignment. *Write a brief essay about the importance of friendship with two illustrations of acts of friendship that illustrate your point. After you have written the essay, reread it. What does your essay reveal about your anticipation of the writing of tenth and eleventh grade students?*

Five student essays follow. They were written by eleventh grade students in a literature class. The students wrote in response to the friendship assignment. Their teacher allowed 40 minutes for the task. She instructed the students to do some prewriting, to write a rough draft, and to complete a revised draft. (This was a significant challenge.) The time and work constraints of the assignment imposed some limitations on the products, but the samples presented here probably represent average high school writing.

Essay 1

I think friendship is important because without friends life would be really boring. You wouldn't have anyone to talk to or help you do something if you didn't have any friends. Friends are fun to do stuff with because you know them and you know what they like to do.

A good friend is someone you can count on to do what they say or keep a secret. Someone who will make you feel better if you're sad or something's wrong. Someone who is loyal and respects you is a good friend.

Like one time me and my friend were at the mall and he didn't have enough money to buy something so I gave him most of my money. I knew he would pay me back and I could count on him. That's what makes us good friends.

Essay 2

The importance of friendship to me is when your friend is going to be there or stick up for you when something happens and you go through bad times, good times, rough times. When you need advice or someone to listen to you.

One example I have is when a friend cheats on his girl friend and you talk about it and never say anything to anyone. My friends know about secrets that they will never tell anyone. My best friend knows my dearest darkest secret.

Also when I get married or before I get married my wife will be my best friend so I can share with her something I have never shared with anyone. And we will both know when, where, and what we like.

That is my idea of friendship and why it is important because it makes you feel good when you have a friend like that.

Essay 3

I think friends are people that you can laugh around. You can have fun with and be comfortable around. A friend is a person you can tell your secrets to and not have to worry if they're going to tell anyone.

Friendship is very important. You need to be around people where you can be yourself. Its important to have people that know almost everything about you. Its nice to know you can call them up anytime and tell them your problems. Without friends I'd be lost because they are the people I depend on.

One example of being a good friend is when they're in a bad situation and you get them out of it. One time they called me really early in the morning to come pick them up. I knew something was wrong so I came with no questions asked. I felt like a good friend afterwards and I knew that if I was ever in that situation I could call them too. Another thing is visiting them when they're sick or hurt. That's especially when they need a good friend, so I try and brighten their day. That's what friendship is all about.

Essay 4

Friends are one of the most important things to have in life. Friends come in all shapes, sizes, and color. They all have different opinions and outlooks on life. I know what it feels to need a friend there and know that you don't have one. I gave all my friends up for my boyfriend, that was one of the stupid decisions I made in life but I learned Boyfriends come and go, but your friends are there forever.

The most important quality in friends is how reliable they are. You should be able to rely on them more than anything else in life. If you tell them you are going to do something, do it without any excuses. And don't lie to your friends. They should mean everything to you, don't betray them.

I need my friends in my life now more than ever. It means the world to me to be able to call them anytime of day to talk to them. I hope that I help them as much as they have helped me. It feels so good to talk to a friend about something that has been on your mind. I don't know how anyone can go through life without a friend.

Essay 5

A friend is one who you may have known for years or just days. A friend is one who you can trust to do anything, even if your life depended upon it. A good friend will go out of his or her way to help or encourage you. You should be able to tell a friend something so secret, that even your parents shouldn't know about. Often, a friend will be the first person you go to tell them what's bothering you, even before you tell your parents. A true friend would give you the shirt off his or her back to help warm you. A friend is someone who more than likely would have much in common with you. A friend is someone who would call if your sick and do anything to help. "What's mine is yours," is what a good friend would tell you. A friend should be the one person you call when all else fails and no one else is dependable. A friend will lend you money or even just a helping hand, so far as to walk through the deepest snow, in sub-zero temperatures, in a raging blizzard to help tow your car out of the snow. And YOU would be a FRIEND to do all of this and more to help someone you care about.

The five essays in the sample treat the assignment fairly generally. However, they all seem to offer honest and even heartfelt responses to the writing prompt. The writers have attempted to comply with the assignments, inasmuch as they have told why they value friendship and supported their reasons with illustrative instances. Even so, the essayists do not offer developed illustrations in support of their theses.

Questions: *What qualities or traits did you accurately "catch" about student writing at this level?*

How do these essays differ from your expectations?

The essays exhibit spelling and grammar and sentence construction errors. Teachers often begin their critical or assessing responses to such student writing by noting errors in the writing. However, the development qualities of the writing may present a more fundamental concern.

Questions: *If the students were to revise these essays, what could they do to make them more satisfying to a reader, more penetrating in their examination of the topic?*

If you were their teacher, what advice could you provide these students that will help them move to a more mature examination of the topic?

Find Constructive Ways of Teaching

One of my strongest beliefs as a teacher of writing is that teachers (and students) need to change the focus of their attention from errors and corrections to diagnosis and constructive criticism. My expectation as a teacher is that when the students were asked to include two illustrations of acts of friendship the student writers would tell stories about friendship. Instead, they mentioned rather general instances, such as loaning money at the mall or keeping one another's secrets or sharing. Students don't think of stories; possibly the things they believe they value in friendship haven't actually happened for or to them. One student writer, the one whose friends called early in the morning to come and get them, did have a concrete experience but related the experience in a very general way. As a teacher, I am disappointed unless I have taken the trouble to place myself in the mind-set of my students. Thus, if I write some of my assignments in the persona of students, I am not in any way ridiculing them or poking fun at them. Rather, I am forcing myself to think as they think. Doing this prepares me to ask questions that may lead them to another stage of development in their writing. I can illustrate this concept further by looking at some essays from slightly more advanced students, students who are writing more extensively and more concretely.

In the essays that follow, Advanced Placement seniors write about autumn. They had been studying literature that speaks of autumn. The essays were conceived, written, and revised in one class setting. These students write coherent sentences with few grammatical and spelling errors (the essays have been typed as they were written with the spelling, grammar, and punctuation of the author).

Essay 1
"I shall smile when wreaths of snow/Blossom where the rose should grow" (Emily Bronte)

Every year it is the same. Leaves wither, flowers die, and the days grow cold. Autumn is a time of many changes. It is also a time of comfort and beauty.

Fall is that time when everything is changing. The plentiful harvest is gathered and the brown stalks are left behind. As children, we return to school and to the duties we left behind. New friendships are made, old ones renewed, and some lost. Children are revealed to have grown during summer.

When we come into Autumn, we leave behind the oppressive heat of summer. The sun does not shine so warmly, the clouds come more readily. It is pleasurable to feel the chill breeze upon your elbows. You can wear a jacket and feel just perfect.

Autumn displays her beauty much better than spring or summer. The nights are brightly lit by stars. Familiar constellations shine from familiar places. The leaves bloom in rich colors of orange, red, and yellow. Green does not seem so important while red is in the trees. The first snow storm comes with the fall stealthy and quick. It leaves behind it fields of white and skies a much brighter blue.

We find such change with the Autumn, everything different and new. But everything is right, and everything is well. And, perhaps, we see that when the Autumn comes, it is the same this year and forever more.

Essay 2

Winter is a time of hibernation, when new life is sprouting where we cannot see, and it is spring that brings birth and new life from the darkness of winter. Summer is a time for living, exploring, and warmth. Autumn is the season that completes the cycle of death and rebirth, it is a time of gathering, preparing, and of winding down.

The gathering of autumn is when family once again comes together giving thanks. We bond as we gather leaving behind the days of summer where in a hurry we missed the closeness found in knowing someone is there for us. In nature the animals gather food and supplies, much like our harvesting the fields before winter's chill. Squirels gather nuts that now are plump and abundant, yet soon there will be none to find. Ants too gather all that they will need to survive, for they will be buried in a few months time. Many other animals such as the bear will be eating and eating to prepare for concealment in their dens. The winged birds and foul are gathered into flocks preparing for their journey to the protecting warmth of the south.

As the days grow shorter the winding down of autumn begins. Trees that so quickly grew, budded, and gave fruit are now decaying. The branches are becoming brittle and are swaying in the breezes, the leaves are waving and their huw are changing. The green fields have turned to gold and rolling like the waves of the ocean. The children have found there way to school again as their schedual continues as before.

Essay 3

Autumn has always been my favorite time of the year. As a child, I loved to gaze out the windows at all the brightly colored leaves as my family and I traveled through Kentucky farmland on our way to church. The leaves ranged in hue from bright yellow to orange to red to brown, and they seemed to create a puffy carpet over the hillside. I also used to play in the leaves with my brother. We would make piles of them in the yard and bury ourselves in them. I loved the way the leaves smelled like a fresh rain and the crunch noise they made. Of course the fun was all over when I found some gross bug or caterpillar!

The worst part of autumn always came when the winds got stronger and started to blow all the leaves off the trees and everything started to die. The air would get colder, and it rained constantly as the sky turned a dismal gray. This part of autumn always seemed very depressing to me.

Essay 4

Autumn is the beginning of an end. Trees go into remission, children go off to school, the first snow of the year falls. The smell of nature is at its peak, and the harvest is collected.

When the colors of red, yellow, and orange come out, so does my family in the family car. We drive around the canyons and look at the sights, smell the freshness of the soil and plant life, and find a cozy place to picnic. The light blue skies and fluffy clouds always set off the different hues of the trees, and the rippling stream is always chilled and fresh.

During autumn the children say their old "good-byes" or their new "hellos" to their schoolmates. Nature walks, hikes, and bike rides become a popular event to take part in. Especially when you will be inside most of the time for the next few months.

The first snow of the year means that all of the bikes and tennis shoes have to be put away. There will be no more colored plants until spring. Only the soft, white snow will cover the earth for the time being. But before the snow, the smell of the world radiates. The scent of the moist soil and leaves create an earthy smell that is so fresh and clean. It livens the spirit and makes you want to dance and sing.

While the snows are beginning to come, the harvest must be collected. All of the covered plants need to be stripped of all good food and taken inside. Some of it is too ripe and so it must be left for the skunks, raccoons, and deer. But the rest is baked, canned, and eaten for the people who provided it with life.

Autumn ushers in a new season. It is a time of enjoyment and sadness. Autumn leaves us with something to look forward to. Life is recycled.

The teacher who assigned these essays provided me with the following criteria for average, above average, and outstanding writing.

1. Average writing meets the assignment for length, topic, etc. There is an introduction, but the thesis is not clear. Examples and illustrations are listed but not explained or clearly connected to the thesis. The conclusion often doesn't really conclude; it just stops. The writing shows little real thought or effort. Grammar and spelling may show areas of weakness. Sentence problems are possible, and vocabulary choices are weak—maybe slang such as "you know" or "like," etc.

2. Above average writing has an introduction that clearly opens the topic. A thesis is present although it is not always strongly or fully stated. The essay supports the thesis, and ideas are developed and/or explained as they connect to or illustrate the thesis. Minimal spelling and grammar errors appear. There is a thorough discussion of the prompt but less creativity than in an outstanding essay. Vocabulary is good, and the conclusion is stated though it may not tie to the thesis. These essays show thought and effort.

3. Outstanding essays begin with introductions that clearly introduce the essay, and the thesis is clearly stated. The conclusion ties back to the thesis. Length goes beyond minimum expectations and shows knowledge of the topic and interest in the topic. Ideas are developed, not just stated. Specific examples support generalizations. These essays are interesting to read and show personal thought—not just a restatement of the teacher or the text. They address the prompt creatively. Vocabulary choices are strong. The writer's voice is clear, and the essay is thoughtful and incisive.

The teacher whose students wrote the four essays I have included here did not rate the essays, so I can only guess at the ratings. I rate all four as average or above, although the third essay is brief and seems unfinished. (I would be hesitant about rating the essays at this stage because all four could be improved, and the third essay has strong promise because of the author's utilization of concrete experience to illustrate her ideas. So a rating of essays written in the time constraints I have described should, in my view, be used only to establish general abilities and possibilities for revision and further development.)

I rate the first two essays as perhaps above average according to the teacher's criteria because their writers use vocabulary effectively, organize coherently, and offer illustrations of the concepts of the essays. However, I find these two essays obvious and not very creative. I find little or no authorial involvement with the topics; rather, I believe the authors have recited many of the often-repeated observations about autumn common to American culture, particularly to suburban or rural culture. Essay 3 caught my interest because the author spoke of a specific place, Kentucky, and specific activities that occurred in the fall—car drives, jumping in piles of leaves. This writer seemed to have paid attention to autumn and to have memories that she or he had filed away, as opposed to having listened to the generalization of others. The author of essay 3 either ran out of time or wasn't able to continue with other specific and concrete memories of fall.

Essay 4 rates as above average and could possibly become outstanding in another version. It begins with its thesis in the first sentence. The conclusion doesn't quite relate back to the thesis, however, because it views autumn as a beginning and not as the beginning of an end. The essay contains specific references to details of fall, such as bike riding and hikes, canning and preparing food, and leaving the overripe food for the raccoons and deer. As a reader, I have the sense that this writer may have real, first-hand experience with and knowledge of the events of fall.

But I am bothered in my ratings of these essays. Although my own rubric (evaluation guide statements) would probably have closely resembled those of my teacher friend for most of my teaching life, I find that these criteria could be interpreted somewhat differently by different readers. And I am also aware that criteria of evaluation often do not help me or my students achieve growth and success as writers. I must ask myself then, "What is it that I want from these students that they have not yet given?" These are serious and sincere students, students who apparently care about writing interesting and appealing essays.

I answer my question by attempting to write an essay in response to the assignment. My essay follows. But I need to say that I made some choices in the way that I wrote my essay, choices that worry me. I based the essay on an actual experience that occurred in my life a couple years ago. No children were involved in the experience. I chose to write my essay in the voice of a girl who is probably a high school student and who could be an Advanced Placement student. I find that I used the vocabulary of an adult, and in a revision I modified some of the word choices, but the language is still that of an adult. I attempted to keep my essay short and to the point, as experience has taught me that student writers are rarely as long-winded as adults who are teachers of writing. Even so, the essay I wrote is almost twice as long as the longest of the student essays, even though I wrote it in less time. Let's read the essay.

Essay 5

Dad had a bad head cold that September, and we didn't get outdoors biking and hiking. As far as I could tell, the entire family felt lethargic and dull. The hustle of our busy summer was behind us, and the excitement of winter and the coming holidays had not yet invigorated us. Something was missing.

One brilliantly sunny day, Mom suggested a drive up into the Black Hills with a stop for lunch at the new log lodge in Spearfish Canyon. Dad and we kids agreed, and about eleven in the morning we headed out. The canyon was elegant. Just above Bridal Veil Falls, there's a hillside covered with aspen trees surrounded by always green spruce. The aspen were at their peak of color, golden orange with some light green touches where a few leaves had not yet turned. As we continued our drive up the fourteen miles of Canyon on the way to Savoy and the Latchstring Inn, the trees regaled us with entertaining colors, and the family mood became one of humor and cheerful banter.

At the lodge, Mom recalled that a new hiking trail had been opened that led from the canyon up to Rough Lock Falls. We kids remembered the falls with excitement for we had always loved to wade up under the shower of the falls on hot summer days. Dad thought he might not feel quite up to the walk, but Mom assured him that it was only a mile and that he could come back to the car and wait for the rest of us if he needed to. "We'll feel more like doing the hike before we eat," she said, and my brother and I both took Dad by the hand and eagerly led him toward the hiking trail.

As we walked, golden leaves cascaded down from the trees like a snowstorm of leaves. The walkway was covered with leaves, so we hiked on a golden carpet. Along the way, we happened upon benches placed about every quarter of a mile, so Dad would sit, and Mom and I would investigate the remaining flowers of summer while my brother explored some of the tiny springs that still ran down the hillside. At the falls, Mom and Dad sat in the warm early October sun while we kids tramped up the rocks that overlook the falls. The roar of the falls was deafening, and we enjoyed the mist that reached our rocks. When we returned to Mom and Dad, we caught them holding hands.

After that we hurried back to the lodge. Dad even walked faster. He was as invigorated as the rest of us by this refreshing and renewing outing. Back at the lodge we enjoyed a delicious lunch on the deck and watched the birds snacking at the feeders placed just off the porch for the pleasure of people as they dined.

When I recall that day, I realize in many ways it contradicts what we most often hear said about fall. It was not a time of decay, and I did not feel the nostalgia that comes with the end of summer. Instead, it was a day I will remember always for it gave me a beautiful mental snapshot of my parents and of the Black Hills that I love. That autumn day is etched in my soul and will comfort me always.

After I wrote my essay, I realized that I probably would not share it immediately with students if I were their teacher. But I did learn something about what I hope these students might achieve in their writing. My essay is based in an experience, and students can achieve greater ownership of their writing by learning to look closely at their own experiences. They can use their stories to help them focus on their own experiences and knowledge, rather than on knowledge that they acquire secondhand. My essay focuses on a single episode that allows some development and detail. Students can attempt to find episodes in their background that would allow similar development. And my essay's thesis reveals a meaningful contradiction, which is that, while common wisdom views autumn as a time of ending, for the persona I posited it was a time of renewing. I find that my essay violates at least one of my teacher friend's expectations. My thesis does not appear until the final paragraph. The topic seems fairly clear to me, although it is possibly left open until the end, too. I am fairly pleased with the essay my assumed persona produced, and I would defend my choices.

Thus, these students can be encouraged to dig more deeply into their own lives and their own experience for strong incidents that illustrate their beliefs. They can take a deeper level of ownership of the topic than all the students whose essays I read for this assignment did. The goal would not be grades; I or any teacher could assign grades to the writing they did. Rather, the goal would be to find new levels for all the students to strive toward. They could benefit from illustrations of what is possible and from encouragement to find their own theses and bases for their theses. Their teacher should avoid holding one model before them as the goal of effective writing, as I think the rubrics teachers so often do. Teachers need to remain sensitive to the dangers of their models, for models can also suggest an ideal. Therefore, teachers should continue writing along with their students and experimenting with different approaches to see which seem to work best. And we want to engage our students in dialogue about what is and what is not effective. Their own writing can provide the basis for this dialogue. Teachers and their students can examine models like the one I wrote for what makes them effective and what prevents them from being effective.

Questions: *For one of the Advanced Placement essays you have just read, excluding essay 5, offer the writer three comments.*

1. *What was something you truly enjoyed or admired about the essay?*

2. *What was something that bothered you about the essay or that detracted in some way from your reading of the essay?*

3. *What is one thing you would recommend that the writer do to strengthen the essay in a revision?*

4. *Which essay did your comments address?*

One of the mistakes we who teach writing make is offering too much advice to our students. Growth occurs slowly and over time. No matter how fine the conversation I have with my students about the goals of their writing and no matter how accurate their comments and observations about the effectiveness of a piece of writing, we will all continue to fall short of our goals. But we can probably help our students by acknowledging that there are positive qualities to what they write. Too often teachers forget to comment on strengths. And we can make our students aware of readers by telling them what bothers us as readers, what interferes with our understanding or our feeling satisfied. And then, if we suggest just one thing that a student writer, or any writer, can do to make a composition more effective and successful, then that one thing may be attainable. The principle may also be remembered in future writing, but we need to expect that change occurs gradually.

And a final illustration: A young woman who was a good student came to talk with me one day. I had never given her a grade higher than a B on essays she wrote in my class. Yet I often complimented the quality of her ideas and the originality of her perceptions. "What," she asked, "must I do to earn an A?" I invited her to review some of her writing with me. We discovered two qualities that I recommended that she work on: First, her vocabulary was filled with slang and adolescent colloquialisms. Second, her paragraphs were very long. Because students commonly compose brief paragraphs of two or three sentences, she had been rewarded by previous teachers for writing more complex paragraphs. But her goal was to appear more mature in her writing. When we collaboratively rewrote one of her paragraphs, selecting the vocabulary thoughtfully, subtle changes occurred. Also, our new version of her paragraph was tighter. Whereas her paragraph had been fifteen sentences in length, the revised version used five sentences to convey the same information. And the sentences were not overly long. We were able to devise a diagnosis: Select vocabulary more carefully and combine and tighten sentences without abbreviating content. Critiques of essays after that day focused on these two areas, and she did eventually receive an A evaluation.

By cooperatively assessing this student's composition, we changed the focus of my evaluations from errors and mistakes and unexplained B-level assessments to two keys to growth and development. *We diagnosed her development as a writer and prescribed ways to move her skills to a higher level, an essential tenet of coaching and teaching writing.*

REFERENCES AND RESOURCES

Dunning, Stephen. *Twenty Poetry Writing Exercises.* Urbana, IL: National Council of Teachers of English, 1992.

Elbow, Peter. *Embracing Contraries: Explorations in Learning and Teaching.* New York: Oxford University Press, 1986.

———. *Writing with Power: Techniques for Mastering the Writing Process.* New York: Oxford University Press, 1981.

———. *Writing Without Teachers.* New York: Oxford University Press, 1973.

Gates, George G. *Ways We Write.* Dubuque, IA: W. C. Brown Book Co., 1966.

Leonard, George. *Education and Ecstasy.* New York: Delacorte Press, 1968.

Macrorie, Ken. *Searching Writing.* Upper Montclair, NJ: Boynton/Cook Publishers, 1984.

———. *Telling Writing,* 4th ed. Upper Montclair, NJ: Boynton/Cook Publishers, 1985.

———. *Uptaught.* New York: Hayden Book Co., 1970.

———. *A Vulnerable Teacher.* Rochelle Park, NJ: Hayden Book Co., 1974.

———. *Writing to Be Read.* Rev. 3rd ed. Upper Montclair, NJ: Boynton/Cook Publishers, 1984.

Moffett, James. *Active Voice: A Writing Program across the Curriculum.* Upper Montclair, NJ: Boynton/Cook Publishers, 1981.

———. *Coming on Center: Essays in English Education.* Portsmouth, NH: Boynton/Cook Publishers, 1988.

———. *A Student Centered Language Arts Curriculum.* Boston: Houghton Mifflin, 1968.

———. *Teaching the Universe of Discourse.* Boston: Houghton Mifflin, 1983.

Stafford, William. "Writing the Australian Crawl." *College Composition and Communication* 15.1 (February 1994): 12–15.

Winterowd, Ross. *English Writing and Language Skills.* New York: Harcourt Brace Jovanovich, 1983–1984.

INDEX